100
Aviation
Facts

Edited by
Mike Machat

**mazing and Little-known Information
About All Aspects of Aviation**

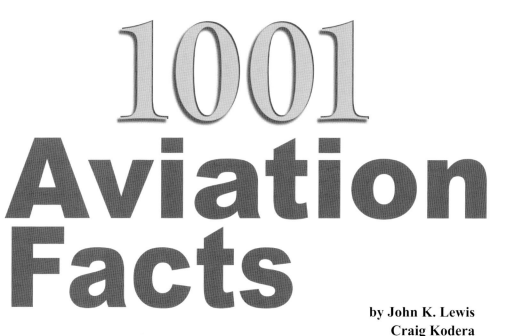

1001
Aviation
Facts

by John K. Lewis
Craig Kodera
Nick Veronico
Jim Keeshen
Hank Caruso
Mark Frankel
and Jon Proctor

Edited by Mike Machat

Amazing and Little-known Information
About All Aspects of Aviation

Specialty Press
838 Lake Street South
Forest Lake, MN 55025
Phone: 651-277-1400 or 800-895-4585
Fax: 651-277-1203
www.specialtypress.com

Edit by Mike Machat
Layout by Monica Seiberlich

ISBN 978-1-58007-244-1
Item No. SP244

Library of Congress CiP Data
https://lccn.loc.gov/2017021373

Written, edited, and designed in the U.S.A.
Printed in China
10 9 8 7 6 5 4 3 2 1

Front Cover: Vought's Mach-2 XF8U-3 by Mike Machat.

Title Page: Lockheed's "Missile with a Man in It." The F-104 Starfighter became the world's first operational Mach 2 aircraft.

DISTRIBUTION BY:

UK and Europe
Crécy Publishing Ltd
1a Ringway Trading Estate
Shadowmoss Road
Manchester M22 5LH England
Tel: 44 161 499 0024
Fax : 44 161 499 0298
www.crecy.co.uk
enquiries@crecy.co.uk

Canada
Login Canada
300 Saulteaux Crescent
Winnipeg, MB, R3J-3T2 Canada
Phone 800 665 1148
Fax: 800 665 0103
www.lb.ca

CONTENTS

About the Authors

HANK CARUSO

An Artist Fellow of the American Society of Aviation Artists, Hank Caruso brings a judicious blend of art and engineering to his imaginative creations. He was trained as both an artist and engineer and is intimately familiar with the technology of flight. As a writer, Caruso brings his depth of experience mixed with a touch of humor to convey salient points about aviation to his readers. Years of flying with the U.S. Navy in support of his artwork has established Caruso as a major player in aviation art. He is the 27th person to be granted the coveted title Honorary Naval Aviator.

MARK FRANKEL

Author Mark Frankel began as a flying aircraft modeler. He competed in Academy of Model Aeronautics national meets as a teenager, which led to his interest in naval aviation. After completing law school, Frankel served as a trial lawyer in Navy JAGC and earned his FAA Private Pilot Certificate. He currently owns a Piper PA-28 Archer and has written two books on aviation subjects: one on the Douglas F4D Skyray and one on post–World War II training aircraft. Frankel remains active in designing, building, and flying large-scale radio-controlled models today.

JIM KEESHEN

The son of a World War II aviator, Jim Keeshen has been involved in aviation modeling since early childhood. Years of flying RC models and attending his father's yearly squadron reunions and Southern California air shows led Keeshen to a lifetime involvement in aircraft modeling. An animator by trade, he attended UCLA and established his own studio, all the while building models and adding to his world-class collection, one of the finest and most comprehensive in the United States today. Keeshen has also written a book on Cold War proposal models for Crecy Publications.

CRAIG KODERA

Former U.S. Air Force pilot Craig Kodera flew the C-130 and KC-10, as well as DC-9 Super 80s for American Airlines. He has written two best-selling books for Specialty Press and is today an active aviation artist, with many published works and originals in museums and galleries. His clients include McDonnell Douglas and Airbus Industrie, and his artwork has been published for many years by the Greenwich Workshop. A lifetime aircraft modeler and vintage model collector, Kodera possesses one of the largest collections of international plastic model kits in the world.

JOHN K. LEWIS

Former U.S. Air Force command pilot John Lewis has flown a wide variety of aircraft in his aviation career, including the North American F-86 Sabre and F-100 Super Sabre, the Boeing B-47 Stratojet, and Douglas C-47 Skytrain. After his Air Force service, he flew DC-3s for a commercial airfreight operator and Gulfstream executive jets for several major U.S. corporations. Lewis entered the aviation literary world working for *Wings & Airpower* magazine, having authored an article on the Grumman Gulfstream family. He is a valued contributor to Specialty Press.

MIKE MACHAT

Mike Machat has dedicated his career to the documentation of aviation history. Beginning as a staff artist for McDonnell Douglas he established his own aviation art studio after being elected first president of the American Society of Aviation Artists. Mike expanded his career to include aviation writing and served as editor-in-chief for *Wings & Airpower* magazine, and acquisitions editor and author for Specialty Press Aviation Publications. He has edited more than 30 books for Specialty and has written three best-selling books on commercial and military aviation.

JON PROCTOR

A seasoned veteran of the U.S. airline industry, Jon Proctor served in various positions with Trans World Airlines for 27 years. He comes from a multi-generational airline family with his father having been a pioneering captain for American Airlines and his brother having flown for TWA. Proctor has a vast background in aviation writing. He was editor of *Airliners* magazine and has written countless articles on commercial airline subjects. Proctor has authored numerous books as well, his most recent being an employee history of TWA.

NICHOLAS A. VERONICO

Nicholas A. Veronico currently serves as a science and technology writer working for the NASA Ames-based Astronomical Society of the Pacific. He has written more than two dozen books about aviation and served as the lead scriptwriter for "Scrapping Aircraft Giants," a Discovery Channel TV documentary covering commercial aircraft scrapping procedures. Veronico also serves as public affairs officer for NASA's Boeing 747SP SOFIA Program (Stratospheric Observatory for Infrared Astronomy), the world's largest flying telescope.

Introduction

Like any specialized subject, aviation is full of interesting but little-known facts, much like trains, ships, and of course cars. As you may know, Specialty Press is a companion company of CarTech Publishing, one of the world's leading producers of books about everything related to the automobile. Several years ago, CarTech launched a series of books with titles all starting with "1001 Facts" on such diverse automotive topics as Muscle Cars, Drag Racing, and NASCAR, and these books were so successful that Specialty decided to embark on a similar project about aviation for its dedicated readers.

To accomplish this feat, a select group of aviation specialists were recruited from a large field of some of the finest pilots, artists, writers, modelers, and historians in the business, many of whom have already distinguished themselves with outstanding books written for Specialty Press. These authors are identified by name after each entry. Additionally, many rare and never-before-seen archival photographs are used throughout this book to bring a visual component to all of the rich history.

Howard Hughes flies the second XF-11 at Culver City, California, in summer 1947.

1001 Aviation Facts brings you an amazing array of information about every facet of aviation, from classic World War II aircraft to exotic experimental rocket planes, luxurious commercial airliners, sport aviation, and even aircraft featured on TV and in the movies. In addition, airplanes would not exist or fly without their designers and pilots, and we've featured numerous facts about those aspects of flight as well. As your captain says aboard an airliner, "Now sit back, relax, and enjoy the flight" through more than 110 years of exciting aviation history.

Editor's Note: Although the authors strive for complete accuracy and authenticity in this book, it should be noted that facts sometimes appear with subtle and innumerable variations. For instance, 17 December 1903 was indeed the date that the Wright Brothers first flew, but what is the MTGW (Max Takeoff Gross Weight) of a Boeing 707? The answer can depend on a number of specifics such as model, engine type, runway parameters, and even airline. With this in mind, we bring you a book of 1,001 facts that are, to the best of our knowledge, accurate and most representative of the information obtained from our vast archival sources.

Publisher's Note: In reporting history, the images required to tell the tale will vary greatly in quality, especially by modern photographic standards. While some images in this volume are not up to those digital standards, we have included them, as we feel they are an important element in telling the story.

Chapter 1

The Beginning

Wilbur and Orville Wright were the world's first test pilots. They not only flew the world's first powered aircraft, but the world's first experimental aircraft at that. Perhaps not a fair comparison to such rocket-powered marvels as the Bell X-1 or Douglas Skyrocket, but certainly just as significant, because everything else that has happened in aviation came after the *Wright Flyer*! Fittingly, we begin this book with a special section of aviation facts about the Wright brothers, courtesy of Jim Keeshen.

THE WRIGHT BROTHERS

1   The first *Wright Flyer* was flown four times on 17 December 1903. The first flight of that day, piloted by Orville, lasted 12 seconds and covered 120 feet. The second flight by Wilbur went for 13 seconds and 175 feet. The third flight by Orville was 15 seconds and covered 200 feet. The final flight by Wilbur lasted 57 seconds and was measured at 852 feet.

2   Although the *Flyer* had the capability to turn and climb, all flights that day were accomplished by flying straight ahead with no attempts to turn the aircraft.

Before the Wright brothers built their trailblazing Wright Flyer *in 1903, they tested aerodynamic theories with an unpowered full-scale glider.*

3 The brothers determined who would fly first by flipping a coin, and Orville won the first toss. After that, they took turns until the fourth flight.

4 After the fourth flight, the *Wright Flyer* was destroyed when a gust of wind picked it up from its resting spot, causing it to tumble end over end for some distance and turning it into a heap of splintered wood and torn linen. It never flew again.

5 After their famous first flight, the Wright brothers returned from Kitty Hawk back to Dayton for the Christmas holidays. They shipped back the heavily damaged Flyer for its historical significance. The *Flyer* was stored for nine years and then, in March 1913, was inundated in the Great Dayton Flood. At one point, Wilbur thought of burning it.

6 Samuel Pierpont Langley strove to beat the Wrights into the air, but a major difference between the *Wright Flyer* and Langley's Aerodrome was the fact that Langley's aircraft had no moveable flying controls. It was launched with the intent to fly only straight ahead.

7 Many newspapers refused to publish the accomplishments of the Wright brothers, thinking that a flight of 59 seconds was not newsworthy. For some time the brothers were ignored by the press and did not get any recognition. In fact, the U.S. Army showed no interest in the *Wright Flyer*. All that changed when the Wrights decided to turn to Europe. They conducted sensational flight demonstrations in France and England and invited the British Military to look over their aircraft. Eventually the U.S. press and U.S. military took an interest.

8 In 1916 the original *Flyer* was brought out of storage and prepared for display at the Massachusetts Institute of Technology. Charlie Taylor, a handyman/mechanic, worked closely with the Wrights from the beginning and was instrumental in helping rebuild the *Flyer*.

After their epic flights at Kitty Hawk, the Wrights were hard-pressed to find fame and adulation anywhere in the United States but were warmly received in Europe.

9 As the Wright brothers developed their *Flyers* from 1904 to 1909, they continuously set world records for duration, height, and distance. And each time they flew, longer or faster or higher, they reset the records, quite literally until their next flight.

10 Later on, the *Flyer* was sent to England to be exhibited at the Science Museum in London. Finally, in 1925, after the Smithsonian agreed to give credit to the Wright brothers as the first to fly, it was copied by the British and the original sent back to the states.

11 While the Wrights and Smithsonian wrestled over the title of who was the first to actually fly a powered, heavier-than-air machine, Henry Ford decided to buy the original Wright family home after the Wrights had moved out. He disassembled the home and reassembled it at his museum in Dearborn, Michigan.

12 Today, the site of the Wrights' original home, 7 Hawthorne Street, Dayton, Ohio, is a vacant lot with a plaque, a sculpture of an early

bike leaning against the front fence, and an odd, small structure, which is a full-size re-creation of the stairs, partial front porch, and front door of the original Wright home. That, along with a picture of what the house looked like in the early 1900s, is all that is left of this historic site.

13 The Wright brothers made their own wind tunnel to test the best angle for wing and propeller shapes. Instead of placing a model in the wind tunnel, they suspended curved metal strips to see which form responded to the wind blown over it. Modern scientific testing showed that the shape of the Wrights' 1903 *Flyer* propellers was extremely efficient.

14 The Wright brothers understood that propellers should be treated as rotating airfoils, not simply flat paddles. As a result, the carefully contoured propellers on their 1903 *Flyer* were capable of 82 percent efficiency. This is a real engineering accomplishment considering that modern propeller efficiencies are around 90 percent. (Veronico)

15 Although 17 December 1903 is considered the date of the first controlled heavier-than-air flight, Wilbur did a short "jump" on 14 December 1903 with the *Wright Flyer* for 4 seconds that went 112 feet. It was discounted by the brothers as an actual flight because the *Flyer* was not launched from level ground. The monorail track from which the *Flyer* took off was set on an 8-degree 50-minute slope at the foot of Big Kill Devil Hill. It has also been described as a failed attempt in which Wilbur pulled up too quickly and stalled the aircraft, causing it to abruptly descend.

16 The early 1902 Wright gliders and their first powered aircraft, including the 1904 *Flyer II*, used wing warping for roll control. These were the only aircraft of the time capable of coordinated banked turns. The Wright aircraft had better roll control than airplanes that used separate surfaces.

17 By 1908, aileron designs had become more refined and it was evident that ailerons were much more practical and effective than wing warping. By 1911 most aircraft were using ailerons rather than wing warping, and by 1915 ailerons were being used on most biplanes and monoplanes as well.

18 Although the Wright brothers used wing warping to control the roll of their airplanes, they eventually changed over to ailerons (French for "little wing") and patented their control systems. This patent has been blamed for stunting the growth of the aviation industry in the United States during the years leading up to World War I because the Wright brothers rigorously sued all U.S. aircraft manufacturers using their invention. The U.S. government eventually stepped in and allowed other aircraft manufacturers to use ailerons. Ironically, there was already a patent on the aileron from the late 1800s, but it was somehow ignored.

19 How many times over the past half century have we seen a helicopter ascend or land on the South Lawn of the White House in

Marine One helicopters may routinely land and take off on the White House South Lawn, but the first aircraft to do so was the Wright "B" Flyer.

Washington, D.C.? Well, the original alighting of an aircraft on that famous landscape was by a Wright Model B flown by Harry Atwood back in 14 July 1911. The then occupant of the famous home, President William Howard Taft, presented Atwood with a gold medal from the Aero Club of Washington. (Kodera)

20 Neil Armstrong took a piece of the *Wright Flyer* with him when he went to the moon on the *Apollo 11* lunar landing mission in July 1969.

THE EARLY YEARS

21 In 1910 Glen Curtiss was issued Pilot License Number 1 while Orville Wright was issued License Number 5 and Wilbur Wright issued License Number 6. The sequence seems out of order, but issuing licenses was in its infancy and in the beginning they were issued in alphabetical order. (Lewis)

22 Spin recovery was an unknown procedure before World War I, and many pilots lost their lives when they inadvertently found themselves in a spin. The usual response was to pull back on the control stick in order to raise the nose of the aircraft to stop it from diving toward the ground. British aviator Lieutenant Wilfred Parke RN (1889–1912) was the first pilot to make an observed recovery from a spin. After his successful recovery, the procedure was named "Parke's Dive" and led to teaching spin recovery prior to World War 1. (Lewis)

23 The first commercial airline to operate in the United States carrying passengers in scheduled revenue service was the St. Petersburg–Tampa Airboat Line. On 1 January 1914 that company inaugurated air service using a Benoist Flying Boat capable of carrying a pilot and one passenger. (Kodera)

24 Juan de la Cierva was a Spanish civil engineer who invented the "autogyro" in 1920. He went on to design an articulated rotor system that led to the first successful rotary wing aircraft. De la Cierva established the Cierva Autogiro Company in England, where he manufactured the rotor systems and contracted with the AV Roe Company to build fuselage sections. (Lewis)

25 The Curtiss NC-4 flying boat was the first aircraft to fly across the Atlantic Ocean in May 1919. Flown by a U.S. Navy crew, it departed from New York and made stops in Massachusetts, Nova Scotia, and the Azores Islands before reaching Lisbon, Portugal, over a period of 19 days. They continued to Plymouth, England, making it also the first flight from America to England. (Lewis)

26 Lieutenant Harold R. Harris was the first man to save his life by using a parachute when the airplane he was flying started to disintegrate over Dayton, Ohio. (Lewis)

27 First Lieutenant Thomas E. Selfridge was the first person to be killed in a heavier-than-air vehicle while on a demonstration flight with Orville Wright when their *Wright Flyer* crashed in Ft. Myer, Virginia, on 17 September 1908. Selfridge had an interest in both lighter- and heavier-than-air vehicles and was one of the first pilots to be trained in U.S. Army dirigibles. He was also the first military officer to solo an aircraft when he flew Aerial Experiment Association's *White Wing* on 19 May 1908 at Hammondsport, New York. (Lewis)

28 In 1910 Henri Coandă of Romania built and flew a controversial aircraft using a turbo-propulseur jet engine of his own design. It flew only once, crashed during the brief flight, and was consumed by fire. Years later his claim was to come under much scrutiny because his turbo-propulseur used a conventional piston engine to drive the compressor and it lacked the combustion of fuel in the air chamber. There was also no proof that it ever flew. (Lewis)

29 Louis Bleriot introduced an enclosed space in his aircraft to protect pilots from both wind blast and cold temperatures. The enclosure resembled the round arena used for cock fighting and led to that portion of an aircraft's fuselage being called a cockpit. (Lewis)

30 The Junkers F.13, built in 1924, has the distinction of being the first cantilevered wing all-metal monoplane passenger aircraft. Made entirely of aluminum, it eliminated the use of external bracing and provided an enclosed heated cabin for four passengers. The F.13 was covered entirely with a stressed corrugated aluminum skin. The four passenger seats had safety belts, a feature that wasn't installed in other aircraft for several years. Although the F.13 had a wheeled landing gear plus a tail skid for ground operations, some models had floats or skis installed. (Lewis)

31 The French Blériot XI aircraft was used by Louis Blériot to make the first crossing of the English Channel in 1909 while in a heavier-than-air vehicle. It was a feat that made Blériot famous and ensured the success of his aircraft company. The Old Rhinebeck Airdrome in Rhinebeck, New York, flies an original Blériot XI in its air shows. Its 1909 Blériot is the oldest flying aircraft registered with the Federal Aviation Administration in the United States. (Lewis)

32 One of the Loughead brothers, tired of people pronouncing his name wrong (Log Head), changed it to Lockheed so it would be pronounced correctly. (Lewis)

33 Henri Pitot (pronounced "pea-tow") was a French hydraulics engineer who invented the Pitot tube in 1732 for use in calculating the flow of water. The invention was later adapted for aircraft to measure and display speeds through the atmosphere. (Lewis)

34 Russian inventor Gleb Kotelnikov designed and tested drogue parachutes in 1912. They were attached to fast-moving vehicles such as automobiles and assisted in slowing them down when deployed. Drogue parachutes have been used on a wide range of aircraft to help in deceleration during landing and are sometimes called drag parachutes, although the application is the same. Many variations of the drogue chute are used on a wide variety of vehicles from drag strip racers to space shuttles. (Lewis)

35 Sir Edwin Alliott Verdon Roe (26 April 1877 to 4 January 1958) and his brother Humphrey founded the A. V. Roe (AVRO) Aircraft Company on 1 January 1910. A. V. Roe was the first Briton to fly an aircraft. (Lewis)

36 The Boeing Model 40 B-4 was the first plane in the Model 40 series to use the two-way radio, designed by Thorpe Hiscock, William Boeing's brother-in-law. It also was the first aircraft built by Boeing to carry passengers. (Lewis)

37 The world's first successful all-metal airplane was built by Hugo Junkers in Dessau, Germany. Constructed of corrugated aluminum skin and flown in 1915, the Junkers J-1 served as the prototype and development airplane for all the Junkers metal aircraft that followed. It had a top speed of 105 mph. (Kodera)

38 The first all-metal airplane built in the United States was the Larsen JL-6 in 1920. The aircraft was actually the Junkers F-13 metal monoplane developed in Germany utilizing corrugated metal aluminum skin. J. L. Larsen, an airplane salesman, negotiated the rights of production in America while on a trip in Europe selling airplanes. Among its customers was the U.S. Navy with an order for three, both land and sea plane types. (Kodera)

39 Everyone knows the aviation prowess of the Southern California region of the United States, so naturally we assume any number of innovations sprang from this hotbed of aeronautical progress. The first all-metal airplane built in those environs was actually not until 1928, and that aircraft was the Crawford C-1 Metalplane, designed by one Harvey Crawford of Los Angeles. It weighed 1,800 pounds and was of a parasol wing monoplane design utilizing the Junkers metal wing. It was powered by a Gnome rotary engine and could fly at 118 mph. (Kodera)

40 Esteemed British aeronautical engineer Sir Sydney Camm once noted that all modern aircraft have four dimensions: span, length, height, and politics. (Frankel)

41 The first human to fly was a Frenchman named Francois de Rozier. He ascended on 15 October 1783 in a 50-foot-diameter Montgolfier balloon that was tethered to the ground, allowing a height of only 84 feet to be attained. The balloon was lifted via heat from a straw-stocked fire beneath. The first free flight took place when de Rozier and companion Marquis d'Arlandes flew 5½ miles across Paris at a maximum height of 1,000 feet on 21 November of that year. (Kodera)

42 The first woman to fly was the Countess de Montalembert, again ascending on a tether on 20 May 1784 in Paris in another Montgolfier balloon. (Kodera)

43 The first balloon flight in the United States took place on 9 January 1793 and was flown, naturally, by a Frenchman, Jean Pierre Blanchard. Interestingly, his ship was lifted by hydrogen rather than hot air. The flight lasted 46 minutes and covered a route from Philadelphia to Gloucester, New Jersey. (Kodera)

44 An American also caught the flying bug and became the first U.S. citizen to fly in a balloon. His name: Charles Durant, of New York, who flew from Castle Garden, New York, to Amboy, New Jersey, and took two hours to do so. (Kodera)

45 The original use of balloons as military devices in the United States was during the great Civil War/War between the States, beginning service on 1 October 1861. The Federal Balloon Corps was formed for such duties as reconnaissance and bombardment under the command of Thaddeus Lowe with five balloons and 50 men. They first saw combat when on 31 May 1862 a Union-tethered balloon piloted by Lowe himself saved Union forces from defeat at the Battle of Fair Oaks in Virginia. (Kodera)

46 A further extrapolation of the balloon, an airship, incorporated power to move deliberately through the atmosphere. Usually long and cigar shaped, there was great potential utility in such an aircraft. The first such ship was built and flown by the Frenchman Henri Giffard, and on 24 September 1852 he began his life as an aeronaut. He flew at a whopping 5 mph, departing the Paris Hippodrome and landing 17 miles later in Trappes, thus proving the concept and opening the door to practical lighter-than-air powered flight. (Kodera)

47 Taking the airship concept to its fullest application, Count Ferdinand von Zeppelin in Germany created the LZ-1, a rigid airship, not a balloon/gas bag/blimp. The Zeppelin, as its later appellation was coined, consisted of an aluminum rib structure with cells installed to hold the lighter-than-air gas. A doped fabric skin was stretched over this structure and a gondola and engines were hung from the cigar-shaped aircraft. The LZ-1 was first flown on 2 July 1900 on a 20-minute flight over Lake Constance in Germany. The ship was 420 feet in length and designed to carry five people. (Kodera)

48 The first person in the world to make a parachute jump was a Frenchman named Andre Garnerin. His plucky deed took place near Paris from an altitude of 3,000 feet on 22 October 1797. (Kodera)

49 The first person to make a parachute jump in the United States was Charles Guille from an exhilarating altitude of 8,000 feet. This display of acumen and daring was staged above Brooklyn, New York, on 2 August 1819, once again from a hydrogen-filled balloon. (Kodera)

50 The first recorded flight of a person becoming airborne in a heavier-than-air craft traces to 1853. The well-known aeronauticist Sir George Cayley, famous for his studies of unpowered gliders and basic flying characteristics, enlisted the aid of a young (and lightweight) 10-year-old boy to accomplish the initial dream of

manned flight. The son of one of the workers on Cayley's estate in Yorkshire, England, our unknown "pilot" was placed into the glider and pulled down the hill by manpower as the aircraft lifted into the breeze and was released. No mention of the child's reaction was given in the written account. (Kodera)

51 The name Otto Lilienthal is synonymous with experiments in manned gliders. His work in Germany heavily influenced the Wright brothers in the United States. Prolific, Lilienthal made more than 2,000 controlled flights in his glider designs between 1891 and 1896, achieving several hundred feet of distance after launching down the hill he had sculpted next to his home in Berlin. Achieving minimal control of his craft was done by shifting his body weight to cause the glider to lean either direction. It took the Wrights to break through and solve the controllability issue by incorporating wing warping into their airplanes. This led, of course, to ailerons in all later airplanes. (Kodera)

52 Lilienthal also holds another distinction of sorts: the first person to be killed in an aircraft. Late in his process of test flying his gliders his craft was one day caught by a strong gust of wind, rendering the airplane uncontrollable. (Kodera)

53 Powered, manned flight came to the United States when Leo Stevens and Edward Boice flew in two airships over Brooklyn, New York, on 30 September 1902. Alberto Santos-Dumont had designed and provided one of his number-6 airships to Boice while Stevens flew one of his own designs. For 45 minutes the pair thrilled thousands of spectators gathered below. (Kodera)

54 As the Wright brothers flew in 1903 and were building follow-on models of their *Wright Flyer* in the years following, the first actual aircraft manufacturing company organized as such and open for business was in France and was known as Voisin Freres. Headquartered in Billancourt in November 1906, the company originally had two employees, Charles and Gabriel Voisin, and they received an order for an ornithopter in December of the same year. The machine never flew, but the next one, a box kite–like biplane, did so successfully in March of 1907. (Kodera)

55 Man in an airplane was a totally new experience in 1903 but by 1907 a newer concept yet had emerged: the helicopter. Once again, France led the way in aeronautical innovation when the Breguet brothers created their Gyroplane I. It flew in September at 2 feet altitude with an intrepid pilot aboard but was actually steadied by four other men on the ground. The next year Gyroplane II flew and had several flights before being destroyed by a storm at the works. (Kodera)

56 Short hops in the new "aeroplane" were common, but when did man start going any distance? That began on 30 October 1908 when Henri Farman flew his airplane from Bouy, France, to Rheims, a total of 14 miles. The flight took 20 minutes to complete. (Kodera)

57 The first woman to fly in an airplane was Madame Therese Peltier of France. She was flown by Leon Delagrange in his commissioned Voisin biplane on 8 July 1908. (Kodera)

58 When one thinks of the early days the idea of airports comes to mind. Where was America's first public flying field designated as such? It was in Mineola, New York, and was operated by none other than the famous flyer and designer Glenn Curtiss. Attracted to the Hempstead Plains of Long Island, Curtiss set up shop there with his *Golden Flyer* in June of 1909, a scant six years after the Wrights' first flight. By July the New York Aeronautic Society had settled on the field and many airplanes were flying or being built within the environs. (Kodera)

59 Glenn Curtiss was quite the icon within the burgeoning aviation world and he had the credentials to prove it, including the first pilot's license in America. The certification came from the Fédération Aeronautic Internationale (FAI) in France (which exists to this day to verify records of aviation activities) and was issued on 7 October 1909. (Kodera)

60 An unusual concept in aerodynamics is the variable geometry swept wing, affording both high- and low-speed advantage to the same airfoil shape. The implementation of such radical thinking began first with the 1931 Westland-Hill Pterodactyl IV tailless design, whereon the slight advancing or retracting of its limited motion wing compensated for the lack of horizontal tail surfaces. (Kodera)

61 England is obviously an island nation and the English Channel between that country and France has historically served as a natural barrier and protection from enemies. It has also served as an impediment; therefore, the significance of the first aerial crossing of the channel was nothing short of gigantic. The honor went to a pilot named Louis Bleriot, who flew an airplane of his own design on 25 July 1909 from Calais, France, to Dover, England. The total flight distance was 22 miles and the elapsed time was roughly 50 minutes. London's newspaper awarded Bleriot the standing prize of 1,000 pounds for his accomplishment. (Kodera)

62 The current annual budget for the U.S. Air Force can make one's head swim. It is interesting to recall that the first airplane acquired by the U.S. government was a follow-on development of the *Wright Flyer*, which was purchased by the Army on 2 August 1909. The total cost for the airplane was a large $25,000 plus a performance bonus of $5,000. Best guess in today's inflated currency would be $758,439, which doesn't account for the extra inflation typically ascribed to defense materiel in the current aerospace industry. (Kodera)

63 The airplane as combat weapon, a natural application of a new technology, got its start on 7 May 1912 at College Park, Maryland, when Charles Chandler of the Army Signal Corps fired a Lewis machine gun from a Wright biplane being flown by Lieutenant Thomas Milling. The gun was fired at fixed targets on the ground and successfully hit them. Thus started the quest for air superiority in military theaters of conflict. (Kodera)

64 An amazing aircraft designer at the turn of the century was Igor Sikorsky from St. Petersburg, Russia. He gave the world its first four-engine airplane, the *Grand*, in 1913. It was a steady and airworthy ship and transformed naturally into a bombing platform. It had a great endurance of more than two hours flying time and could carry eight people. Leaving mother Russia for America after the communist revolution, Sikorsky made much more aviation history in the following seven decades. (Kodera)

65 Among the competitive relationships between aviation pioneers in the United States none was more fever-pitched and contentious than that of the Wright brothers and Glenn Curtiss. Direct allegations by the Wrights toward Curtiss involving thievery of their patents for their unique three-axis control system escalated to the point of precipitating the first-ever lawsuit in aviation. The battle raged from 1909 to 1917, prescient of what today's legal system produces. The whole thing finally ended when a cross-licensing agreement was negotiated between the parties. Ironically, it was Curtiss who eventually procured the entire business from the brothers of Dayton, the final amalgamated company being known forever more as Curtiss-Wright Aircraft. (Kodera)

66 Air commerce involves both the carrying of passengers and freight, or air cargo. Today we have entire airlines around the world that specialize in nothing but the flying of packages and items. Our current air cargo businesses started all the way back in 1910 when pilot Phil Parmalee flew the first such mission on 7 November, hauling two bolts of dressmaker's silk fabric from Dayton, Ohio, to Columbus, covering a distance of 65 miles. (Kodera)

67 As an adjunct to air cargo is the imperative of air mail. The first demonstration of this vital concept was performed by pilot Earl Ovington, who was noted as Air Mail Pilot #1, as he flew a 30-pound sack of mail from Garden City, New York, to Mineola, New York. Keeping the bag on his lap while flying, Ovington dropped the cargo from his airplane as he overflew the post office. (Kodera)

68 In America, the first sustained air mail operation began on 15 May 1918 when two Curtiss Jenny airplanes departed from cities on the East Coast. One of the planes left Washington, D.C., heading north while the other departed Belmont, New York, heading south, trading each other's city with mail delivery. (Kodera)

69 Man always wanted to fly, but he also always went to sea. It wasn't long after the first pioneering flights that airplanes were made seaworthy by placing pontoons under them or crafting a hull with wings attached. The first seaplane was built by Henri Fabre of France and flown for the first time on 28 March 1910. He designed his airplane for water landings not because of utility but rather because "crashing on the water would be gentler on the pilot than doing so on land." (Kodera)

70 The first practical seaplane design is credited to Glenn Curtiss in 1911. Known as the Model E, it first flew at San Diego in January of that year. (Kodera)

71 Curtiss went on to sell the Model E seaplane to the U.S. Navy, which designated the craft the Curtiss A-1. Fourteen airplanes were eventually procured and were given the designations A-1 through A-4. This was the first purchase of aircraft by the Navy. Curtiss produced seaplanes for the naval forces of the United States for decades after this first buy and his products are noted for many significant achievements in naval aviation. (Kodera)

72 Moving motor vehicles by air is not a recent invention. The first such upload was in 1925 as a Burnelli RB-2 carried a Hudson Motors Essex automobile on a national sales tour. (Kodera)

73 The first airplane to take off from a warship was a Curtiss pusher departing from a makeshift platform on the USS *Birmingham* on 14 November 1910. The pilot was Eugene Ely, who then flew the airplane an additional 2 miles before landing on a beach. On 18 January 1911 Ely again made history with the first landing on a ship, the USS *Pennsylvania*, moored in San Francisco Bay. (Kodera)

74 The first naval aviator in the United States was Theodore Ellyson who began his career in 1911 along with the Curtiss machines. Among his other achievements, he was the first to fly off a ship by being catapulted. He eventually became an admiral and served with distinction. (Kodera)

Auto racing legend Eddie Rickenbacker became an ace during World War I, and is shown here with his faithful SPAD fighter.

75 In 1924, the U.S. Army Air Service succeeded in circumnavigating the world using four Douglas World Cruiser aircraft powered by Liberty L-12 engines. Based on the Douglas DT torpedo bomber, they were completed in just 45 days. On 6 April 1924 the four DWC aircraft, *Boston*, *Chicago*, *New Orleans*, and *Seattle* left Sand Point, Washington, for the around-the-world flight. One crashed in Alaska, another sank in the Atlantic Ocean near Faroe Islands, but the remaining two completed the six-month journey on 28 September 1924 after covering 23,942 miles in 371 hours, 11 minutes at an average speed of 70 mph. (Lewis)

76 The first notable endurance record was accomplished by a Curtiss Robin aircraft, which set that record by staying in the air for 17 days in 1929. (Keeshen)

77 The first airplane to overfly the North Pole was the *Josephine Ford*, a Fokker Trimotor commanded by Lieutenant Commander Richard Byrd, and assisted on the expedition by pilot Floyd Bennett. The date of the flight was 9 May 1926 and the group had departed from their home base at the time, Spitsbergen, Norway. Coincidentally, the Italian-built airship *Norge*, with Lincoln Ellsworth flying, crossed the pole on 12 May. Great dispute continues to this day claiming that the airship actually made the first flight over the northern pole location. (Kodera)

78 Leaving no pole undiscovered, Richard Byrd, along with pilot Bernt Balchen and a small team of men, headed to the southernmost reaches of our planet and crossed the South Pole on 28 November 1929. This time they were flying in a Ford Trimotor and operated from their base camp in Little America, Antarctica. (Kodera)

79 Coincident with the development of piston engines as airplane powerplants came rocket propulsion. The Germans were early pioneers in Europe, while in America Robert Goddard led the "colonies" in hot pursuit of a new and immense thrust source for airplanes. The first airplane to be powered by rockets was the Teutonic Rhon-Rossitten–built glider known as the *Duck*. On 11 June 1928 the airplane made its first flight and covered just short of a mile while cruising at 70 mph using two Sander solid-fuel rockets. Just a couple of months later on 30 September, Fritz von Opel flew his *Opel* glider and is more commonly, but erroneously, associated with this airplane as the first to fly with rockets. (Kodera)

80 Germany created the world's first airline operation. Of course, the mode of transport was five of their very own 500-foot-long-ships, the Zeppelins. They named the carrier DELAG (Deutsche Luftschiffahrts-Aktiengesellschaft, or German Airship Transportation Corporation Ltd), which was established on 16 November 1909 as a subsidiary of the Zeppelin Company. It began commercial activity in 1910. Each of the airships carried 24 paying customers on local jaunts of a couple of hours, and later, between Baden-Baden and Frankfurt, Düsseldorf, and eventually to Berlin. By the time the airline stopped operating in 1914 (due to World War I) it had carried more than 34,000 passengers. (Kodera)

81 The first and only around-the-world airship flight occurred between 8 and 29 August 1929. The LZ-127 Graf Zeppelin, more than 700 feet long and based upon the earlier design for the U.S. Navy, the LZ-126 *Los Angeles*, began its journey thanks to the financial backing of publisher William Randolph Hurst. Hence, it departed America at Lakehurst, New Jersey, stopping at Friedrichshafen, Germany, Tokyo, Japan, and Los Angeles, California. It was piloted by airship designer and visionary Dr. Hugo Eckener. Finishing once again at Lakehurst, the airship completed the journey in 21 days and 7 hours. The flight from Japan to Southern California also marked the first time an aircraft of any type had flown nonstop across the Pacific Ocean. Also, the first woman to circumnavigate the globe was aboard the ship, at the request of Hurst. Her name was Lady Grace Drummond-Hay, a correspondent for the newspapers. (Kodera)

82 Ships carry airplanes all the time and for important tactical reasons. What if a ship of the air could do the same, with the same desired effect? Well, the clever people of the United States Navy planning department put the question to the test. They took the two Navy 1932 airships, the *Macon* and the *Akron*, and installed a hangar deck structure as well as a swinging hook "trapeze" device for lowering and retrieving small biplane fighter airplanes from inside the airship's hull. Using the Curtiss F9C-2 Sparrowhawk, these flying aircraft carriers could manage five airplanes onboard at any given time. The experiment lasted only as long as the airships remained flying, which was about another three years. (Kodera)

83 Earlier than imagined, Lawrence Sperry, inventor and son of famous inventor Elmer Sperry, conceptualized and manufactured the world's first automatic pilot. How early? 1913 to be exact. The heart of the system lies within the gyroscope developed for aviation use. First demonstrated on a Curtiss Model F seaplane, Sperry's invention was awarded a prize for the first automatically stabilized aircraft in 1914 when Sperry took it to France. (Kodera)

84 When the Western world went to war in Europe in 1914, the new aeroplane was exploited as a weapon of combat, and with astounding results. Employed in aerial combat, the first "shoot down" of one airplane by another in the war period took place on 5 October 1914 over Rheims, France. A German two-seat Aviatik was downed by Frenchman Joseph Frantz in a Voisin pusher airplane utilizing a Hotchkiss machine gun mounted in the front cockpit. (Kodera)

85 The United States managed to stay out of World War I for several years but had its own conflict at home along the Texas-Mexico border. Pancho Villa was making incursions into U.S. territory, and as a remedy the U.S. government detached the 1st Aero Squadron to the border lands. Eight Curtiss JN Jennys were placed under the command of General John "Blackjack" Pershing in March 1916. This represented the first use of American aircraft in a combat scenario. (Kodera)

86 The initial United States aircraft to see service in World War I was the LWF V-1 of the Lowe, Willard, and Fowler Company, and their first product was the Model V, a large two-seat training and observation biplane. The manufacturer was based in Queens, New York. The Army sent the V-1s to the Eastern front to aid the Czech air force in their efforts against Communist Russian troops in the summer of 1917. (Kodera)

87 Once the United States entered the Great War it wasn't long until they began amassing aerial victories like their European brethren. The first aerial victory for a Yank in an American unit came on 5 February 1918 over Saarbrucken, Germany, and was credited to Stephen Thompson of the 1st Aero Squadron. (Kodera)

The Cloudster *was the first of tens of thousands of all types of aircraft built* by the Douglas Aircraft Company and McDonnell Douglas Corporation.

88 One of the more famous French fighter aircraft of World War I was called a SPAD, an acronym for *Société Pour L'Aviation et ses Dérivés*. When translated to English SPAD means Society for Aviation and Its Derivatives. Captain Eddie Rickenbacker, who received the Medal of Honor for his bravery, was America's most successful fighter ace of World War I, shooting down 26 enemy aircraft while flying the SPAD design. (Lewis)

89 Early as it may seem, the world's first female military pilot hailed from pre-revolution Russia. She was Princess Eugenie Mikhailovna Shakovsaya, who had learned to fly in Germany in 1911. Once war broke out in Europe she pleaded with Tsar Nicholas to allow her to participate in combat operations. He agreed and sent her to the 1st Field Air Squadron where she performed as a reconnaissance pilot. She did survive the war. (Kodera)

90 World War I made very clear that aerial combat was the way of the future. The challenge was to fire a gun, preferably a rapid-fire machine gun, at your opponent without inflicting damage on your

own airplane, thus shooting yourself down! The best location for the gun was in front so that the pilot could point the airplane in the direction of fire, but this was difficult to do without shooting apart the propeller. The first solution to this dilemma appeared on the French Morane-Saulnier monoplane fighter, which utilized metal deflector plates on the back of the propeller blade. The year was 1915. (Kodera)

91 The bullet deflector concept for firing a machine gun from an airplane was inadequate in that the constant pounding of the machine gun ammo on the prop blades actually bent the crankshaft of the engine. The Germans had captured one of these French airplanes and asked their genius designer, Anthony Fokker, to replicate the concept for use on their own fighters (first on one of Fokker's Eindecker monoplanes). (Kodera)

92 Fokker had a much better idea: noting that the engine turned at 1,200 rpm and the machine gun fired 600 shots per minute, why not allow the engine/propeller to fire the gun sequence? Every other turn of the prop would fire the gun, disallowing bullets from ever hitting the blades. The invention was known as the Fokker Interrupter. In the Allied camps it was called the Fokker Scourge since it helped German pilots down thousands of enemy pilots in the second half of the war. (Kodera)

93 Lest we forget that various naval air arms around the world also wanted to employ their airplanes in combat roles, we find the first use of a Navy airplane in such a role was given to us by the Japanese. On 1 September 1914 Farman biplanes from the Japanese seaplane tender *Wakamiya* attacked German sea forces at Kiachow Bay, China. They dropped improvised bombs made from naval ship gun shells. Indeed, they actually managed to sink a minelayer in the harbor. (Kodera)

94 Can land planes be placed on a ship and their force projected at an enemy from any ocean in the world? Yes, as long as the ship is designed to carry and launch such aircraft from its deck. Known commonly as an aircraft carrier, the first such purpose-designed ship was HMS *Furious* of the English Royal Navy. Starting life as a cruiser, the ship's design was altered while being laid down at the ship works, and a flight deck plus below-deck hangar space were added. The ship took a complement of six Sopwith Pup fighters plus four seaplanes. She entered service in June 1917 and was modified in the 1920s and again during World War II. Her career ended in late 1945 having seen combat and ferrying operations throughout the war period. (Kodera)

95 The first purpose-built ship designed as an aircraft carrier from its outset was the Japanese *Hosho*, initially laid down in December 1919 with sea trials in November 1922. She was 168 feet long and could carry 21 aircraft at 25 knots. She was a small ship, used for backup combat operations during World War II as well as for training. She was decommissioned in 1946. (Kodera)

96 The leading ace of World War I was the German Manfred von Richtofen, aka, the Red Baron, with whom many are familiar. His flying acumen and cold, calculating dedication to duty allowed him to amass 80 victories between September 1916 and April 1918. His airplane of choice was a Fokker DR1 Triplane painted in his signature gloss red, thus engendering his enigmatic title. (Kodera)

97 The man credited with shooting down the then-greatest flying ace of all time, the Red Baron, was Royal Flying Corps (RFC) Captain by the name of Roy Brown, doing so on 21 April 1918. Controversy surrounds the claim by the Canadian's squadron commander that Brown finished off von Richtofen since the baron crashed much later in the mission after having flown into the machine gun fire of Australian anti-aircraft gunner Sergeant Cedric Popkin, well inside Allied lines. (Kodera)

98 The leading ace for the Allies and number two in total kills was French pilot Captain Rene Fonck with 75 victories. A possible additional 25 unconfirmed would make him the leading ace, but

such are the fortunes of war. Known for his clinical professional-
ism, he applied mathematical principles to combat flying and engineering knowledge regarding the capabilities of the aircraft he flew.
Fonck took few chances, patiently stalking his intended victims
from higher altitudes. He then used deflection shooting with deadly
accuracy on enemy pilots at close range, resulting in an astonish-
ing economy of ammunition expended per kill. More often than
not, a single burst of less than five rounds from his SPAD's Vickers
machine gun was sufficient. (Kodera)

99 The largest airplane of World War I was the German bomber Sie-
mens-Schukert R VIII. The aircraft had a huge, 157-foot wingspan
and was powered by six engines buried in the fuselage linked to
four propellers between the wings, two tractor and two pusher. The
gross weight for this giant was 35,000-plus pounds (estimated), and
the top speed a lumbering 78 mph, again estimated. The bomber
never flew because it was completed in 1919, after the end of hos-
tilities. (Kodera)

100 Fledgling aviation was challenged for decades to conquer inhospitable natural expanses of the globe, and no prize loomed as
large as crossing the Atlantic Ocean. Immediately following the
accomplishments of the U.S. Navy NC flying boats in 1919 a month
earlier, the first nonstop crossing of the ocean was achieved by British aeronauts Captain John Alcock and Lieutenant Arthur Brown
on 14–15 June. They flew a Vickers Vimy bomber on a route that
spanned St. John's, Newfoundland, to Clifden, Ireland. Total flight
time totaled nearly 16 hours. (Kodera)

101 The spring and summer of 1919 was a busy time in the airspace
over the Atlantic as another set of firsts took place beginning
2 July: the first crossing from east to west (against the prevailing
winds) in the British airship R-34, which also marked the first
crossing by any lighter-than-air craft. The initial leg lasted until 6
July when the craft alighted at Roosevelt Field on Long Island, New
York. Two days later R-34 returned to Great Britain, which thus
completed the first roundtrip crossing of the Atlantic. The most

foreboding body of water for the Western world had finally been conquered by aviation. (Kodera)

102 The Dayton-Wright RB-1 (Rinehart-Bauman model one), known simply as the Dayton-Wright Racer, was a very advanced racing aircraft developed in the United States to participate in the 1920 Gordon Bennett Cup competition. Among its many forward looking features, the aircraft had a monocoque fuselage and high monoplane cantilever wing (built of solid balsa wood covered in plywood and linen) that incorporated mechanisms to vary its camber in flight by moving the leading and trailing edges. (Kodera)

103 The RB-1 also featured what is believed to be the first retractable undercarriage on an airplane. Its sleek, fish-like shape allowed it to fly at 200 mph. The pilot could not see forward and so designers incorporated large side view windows containing clear celluloid, which was flexible. The pilot entered through a hatch above the cockpit area. All in all, the RB-1 looked and acted more like an airplane from the 1930s than immediately after World War I. (Kodera)

104 The German Zeppelin D.I, or Zeppelin-Lindau D.I, or Zeppelin D.I, pick a title, was the first all-metal stressed-skin aircraft in the world, flying first in 1918. Stressing the metal rather than just laying duralumin over the base structure makes for far greater rigidity and, therefore, rugged strength throughout the airframe. The D.I was ordered into production just prior to the end of World War I and then canceled after 50 airframes were on the production line. The United States Navy and Army acquired specimens of the follow-on airplane, the Do H Falke, in order to assimilate the technology. Meanwhile, in Britain, the Short brothers of Ireland designed and flew the Short Silver Streak in 1919, the UK's answer to stressed skin aircraft. (Kodera)

105 Following World War I, aviation really started to blossom around the world. In the United States, for example, air transportation of passengers was becoming an established business concept, and one of the first airlines to operate in the states

was Aeromarine West Indies Airways, which operated from 1920 to 1924. It was reorganized as Aeromarine Airways in 1921. The fledgling air carrier enjoyed many firsts: the first U.S. international air mail service and first scheduled U.S. international passenger service (Key West to Havana, 1 November 1920); first total-service U.S. airline (passenger, mail, express cargo); perhaps the first in-flight movie (Chicago, August 1921); first airline baggage label (1921); and the first U.S. airline ticket office (Cleveland, July 1922). (Kodera)

"First Around the World" became the company slogan after the Douglas World Cruisers completed the first circumnavigation of the globe in 1924.

106 To meet the growing demand for air transportation, even in its infancy, a growing number of aircraft manufacturers were formed in the early 1920s. One such organization was the Davis-Douglas Company, founded by an MIT-educated

engineer named Donald Wills Douglas and a wealthy industrialist named David Davis. The fledgling airplane company built its first airplane in 1921, *The Cloudster*. The large biplane was powered by a Liberty V-12 engine and carried 12 passengers. *The Cloudster* was the world's first airplane to carry a useful load equal to its own empty weight. (Machat)

107 Human beings' physiological necessities remain a consideration even in flight. Therefore, thanks to the clever designers at de Havilland aircraft of England, their eight-passenger DH-34 biplane airliner of 1920 contained the world's first toilet installed on an airliner. The airplane type was used by the precursor to Imperial Airways (later BOAC and British Airways), Daimler Airlines, and flew daily trips between London and Paris. (Kodera)

108 The advent of aviation and accessibility to it by regular folks in the early twentieth century made it inevitable that an innovative young couple would be married aboard an airplane in flight. The first recorded event of this type took place on 31 May 1919 over Ellington Field, Texas, in a converted Handley Page bomber. The lucky couple was Lieutenant R. W. Meade and Miss Marjorie Dumont. The ceremony was officiated by the local Army chaplain. Over the ensuing years aviation has witnessed the Mile High Club of activities, including onboard births and anniversary celebrations between marrieds. No word yet on who claims to be the first to secure a divorce while stratospheric. (Kodera)

109 Weight is the enemy of an airplane; therefore, only so much human and inert cargo can be carried aloft. The same is unfortunately true of the fuel to run the engine. Thus, the answer would be in-flight refueling. The first successful venture in this regard took place on 27 June 1923 over San Diego, California. Pilots Captain L. H. Smith and Lieutenant J. P. Richter flew a de Havilland DH-4 while an additional de Havilland lowered a hose and pumped fuel to the receiver aircraft. (Kodera)

110 During the total solar eclipse of 10 September 1923, a British-designed, U.S. Naval Aircraft Factory–built Felixstowe FL-5 Flying Boat was one of a number of aircraft used to determine the centerline of an eclipse from the air. In addition to the FL-5, de Havilland DH-4Bs were flown at altitudes between 5,500 and 16,500 feet to take observations and images of the eclipse. (Veronico)

111 In the early days of flying, instrument navigation had yet to be invented. Visual landmarks were a pilot's only help in determining location. Limited to daytime flying, a way had to be found to enable aviating in the dark of night. Starting in August 1923, the lighted airway was introduced on its first route, Chicago, Illinois, to Cheyenne, Wyoming. Forty-two landing fields were augmented by 30 rotating beacons mounted high on derrick-style metal platforms. Each beacon could be seen for some 50 miles. Eventually the entire continental United States was illuminated. (Kodera)

112 The first nonstop transcontinental flight by airplane was accomplished 3 May 1923 by Army pilots O. G. Kelly and J. A. Macready. They were flying in a Fokker T-2, a big airplane for the time, which they had modified with an extra 725-gallon fuel tank and additional oil and water tanks. The flight started at Roosevelt Field in New York and ended at Rockwell Field in San Diego, California. Total elapsed time was 26 hours, 50 minutes, and it created a media frenzy for weeks afterward. The airplane was then delivered to the Smithsonian Institution, where it lives today. (Kodera)

113 What about flying for the first time from the West Coast of the U.S. to Hawaii? Surely someone could accomplish such a feat. Indeed, on 29 June 1927 the *Bird of Paradise*, a Fokker C-2 Trimotor of the United States Army, touched down in Honolulu after a 25-hour, 50-minute flight from Oakland, California. Pilots on the momentous 2,400-mile trip were Lieutenants Albert Hegenberger and Lester Maitland. (Kodera)

114 The vastness of the Pacific Ocean certainly seemed daunting to 1928 aviators, but one gallant man stepped up to tackle the challenge of the ultimate water-crossing trip. Captain Charles Kingsford Smith and his crew of the airplane known as the *Southern Cross* (named for the celestial star array) managed the first crossing of the Pacific Ocean by flying a Fokker F. VIIB-3 Trimotor from San Francisco, California, to Brisbane, Australia. It took them from 31 May to 9 June owing to four planned stops along the route. (Kodera)

115 Kingsford Smith was quite prolific in his long-distance flying: He also made the first nonstop crossing of the Australian mainland, the first flights between Australia and New Zealand, and the first eastward Pacific crossing from Australia to the United States. He also made a flight from Australia to London, setting a new record of 10.5 days. (Kodera)

116 On 10 October 1928, Air Service Captains St. Clair "Bill" Streett (1893–1970) and Albert W. Stevens (1866–1949) departed Wright Field, Ohio, to study how to determine an aircraft's exact altitude from photos it takes of the ground. Although they did not set an altitude record, the pair flew their Engineering Division XCO-5 biplane to a height of 37,854 feet. Built at McCook Field, this aircraft's wings were built for high-altitude flight. At more than 37,000 feet, the outside air temperature was -76 degrees Fahrenheit (-60 degrees C), and it took 1 hour and 40 minutes for the biplane to climb to altitude. (Veronico)

117 The first transcontinental airplane flight to cross the United States in under 24 hours occurred on 4 September 1922 and was flown by that inimitable pilot, James H. Doolittle. The airplane used in the flight was a modified DH-4 biplane from the 90th Aero Squadron and the westbound route was from Pablo Beach near Jacksonville, Florida, nonstop to Kelly Field in San Antonio, Texas, and thence nonstop to Rockwell Field near San Diego, California. Total elapsed time was 22 hours, 30 minutes. (Kodera)

Shown here with the speedy but volatile Gee Bee racer, James H. "Jimmy" Doolittle set many records and achieved fame in the 1930s.

118 The first time a pilot flew an airplane without reference to the outside world, essentially a "blind" flight, occurred on 24 September 1929 from Mitchel Field, Long Island, New York. Flying a modified Consolidated NY-2 biplane, James H. Doolittle flew by reference to a flight instrument mounted in the cockpit by its inventor, Elmer Sperry. This gyroscope-powered and -stabilized instrument was known as the first "artificial horizon" and became the single most important advancement in all-weather flying ever. (Kodera)

119 Wiley Post was famous for many aviation feats, including a round-the-world flight with Harold Gatty in 1931, a flight they completed in just eight days, and a solo round-the-world flight in 1933 in his classic Lockheed Vega *Winnie Mae*. He won the coveted National Air Race Derby from Los Angeles to Chicago in 9 hours, 9 minutes, 4 seconds. Post was also instrumental in developing a pressure suit used on a record-breaking flight into the stratosphere that pioneered the use of space suits in later altitude and speed records and went on to become the basis for those worn by astronauts. Sadly, he lost his life when he and humorist Will Rogers crashed near Point Barrow, Alaska, in 1935. (Lewis)

120 No one likes snarled traffic on the highways. To aid the motorist, airborne "eyes in the sky" monitor and report on congestion in cities all across the nation today. The first such bird's eye view on the radio was from a Goodyear blimp operating from Holmes Airport in Queens, New York, during the summer of 1936. (Kodera)

121 In 1936, the Douglas Dolphin first took to the air, ushering in a new era for twin-engine piston-powered seaplanes and amphibians operated for airline, military, and executive purposes With its twin Pratt & Whitney R-1340 Wasp radials mounted on struts high atop the wing and away from performance-robbing water spray, the Dolphin excelled operating from both oceans

and runways. Top speed was 156 mph with a range of 720 miles. (Machat)

Representing the best in sea and air transportation during the Golden Age, a Douglas Dolphin and Catalina steamer share dock space at San Pedro, California.

Chapter 2

Military Aviation

It is hard to fathom that today's digital-age military aircraft with all their electronic wizardry are direct descendants of what were essentially box kites with engines during World War I. In that conflict, bombardiers dropped their charges by hand from open cockpits. Today, a single B-2 Stealth Bomber possesses more lethality than multiple squadrons of World War II B-17s. The goal of high speed has come full circle, with stealth capability negating the need for aircraft that can fly three times the speed of sound. Most amazingly, since the early days of flight, technical advances developed in military aviation have entered the civilian arena. Just look at the side-stick controller, digital "glass cockpit," and GPS Nav system in a modern homebuilt aircraft next time you attend the EAA Airventure at Oshkosh.

THE WAR YEARS

122 The Douglas XB-19 was larger than the Boeing XB-15 and remained the largest bomber aircraft built for the U.S. Army Air Forces until 1946. Although it was obsolete before it was completed the USAAF wanted to use it for testing. Its first flight was on 27 June 1941 after more than three years under construction. The original Wright R-3350 engines were replaced with Allison V-3420 engines. Plans to convert it to a transport aircraft were never completed and it was eventually scrapped in 1949. Two huge main gear tires were saved; one is on display at the National Museum of the U.S. Air Force and the other at Hill AFB, Utah. (Lewis)

When asked to name their all-time favorite aircraft, Bob Hoover, Chuck Yeager, and "Pete" Everest all answered without hesitation, the F-86!

123 The first combat mission flown by the Boeing B-17 Flying Fortress took place on 8 July 1941 and was successfully carried out by camouflaged aircraft wearing the large red, white, and blue roundels of the Royal Air Force (RAF). The raid attacking strategic targets in Wilhelmshaven, Germany, was flown at 30,000 feet by aircraft assigned to the 90th Bomber Squadron R.A.F. The bombers, 20 of which were delivered to England and designated as Fortress I, were the equivalent of the Boeing B-17C, powered by four Wright R-1820 engines and carrying a payload of 4,000 pounds. (Machat)

124 One of the more unusual jobs the Douglas C-47 Skytrain was tasked to do during World War II was to be employed as a mobile laundry. Washing machines were mounted in the cabin of the C-47 aircraft so it could fly from one location to another allowing troops in the field who had no other means available to get their clothes washed. (Lewis)

125 The man who shot down a Mitsubishi Zero fighter with a .45-caliber pistol was Army Air Forces Lieutenant Owen J. Baggett of the 7th Bomb Group. On 31 March 1943 his B-24 Liberator was attacked by a flight of Zeros over Burma. Baggett's crew was ordered to bail out from the stricken bomber, and while hanging from their parachutes, were shot at with two men killed by the same marauding Zeros. Baggett, shot in the arm, played dead while descending. The offending Zero pilot wanted to verify his dastardly deed and so slowed to near stall speed to survey Baggett in the straps. Floating past the Lieutenant, the pilot opened his canopy for a closer look, at which time Baggett sprang to life, shooting four rounds into the cockpit of the Zero. One round hit the pilot in the head and the Zero spiraled out of control and crashed, making Owen Baggett the only man in World War II who shot down an airplane in midair with a pistol. (Kodera)

126 Not every country used the same name for aircraft engine types. During the 1930s and 1940s, Germans referred to piston engines as *Ottos*, after Nikolaus Otto, inventor of the first practical internal-combustion engine. Similarly, during World War II,

German designers referred to ramjet engines as *Lorin* jet tubes, after the engine's inventor, Frenchman René Lorin (1913). The British referred to ramjet engines as *athodyds*, a contraction of AeroThermODynamicDuct. (Veronico)

127 In the process of naming airplane types, it is inevitable that different airplanes may coincidentally wind up with the same name, especially over several generations. A number of World War II Army Air Corps and U.S. Army Air Forces aircraft names were re-used years later. These would include the Douglas P-70 night fighter version of the A-20 Havoc, and the Lockheed F-117 first-generation stealth fighter, both formally named Nighthawk. (Lewis)

128 Another example of the "name game" would be North American's dive-bomber variant of the P-51 Mustang and the McDonnell Douglas (now Boeing) AH-64 attack gunship helicopter, both named Apache. (Lewis)

129 Our final example of the recycling of aircraft names includes the World War II Curtiss A-25 USAAF version of the Helldiver and the Rockwell executive light-twin made famous by air show legend R. A. "Bob" Hoover, the "Shrike," and the World War II Medivac transport, Howard NH, and its Jet Age counterpart, the Douglas C-9B, both named "Nightingale" to reflect their respective mercy missions. (Lewis)

130 Bed Check Charlie or Washing Machine Charlie were names given to enemy aircraft that flew over U.S. troops at night to conduct reconnaissance, spot artillery, drop flares to assist their ground troops, or just to harass U.S. personnel by making it difficult to obtain adequate rest with the constant noise. When twin-engine aircraft were employed they would intentionally adjust their engines to run out-of-synchronization to make the engine noise even more disturbing. When night fighter aircraft became available they helped in eliminating the harassment. (Lewis)

131 General Lesley James McNair was an American U.S. Army officer who served during both World War I and World War II. He was the highest ranking American officer killed during World War II. Employment of heavy bombers in close air support of infantry operations as part of the Battle of Normandy proved to be ill advised. He died from friendly fire when an 8th Air Force bomb landed in his foxhole. General Eisenhower refused to employ the use of heavy bombers against tactical targets for the remainder of the European campaign. (Lewis)

132 The phrase "give him the whole nine yards" is attributed to the 27-foot length of ammunition belts in World War II fighter aircraft. When someone said "give him the whole nine yards" it meant you were supposed to empty your guns and use every round of ammunition available to shoot him down. (Lewis)

133 Ammunition belts were loaded with a tracer bullet in every fifth position. They were supposed to help aim guns at enemy aircraft. In reality the trajectory of tracer bullets was different from the rest of the ammunition, so when tracers were hitting the target, 80 percent of the bullets were missing. Tracers also alerted an enemy that someone was shooting at them. The practice of loading a row of tracers at the end of each belt not only announced to the pilot that he was out of ammunition but also told enemy pilots he was out of ammunition! (Lewis)

134 Of the 7,377 Avro Lancaster bombers built during World War II almost half (3,299) were lost. That's more than 23,000 crewmen who either bailed out or were killed in action while flying mostly night operations. As bad as losses were during trench warfare in World War I, this wasn't much better. (Lewis)

135 Boeing B-29 Superfortress *Kee Bird* was forced to make an emergency landing in Northwestern Greenland after becoming lost well north of the Arctic Circle during a reconnaissance mission. Although all crew members were successfully rescued, the aircraft was abandoned. In 1994 a crew flew to the site to restore and recover

the aircraft. Progress was made during the first summer, but it was necessary to abandon the project when a crew member became ill and bad weather moved into the area. During the second summer the B-29 was almost ready for flight when a fuel tank used to supply the auxiliary power unit (APU) broke loose from its mount and the resultant fire gutted the aircraft. (Lewis)

136 The twin-engine Douglas B-23 Dragon and de Havilland DH.84 Dragon share the same name. (Lewis)

137 The Japanese Aichi M6A Seiran aircraft, powered by a German Daimler-Benz engine, was designed to be launched from a submarine that had an aircraft hangar attached to its hull. The Seiran was fitted with folding wings and empennage so it could be enclosed entirely within the submarine hangar. Once removed from the hangar and unfolded it was supposed to bomb the Panama Canal. The aircraft were operational but the special submarines were never completed before the war ended. One example of the Aichi M6A Seiran is part of the Smithsonian museum's aircraft collection. (Lewis)

138 Developed as an aerial troop transport to carry personnel and supplies by air, thus avoiding the shipping lanes being attacked by submarine, the Hughes-Kaiser HK-1 "Hercules" was the largest

Powered by eight Pratt & Whitney R-4360 radial engines producing 3,500 hp each, the Hughes HK-1 flew for one mile on 2 November 1947.

airplane in the world at the time. Constructed from laminated wood to save on precious war materials, the mammoth flying boat was nicknamed the "Spruce Goose" despite being built out of birch. The craft's 300-foot 11-inch wingspan is still the longest of any aircraft ever flown. (Machat)

139 Anyone who either knew or worked for Howard Hughes was well aware of his penchant for 100-percent perfection. Despite the immense size and sheer complexity of the eight-engine HK-1, typical Hughes Aircraft Company workmanship and attention to detail was employed to the fullest with all the many thousands of single-slotted screws used to fasten the wood floor panels in the main cargo cabin installed so that every single slot aligned perfectly fore-and-aft. (Machat)

140 USAAF Consolidated B-24D Liberator *Lady Be Good* and its crew were thought to be lost in the Mediterranean Sea while returning from their first bombing mission against targets in Naples, Italy, from Soluch field in Libya. Years later the aircraft was discovered virtually intact in the Libyan desert by a British Petroleum survey crew. An investigation revealed the new crew had overflown Soluch field and continued out across the Libyan Desert until their fuel was exhausted, at which time they were forced to bail out. All the crew members perished while trying to walk to safety. The bodies of all but one of the crew were recovered. (Lewis)

141 Boeing's Model 299 (predecessor to the production B-17) had not been officially named yet when the prototype aircraft was rolled out of Boeing's Seattle plant in 1935. *Seattle Times* reporter Richard Williams saw the giant airplane bristling with guns that could fire in every direction to protect the mammoth bomber and exclaimed, "Why, it's a flying fortress!" Boeing executives liked the name and immediately filed for its trademark. So began a legend! (Lewis)

142 Although the Boeing B-17 Flying Fortress named *Memphis Belle* was credited with being the first U.S. bomber to complete 25 missions, research has shown that it was actually the third. The first bomber to reach the magic number of 25 missions was Consolidated B-24 Liberator *Hot Stuff*, but the aircraft was lost when it crashed in Iceland. A second Boeing B-17, *Hell's Angels*, completed 25 missions six days before *Memphis Belle*, but due to the crash of *Hot Stuff* and the impact of using the name *Hell's Angels*, *Memphis Belle* was selected for the honor. (Lewis)

143 Companies with no aviation experience have often been responsible for significant developments in aviation. The Link Trainer, a device used during World War II to teach instrument flying to thousands of student pilots, was developed in the 1920s by a piano and organ manufacturer. Pneumatic organ bellows were used to move a simulated airplane in response to control inputs from its student pilot. Regarded as a novelty at first, the Link Trainer became standard equipment at every flight school in the United States and most allied nations. A total of nearly 10,000 units were produced during the war. (Frankel)

144 Harvard, Yale, and Cornell (AT-6, NA-64, and PT-26). In Canadian service North American's AT-6 Texan was known as a Harvard, NA-64s as Yale, and PT-26s were designated Cornell for use by the British Commonwealth Air Training Plan. (Lewis)

145 Speaking of British and Canadian names for American military aircraft, the British name for the famed Douglas C-47 Skytrain

The Douglas C-47 was named by General Dwight D. Eisenhower as one of the five most important machines in the Allied victory of World War II.

was "Dakota." A fitting moniker by itself, there was also a double-meaning if that word was considered an acronym: DAKOTA also stood for <u>D</u>ouglas <u>A</u>ircraft <u>KO</u>mpany <u>T</u>ransport <u>A</u>ircraft. (Lewis)

146 The Boeing XB-15 was the largest aircraft built in America when it was completed in 1937. During its test phase it managed to lift a 31,205-pound payload to 8,200 feet altitude and was capable of flying 5,000 miles at 152 mph. It was converted into a transport aircraft and flew numerous relief and cargo missions in support of the war effort. When spare parts were no longer available it was ordered to be scrapped at Albrook Field in Panama, its engines and internal parts removed along with its vertical stabilizer and rudder. The remaining airframe was deposited at Diablo dump. (Lewis)

147 An early model of the Boeing B-17D Flying Fortress, the *Swoose*, is the oldest surviving B-17 aircraft in existence. It still has the shark-fin tail and original belly turret that preceded later models of the B-17. The *Swoose* flew many missions in the early days following Pearl Harbor before more modern versions of the Boeing B-17 arrived in the Pacific Theater. The pilot's daughter, actress Swoosie Kurts, was named after the aircraft. (Lewis)

148 The Messerschmitt Me 323 Gigant was a six-engine German transport aircraft originally designed as a glider (Me 321). Originally planned for the invasion of England it saw service in support of Operation Barbarosa in Russia. With a wingspan of 181 feet, powered by Gnome-Rhone engines, and capable of carrying 130 troops or 10 to 12 tons of cargo, it was the largest aircraft to see service during World War II. (Lewis)

149 The first jet-powered airplane to fly was the German Heinkel He 178, on 27 August 1939. Erich Warsitz was the test pilot of the privately funded project from designer Ernst Heinkel and the airfield was at Marienehe. A young designer by the name of Hans von Ohain developed and patented the turbine jet engine in Germany in 1936 and a version known as the HeS 3 was the powerplant used on the -178. At that time, and as is customary of most any jet engine, which is noted to burn just about anything, the fuel used was diesel oil. (Kodera)

150 The Heinkel He 176 rocket plane was the first airplane in the world to be fitted with an ejection seat. The first production aircraft to have ejection seats from the outset of design were the Heinkel He 280 jet fighter and the He 219 Uhu night fighter. The first recorded live emergency ejection from an airplane took place on 13 January 1943 from one of the Heinkel 280s. (Kodera)

151 At the end of World War II, England was undoubtedly the world leader in turbine technology and its esteemed manufacturer, Rolls-Royce, was the most prominent producer of turbine engines. Many early American jet engines were license-built versions of British design. (Frankel)

152 The Rolls-Royce Nene was so highly regarded that the U.S. Navy purchased the license and funded the development cost for Pratt & Whitney to mass produce the engine as the J42 in the United States. Further refinements by Rolls-Royce led to the Tay engine, which produced a 25-percent increase in thrust. Pratt & Whitney manufactured the Tay as the J48, and in 1954 a J48-powered Grumman F9F-6 Cougar broke the sound barrier, one of the rare times that a centrifugal flow turbojet flew beyond Mach 1. (Frankel)

153 In 1950 the Tay turbojet was used to conduct the first successful afterburning tests in the prototype Lockheed YF-94C. The joint venture with Rolls-Royce allowed Pratt & Whitney to enter the jet engine business quickly and gain important jet experience at minimum risk. Ultimately, Pratt & Whitney produced 5,250 Rolls-Royce–designed engines for the U.S. Navy and Air Force. (Frankel)

154 Although the Boeing B-47 Stratojet is often considered the first six-engine swept wing jet bomber, the German/Russian OKB-1/Junkers EF-131, produced in both Germany and the USSR, was first. Unlike the B-47 the OKB-1/EF-131 wing was swept forward and

the engines housed in two pylons below the wings that contained three engines each. Components of the Junkers Ju 287 V2 and V3 were obtained by the Russians and used in the construction of the OKB-1 jet bomber. (Lewis)

155 The famous U.S. Eighth Air Force of World War II was constituted specifically for the war effort in January 1942, in Savannah, Georgia. After positioning aircraft, men, and material overseas in England, the Air Force was ready to fly its first mission of the war, using its own aircraft, on 17 August 1942. A flight of 12 B-17s flew a bombing mission to Rouen, France, to attack railway yards. The mightiest air force of all time was now in business. (Kodera)

156 The first time American forces bombed Germany was 27 January 1943. Using proven daylight bombing techniques, which included the top secret Norden bombsight, the aircraft attacked Wilhelmshaven and Emden. (Kodera)

157 The first use of instruments and equipment designed to identify and drop bombs on a target under cloud cover took place on 27 September 1943 when Eighth Air Force bombers attacked Emden, Germany. (Kodera)

158 The single largest bombing mission ever to take place during aerial warfare commenced on Christmas Eve 1944 and involved aircraft from the Eighth Air Force. More than 2,000 B-17 and B-24 aircraft partook in the raids and were escorted and augmented by more than 900 fighters. Targets included rail yards and communications centers behind enemy lines. (Kodera)

159 At the height of World War II, the total weight of bombs dropped by the prolific Eighth Air Force for one month, June 1944, was a record 60,504 tons. This nearly equaled the total tonnage dropped by the Luftwaffe on Britain over a *three-year* period, 1940–1942. (Kodera)

160 The critical factor in bomber escort by fighter aircraft in World War II was range. To see just how far aeronautical design and innovation had come in a very short period of time, consider these stats: In 1942 the Republic P-47 managed to reach approximately 200 miles distance from its bases in England. By spring 1944, North American P-51 Mustangs were ranging over a distance of 800-plus miles and back from British facilities. This made strategic bombing completely viable and allowed U.S. strategic forces to affect the German homeland directly, helping end the war earlier than otherwise would have been possible. (Kodera)

161 The most produced combat aircraft of World War II was the Russian Ilyushin IL-2 Sturmovik fighter: 36,183 airframes were constructed. (Kodera)

162 The most produced combat airplane built in the United States during World War II, and sixth most produced worldwide, was the Consolidated B-24/PB4Y Liberator/Privateer at 18,482 airframes. The B-24 family of airplanes was constructed at both Fort Worth, Texas, and Willow Run, Michigan. The Liberator was manufactured in greater quantity than the more romanticized Boeing B-17, contrary to popular belief. (Kodera)

163 The total number of aircraft produced in the United States during World War II was slightly greater than 276,000 airframes. This staggering amount of aeronautical product outstripped all the other involved countries around the globe and secured the hard-won victory for the Allied powers. (Kodera)

164 The Martin B-26 Marauder and Douglas A-26 Invader were both twin-engine medium bombers used in World War II. The Martin B-26s were retired after the war, but the Douglas A-26s were mothballed and used again in Korea and Vietnam. When the "A" attack designation was dropped, the Invaders became B-26s. Since bomber aircraft were not allowed in Vietnam during the early days of the war, the Douglas B-26s were re-designated as A-26s. Later in the war when other bomber aircraft were introduced, the

Invaders once again became B-26s. To this day, the two aircraft are often confused. (Lewis)

165 Some Boeing B-17 Flying Fortress and Consolidated B-24 Liberator aircraft were painted with polka dots or stripes in bright colors and then used as formation assembly aircraft to join bomber group aircraft over England before proceeding to their targets. The distinctive paint made it easier to identify the lead aircraft when assembling a group of bombers. (Lewis)

166 A Douglas C-47 crew had a bad oil leak in one engine over the Pacific Ocean during World War II but managed to land on one engine at a forward airfield. They repaired the leak but no oil was available, and they would be stuck on this atoll until oil could be found. The mess tent was serving rice with grape jelly! The cook said the only thing he had plenty of besides rice and jelly was grapefruit juice and Wesson oil. The news made them all wonder if it would work. After their tank was filled with Wesson oil they started engines then took off for home. (Lewis)

167 The first U.S. Army Air Forces bomber to reach the coveted 25 missions was the Consolidated B-24 Liberator *Hot Stuff*. The aircraft was subsequently lost when it crashed in Iceland while returning home from England. Due to the tragic news of the crash it was decided that *Hot Stuff* should not be used in recognition of completing 25 missions and the honor was given to *Memphis Belle*. Andrews AFB, Maryland, was named in honor of Lt Gen. Andrews, who died in the crash of *Hot Stuff*. (Lewis)

168 Propellers on twin-engine aircraft that rotate in opposite directions are called counter-rotating propellers. The advantage of using counter-rotating propellers is the elimination of torque, or P-factor, that causes an aircraft to swerve from flying straight ahead when power is applied. One of the best-known aircraft with this feature is the Lockheed P-38 Lightning, and even the original *Wright Flyer* used counter-rotating technology. The modern-day Bell Boeing V-22 Osprey also uses counter-rotating propellers. (Lewis)

Lockheed's P-38 Lightning was the most successful U.S. twin-engine fighter of World War II, helping many pilots achieve ace status.

169 Contra-rotating propellers are a combination of two propellers mounted on the same engine that rotate in opposite directions. They are often employed when an engine is capable of developing more power than a single propeller can absorb or the ground clearance when using a larger diameter single propeller is impractical. Examples of contra-rotating propellers can be found on the Northrop XB-35 flying wing, Fisher P-75 Eagle, and both the Lockheed XFV-1 Salmon and Convair XFY-1 Pogo VTOL aircraft. (Lewis)

170 How about a four-blade balsa-wood propeller with no pitch to the blades whatsoever? Yes, absolutely true! The catch, of course, is that it was only used as a decoy, mounted to the nose of the then super-secret Bell XP-59 Airacomet, America's first jet-powered aircraft, flown in October 1942 at Muroc. When the airplane was towed to and from its hangar adjacent to Rogers Dry Lake, that wooden prop was affixed either in plain view or under a tarpaulin, all to fool prying eyes on the new jet. (Machat)

171 The XP-59 was not only the first U.S. jet, it was America's first (and only) open-cockpit jet aircraft as well. Although the pilot flew in his fully enclosed station, provisions for a Flight Test Engineer station were built into the aircraft's nose cone complete with a small windscreen reminiscent of a World War I fighter. NACA Engineer Jack Russell was the first to strap on a parachute and occupy what had to be a cold and windy environment while airborne. Bell Aircraft's CEO Larry Bell was flown in that open cockpit as well. (Machat)

172 Alternating black and white invasion stripes were painted on Allied aircraft just prior to the Normandy Invasion (D-Day) to prevent Allied aircraft from being fired upon by friendly forces. The stripes were applied to the top and bottom of both wings and around the aft fuselage. Although the stripes proved effective for the D-Day invasion, they became a dangerous legacy afterward since it became easy for German forces to spot Allied aircraft from a distance. (Lewis)

173 A total of 821 C-47 Skytrain aircraft were used to drop airborne troops and tow gliders across the English Channel in support of the Normandy Invasion on D-Day, 6 June 1944. Of these, 800 returned from the mission to fly another day. (Lewis)

174 The dreaded German Messerschmitt Me 264 was theoretically a six-engine long-range "Amerika Bomber," allegedly capable of bombing New York City. The Luftwaffe ultimately decided it wasn't worth the effort and the aircraft was never employed. (Lewis)

175 RAF pilots strapped kegs of beer to the bottom of both wings of a Supermarine Spitfire fighter and climbed to altitude to cool the beer when no other means was available to lower the temperature. The aircraft would climb to altitude, loiter long enough to ensure cooling, and then descend to a waiting crowd. (Lewis)

176 The Fairey Aviation Company's T.S.R. I Swordfish aircraft was a fabric-covered biplane torpedo bomber with a 645-hp Bristol Pegasus IIM radial engine. Because it was capable of several other duties besides torpedo delivery (including dive bombing), it earned the nickname Stringbag. Even though the 90-mph Swordfish was obsolescent at the beginning of World War II, it served throughout the conflict with distinction. Among many other accomplishments, it was instrumental in sinking the German battleship *Bismarck* by damaging its rudder and leaving it vulnerable to further attack by British warships. (Lewis)

To this date, the world's fastest multi-engine piston-powered airplane remains the Luftwaffe's "pusher-puller" Dornier Do 335, which was capable of a 475-mph top speed.

177 The Dornier Do 335 Pfeil (German for "Arrow"), a World War II twin-engine heavy fighter, was the fastest piston-powered fighter of World War II and the fastest multi-engine piston-powered aircraft ever flown. With its conventional engine installation in the nose and a pusher engine in the tail, the ultra-streamlined aircraft was capable of a top speed of 475 mph. The AVRO CF-105 Arrow was a Canadian-built twin-engine delta-wing jet fighter interceptor prototype capable of Mach 2-plus speed that shared the same name as the Dornier twin. (Lewis)

178 Because of its intense secrecy, the He-178 was initially *not* listed officially as the first jet in the world to fly. That honor went to the Italian Caproni Campini N.1 motorjet, an ungainly looking thing that took to the air on 27 August 1940 and was pronounced primary by the *Fédération Aéronautique Internationale*. Mario de Bernardi was the pilot that day and for most N.1 flying thereafter. The N.1 was called a motorjet because, unlike most jet engines, the fan compressor in this airplane was operated by a liquid-cooled piston aircraft engine. (Kodera)

179 The only American combat airplane to fly missions in three wars was the Douglas A-26/B-26 Invader. Its first use was with the 9th Air Force in Europe in November 1944; the airplane concluded its tours of duty in the Vietnam War in Southeast Asia. (Kodera)

180 Throughout aviation history, design crossover from military aircraft to commercial airliners, and vice versa, has been used to great advantage. First there was the Douglas DC-2, which became the Army C-39, and during World War II, Douglas built the C-47 Skytrain transport from the 1935 DC-3 airliner. In turn, the four-engine military C-54 of Berlin Airlift fame became the DC-4 airliner that helped establish many global commercial airlines in the postwar years. (Machat)

181 On 22–23 March 1944, 74 B-25s of the 340th Bomb Group at Pompeii Air Field, Italy, were damaged so badly they had to be stricken from active records—14 more were eventually repaired. It was an "air raid" when Mount Vesuvius erupted, raining down rocks and volcanic debris on the base 5 miles away, accounting for more USAAF aircraft destroyed than in any single enemy action during World War II. At Pearl Harbor, 7 December 1941, 64 planes were lost; on the Regensburg-Schweinfurt mission, 17 August 1943, 60 planes were lost; and in bombing Ploesti, 1 August 1943, 54 planes were lost as our troops heard Nazi broadcaster Axis Sally report "the 340th was knocked out of the war" in "a clear sign that God had sided with the Axis." However, the 340th moved to Paestum, 40 miles away, was re-equipped and back in action five days later, and Vesuvius settled down to its picturesque former self. (Lewis)

182 On Sunday, 28 July 1945, a twin-engine North American B-25 Mitchell bomber crashed into the Empire State Building in downtown Manhattan. Pilot William Smith Jr. became disoriented in heavy fog on a flight from Bedford Army Air Field, Massachusetts, to Newark airport in New Jersey, mistaking the East River for the Hudson, thinking he was over the flatlands of New Jersey. Instead, he flew into the building between the 78th and 80th floors. The 14 casualties included the B-25 passengers and crew and civilians working in the Empire State Building. Several civilians killed were women employed by the National Catholic Welfare Conference, which had offices on the 79th floor. (Lewis)

183 It is both sobering and somewhat unbelievable that many operational and/or prototype aircraft built for the U.S. Navy were either lost in accidents or scrapped at the end of their careers with not even one example left anywhere in the world today. Paramount among these aircraft types are the Lockheed R6V-1 Constitution transport, Convair R3Y Tradewind flying boat, and Vought XF8U-3 Super Crusader, with not one airplane having survived! (Lewis)

184 Many prototype and operational aircraft built for the U.S. Army Air Corps (pre-1942) and U.S. Army Air Forces (1942–1947) are now extinct, with not even one example left anywhere in the world. Notable among the aircraft types lost to either accident or the scrap pile are the Boeing XB-15 and Douglas XB-19 experimental bomber prototypes, the Convair B-32 Dominator, and Douglas C-74 Globemaster. (Lewis)

185 The McDonnell XP-57 Moonbat was a radical design offered in response to a request for a long-range interceptor. Early Models I and II were rejected, which led to the Model IIa, which featured twin Allison inverted V-12 engines. The engines suffered from overheating and failed to provide the anticipated power output. The XP-67 reached a confirmed top speed of only 405 mph, well below the planned 500-mph speed that was expected. The single prototype suffered an engine fire and efforts to save it were unsuccessful. The prototype was abandoned and the second example was never completed. (Lewis)

U.S NAVY/MARINE CORPS IN WORLD WAR II

186 The Navy always understood the value of airplanes as scout craft and welcomed them aboard the large ships of the day prior to and through World War II. The concept being a sound one, airplane carriage was even attempted on submarines. The first such experimental use was in 1923, enacted at the Washington Navy Yard near the nation's capital. The airplane chosen was the Cox-Klemin XS-1, a diminutive aircraft with folding wings and pontoons, designed as such to fit in a watertight capsule or "hangar" on the deck of the sub. The Imperial Japanese Navy was also quite enamored of the idea and actively engaged in its use during World War II. (Kodera)

187 In the 1930s, the Navy kept a dedicated Douglas RD-2 Dolphin amphibian at Anacostia Naval Air Station for special services for the president, but Franklin Delano Roosevelt never flew in it. A Douglas C-54 named the "Sacred Cow" and discretely fitted with an elevator for the wheelchair-bound president became the first of a long fleet of special presidential aircraft, a tradition that has continued to this day. (Kodera)

188 The fuel tanks of Shigenori Nishikaichi's Mitsubishi A6M Zero fighter that attacked Pearl Harbor on 7 December 1941 had been punctured during the raid. When he realized he didn't have enough fuel to reach his carrier *Hiryu* he elected to land on Niihau Island off the northern coast of Oahu. His intelligence

briefing indicated the island was uninhabited, but as he approached for landing he spotted buildings and a village. The Niihauans captured him after he crash-landed in a freshly plowed field, and although some of Japanese ancestry tried to help, others intervened and he was eventually killed. (Lewis)

189 Think the United States mainland was never attacked in World War II? Think again, as two distinct aerial missions from the Japanese submarine I-25 allowed its deck-launched Yokosuka E-14Y Glen to disperse a total of nine phosphorus bombs on the woods of Brookings, Oregon. On 9 and 25 September, IJN pilot Nobuo Fujita attempted to start forest fires near the coastal Oregon hamlet, but thanks to quick response from the town fire department, the flames were knocked down immediately. Following the war Fujita visited the town and apologized for his sorties. On a later trip he was made an honorary town citizen. (Kodera)

190 The first official Navy Flight Demonstration Team, the Three Flying Fish, was created in 1930. Their demonstration program, including loops and rolls, was flown with the wing struts on their aircraft tied together with ribbons from takeoff to landing. The team consisted of LTs Frederick Trapnell, Matt Gardner, and Putt Storrs flying Curtiss F6C-4 Hawk biplanes. (Caruso)

191 The process for naming U.S. Navy aircraft was such that different airplanes coincidentally wound up with the same name over the generations. Several World War II naval aircraft names were re-used years later, including the Consolidated PB2Y patrol bomber and 1960s Convair 990 jetliner, both named the "Coronado," and the Curtiss SNC-1 dive bomber and McDonnell F3H-1 carrier-based jet fighter, both named the "Demon." (Lewis)

192 Other examples of the Navy aircraft "name game" would be Grumman's famed TBM torpedo-bomber and the still-born McDonnell Douglas (now Boeing) A-12 attack jet, both named "Avenger." (Lewis)

193 Our final example of the recycling of Navy aircraft names includes a pair of experimental aircraft: the twin-engine, twin-tail World War II Grumman XF5F-1 and Douglas research aircraft the D-558-2, both named "Skyrocket" to reflect their respective advanced performance. (Lewis)

194 The Grumman F8F Bearcat, first flown on 21 August 1944, was originally designed with wingtips that would break off if the aircraft exceeded predetermined G-loads during maneuvers, thereby alleviating excessive stress on the rest of the wing structure. If only one wingtip broke away, the pilot could jettison the remaining wingtip by means of explosive bolts to keep control forces balanced. This design feature was eventually removed. (Veronico)

195 During World War II, QANTAS PBY Catalinas operated from Western Australia to Lake Koggala in Ceylon and later Karachi, where connections with BOAC aircraft could be made between Australia and England. The 3,500-nautical-mile flights took from 27 to 33 hours and two sunrises were observed on each flight. They were the longest nonstop air routes flown at the time. Passengers who flew on flights that exceeded 24 hours were given a certificate: the Rare and Secret Order of the Double Sunrise. By the time the operation ended on 18 July 1945, 271 crossings of the Indian Ocean had been completed. (Lewis)

196 The last biplane combat aircraft produced in the United States was the Curtiss SBC Helldiver, which was in production starting in 1934 and continued in Navy service even as World War II was breaking out. (Kodera)

197 Ensign George Henry Gay Jr. was the only survivor out of 30 men from Torpedo Squadron VT-8 who flew their Douglas TBD Devastator torpedo bombers from the aircraft carrier USS *Hornet* (CV-8) against Japanese ships during the Battle of Midway. The U.S. Navy managed to sink four Japanese aircraft carriers during the battle, which changed the course of the war in the Pacific, but at a terrible cost to VT-8. (Lewis)

198 The name for the aircraft carrier USS *Shangri-La* (CV-38) was coined well outside normal channels for naming U.S. Navy ships. They were normally named after battles or former U.S. Navy ships. This ship received its name as a result of President Roosevelt's response to the press when asked where the Doolittle Raiders launched from in order to bomb Japan. He told the press the Raiders launched their B-25 Mitchell bombers "from Shangri-La." The *Shangri-La* was involved in several campaigns during World War II in the Pacific and went on to serve again during the Vietnam War. (Lewis)

The North American P-51D was one of two USAAF aircraft evaluated for carrier operations. Neither was selected, however.

199 A North American P-51 Mustang was carrier qualified aboard the USS *Shangri La* by Navy test pilot CAPT Bob Elder in November 1944. In a clever bit of marketing prowess, the Navy renamed the P-51 the "Seahorse" for its brief naval operations. A North American PBJ (Navy B-25) and Grumman F7F-1 Tigercat were also flown out to the carrier off the Atlantic coast from the

naval base at Philadelphia for quals that day, but none of the three aircraft were ever adopted for carrier-based service. (Machat)

200 When the American aircraft industry responded to the clarion call of World War II it did so in a full-throated way, stunning our enemies with our production prowess. Of singular importance was the fighter airplane, and one of the absolute stand-outs on that list was the Vought F4U Corsair for the Navy/Marine Corps. Interestingly, the Corsair holds the record for the longest running production of any of the war-designed airframes. First flying in May 1940, the last airplane off the line emerged from the Dallas factory in December 1952. As with many other types from the previous war, the F4U was utilized in the Korean conflict. (Kodera)

201 World War II saw a major paradigm shift in the minds of the old and entrenched "Battleship Navy" officers and planners. The service discovered that air power was the key to naval supremacy, with this hard-learned lesson applied for the first time in earnest at the Battle of the Coral Sea in the South Pacific. Here was a naval battle between ships, to be sure, and on the open sea (blue water ops), but the weapons used to attack and render the enemy moot were airplanes, hurled effectively by both sides at each other. Each country lost ships, including aircraft carriers, but the Japanese suffered a greater overall loss and so the United States is credited with the victory. (Kodera)

202 Non-rigid airships had been a part of naval aviation since the World War I period and they shined brightly in World War II, having sunk/deterred/helped sink many German submarines operating in both the Atlantic and Mediterranean. Not an intuitive concept of battle strategy, blimps were surprisingly adroit at protecting convoys and shipping in general. As verification of their resiliency in combat, only one blimp was lost during the war due to being shot down. (Kodera)

203 The airship K-74 was operating at night along the coastline of Florida on 18 July 1943 and spotted on its radar a surfaced

German submarine, the U-134. Unfortunately, the sub also saw the airship and opened fire using its deck gun. The stricken craft deflated to the surface of the ocean never having gotten its depth charge loosed toward the sub. All but one crew member was recovered the next day; the submarine was eventually destroyed in August 1943 near Spain. (Kodera)

204 Fighter pilots are a different breed from the rest of aviators. One of the best examples of one of these knights of the air was Navy CDR David McCampbell, Air Group Commander of VF-15 flying Grumman Hellcats from the USS *Essex*. He holds the distinction of being the one American ace to have downed the most airplanes in a single day, five Mitsubishi A6M Zekes, two Mitsubishi A6M3 Hamps, and two Mitsubishi Ki-43 Oscars during the Battle of Leyte Gulf, 24 October 1944. He was presented with the Medal of Honor personally by President Franklin Roosevelt. Other medals and awards in the man's naval career included the Navy Cross, the Silver Star, the Air Medal and the Distinguished Flying Cross. (Kodera)

205 Old habits die hard, and in the air arm of the United States Navy, the biplane was the enduring symbol of prewar naval aviation. So the question naturally arises, which airplane hung on to be the last biplane fighter for the Navy? It turns out that the Curtiss SBC Helldiver owns the distinction. First flying in 1934, production of the final model finished in 1941. Biplanes did continue arriving in Navy inventory throughout the war in the form of Grumman J2F Ducks for peripheral combat chores and the Naval Air Factory N3N basic trainer for pilots. (Kodera)

206 Who was Japan's first kamikaze (devine wind) pilot of World War II? Navy Lieutenant Yukio Seki formed the first unit in October 1944 and successfully attacked and sank the American aircraft carrier *St. Lo* on the 25th of that month. The Mitsubishi Zero fighter he used for the deadly deed was equipped with a single 250-pound bomb. (Kodera)

207 Naval aviation in World War II was nearly synonymous with the name *Grumman*. After a string of successes over a nearly 20-year period, the "Ironworks" at Bethpage, Long Island, cranked out yet another winner with its F7F Tigercat. The F7F was the first twin-engine fighter accepted by the Navy and was also the first operational Navy fighter with tricycle landing gear. Utilizing the consummate radial engine of our time, the Pratt & Whitney R-2800, the latest cat from Grumman had a top speed of nearly 460 mph. Because of its size and speed, the airplane just didn't fit the *Midway* class carriers of the late war period and so became an outstanding land-based fighter with the Marine Corps, specializing in nighttime operations. (Kodera)

208 Grumman Aircraft holds another World War II distinction: the most airplanes produced in a single month. The builders at Bethpage, New York, constructed 605 F6F Hellcats in the month of March 1945, a record that stands to this day. The Arsenal of Democracy surely had hit its stride when a factory turned out almost one airplane per hour! (Kodera)

U.S. AIR FORCE

209 Following World War II, the Army Air Forces found themselves so distant from their U.S. Army mother command that a vocal movement sprang up to separate the air branch from the rest of the Army. On 18 September 1947 hopes became reality when President Truman signed the order creating the United States Air Force as a separate branch of the U.S. Armed Forces. (Kodera)

210 Designed too late to see action in World War II, one of the first new postwar aircraft for the fledgling U.S. Air Force was the North American F-82 Twin Mustang. At first thought to be simply two P-51s joined with a common center wing section, nothing could be further from the truth. Although visually similar in appearance, the F-82 was powered by twin inline Allison engines, whereas the Mustang had a Rolls-Royce Merlin

powerplant. The pilot occupied the left fuselage's cockpit while the radar intercept officer (RIO) or navigator sat in the right-hand fuselage. (Machat)

211 During the Berlin Airlift a Douglas C-47 Skytrain was scheduled to haul pierced aluminum planking (PAP) from Wiesbaden, Germany, to Templehoff airfield in Berlin. During takeoff, the aircraft wasn't gaining flying speed at the usual rate although engine instruments looked normal. After a longer than normal takeoff roll it finally became airborne, but the climb rate was low and after level-off the cruise speed was also below normal. Extra power was needed to maintain airspeed on final and on landing at Templehoff the tail of the C-47 slammed down hard. The pilot checked his load after parking and was astounded to learn he had carried not PAP but pierced *steel* planking (PSP) to Berlin and set a new world record. The cargo load came to 13,500 pounds, twice the normal payload for a C-47. (Lewis)

212 Two USAF pilots flew a C-47 Skytrain from coast to coast on one engine. They were on a training mission with plans to shut down an engine for practice. One step in the emergency procedure was to pull a T-handle that shuts off fuel, oil, and hydraulic fluid to the engine. During the restart procedure, the T-handle was pushed back down but the linkage failed. This wasn't detected until attempts to start the engine proved unsuccessful so they headed for their home base on one engine. Starting at the Atlantic Ocean they proceeded west until arriving at Howard Air Base on the Pacific side of the Panama Canal Zone and landed safely. (Lewis)

213 As with Navy aircraft, different U.S. Air Force airplanes were given the same name unintentionally, such as the McDonnell F-110A, original Air Force designation for the F-4 Phantom II, and cannon-equipped Lockheed-Martin AC-130H gunship, both formally named Spectre. (Lewis)

While the name "Republic Aviation Corporation" is painted on Building 17 at Farmingdale, a new F-84G Thunderjet poses on the east ramp.

214 Although the subsonic straight-wing Republic F-84 Thunderjet lived in the shadow of North American's F-86 Sabre during the Korean War, it was the first U.S. jet fighter fitted with the capability to accomplish in-flight refueling. The F-84 was also the first jet fighter able to deliver nuclear weapons carried on its external pylons. (Lewis)

215 Douglas A-26 Invaders, mothballed after the Korean conflict, experienced wing failures when placed back in service during the early days of the Vietnam War. The U.S. Air Force, wishing to return the Invaders to operational status, contracted the On-Mark Engineering Company to refurbish the aircraft. Upgrades included new engines, propellers, and brakes along with extensive modifications to the wings with fuel tanks added to the tips. The upgraded aircraft received a new B-26K designation. (Lewis)

216 The first four-engine Royal Air Force bomber to deliver ordnance to strategic targets in Germany was not the AVRO

Lancaster. That dubious distinction goes to the Handley-Page Halifax, which delivered its lethal payload during a raid on Hamburg, Germany, during the night of 12/13 March 1941. (Machat)

217 During World War II, the secret P-13A delta-wing aircraft was designed as an interceptor to attack Allied bombers. The concept was never developed any further than the DM-1 test glider, but after the war designer Alexander Lippisch began working with engineers of the American manufacturer Convair. This unusual partnership produced the experimental delta-wing XF-92 prototype, which eventually evolved to become the supersonic F-102 Delta Dagger and its successor, the Mach-2 F-106 Delta Dart. (Lewis)

218 North American F-86A Sabre 48-178 is the oldest airworthy jet fighter aircraft on record. Manufactured in Inglewood, California, in 1948 it saw service with the Strategic Air Command, Air Defense Command, and California Air National Guard before it was retired from military service. Slated to become a "Gate Guard," it changed hands several times and eventually ended up in England where it was seen performing in air shows for several years. 48-178 has been shipped back to America where it continues to fly in air shows around the United States. (Lewis)

219 Lockheed's P-80A, America's first tactical jet fighter, was introduced into service in 1945. Since there was no two-place jet trainer at that time, a pilot's first jet flight was also his first jet solo. Needless to say, the accident rate was unacceptable. In 1947, the "Captivair," a fully functional P-80A anchored to cement pylons, was developed. This training device allowed student pilots to become familiar with all P-80A systems without having to leave the ground. An instructor was stationed in an adjacent control house where he could simulate any flight condition or emergency on the cockpit instruments. Transitioning jet pilots received about 25 hours of "dual instruction" in the Captivair before actually flying the P-80A. (Frankel)

Although operated by transport and systems commands today, the Lockheed C-130 Hercules initially served with the Tactical Air Command.

220 The longest continuous production military airplane in the world today is the Lockheed C-130 Hercules, which first flew in 1954. The airplane has been built in some 40 different versions and has surpassed 2,500 total number built as of publication of this book. The airplane has been and is used both commercially as well as militarily, and, like the Douglas DC-3, seems to have no competing replacement aircraft to threaten its longevity. (Kodera)

221 The "Pardo Push" was a maneuver performed by Capt. Bob Pardo to save his wingmen Capt. Earl Aman and back seater 1st Lt. Robert Houghton from certain capture when their F-4C Phantom jet fighter was severely damaged by ground fire over Hanoi, North Vietnam. When Pardo realized his wingmen weren't going to make it back to base he had Aman lower his tailhook, which he placed against his windshield to push their F-4 out of harm's way. Although the effort was successful it exhausted their remaining fuel and both aircraft were subsequently lost when all four crewmen ejected over friendly territory. (Lewis)

222 The term "Hangar Queen" may seem like a royal compliment, but in actuality, aircraft that habitually end up needing additional maintenance, requiring more time in a hangar than the rest of the aircraft in a unit, are referred to as Hangar Queens. (Lewis)

223 British Royal Air Force crews were the only ones besides USAF personnel to fly the North American Aviation RB-45C Tornado. When Winston Churchill and his Conservative Party returned to power he agreed to conduct reconnaissance flights probing the Soviet Union using our RB-45C aircraft. The United States had promised the USSR that it would not spy on Russia. Operation Jujitsu flights originated from RAF Sculthorpe and flew deep into the USSR to gather much needed photographic and electronic intelligence. On one mission, Soviet ground radar tracked a flight of three RB-45s and dispatched night fighters to intercept them. Fortunately, the RB-45s were able to exit Russian airspace before they could be intercepted. (Lewis)

224 According to the *Guinness Book of Records* a maintenance hangar at Kelly AFB, San Antonio, Texas, is the largest free-standing aircraft hangar in the world. (Lewis)

225 The Convair XB-46 was a four-engine jet medium bomber designed to compete with both the Boeing XB-47 and Martin XB-48. Stability and control were excellent but vertical oscillations caused by harmonic resonance between the wing and spoilers were found to be a problem. The fuselage turned out to also be a problem as it distorted under flight loads. The unusual flight control system utilized pneumatic piping to transmit the pilot's control inputs and actuate various systems rather than conventional hydraulic, manual, or electrical control lines and systems. In the end, it lost out to the Boeing B-47 and was canceled. (Lewis)

226 The Martin XB-48 was a six-engine jet medium bomber built to compete with the Boeing XB-47 Stratojet. It had a bicycle-type landing gear with two outriggers that was developed using a modified B-26. It was 50 mph slower than the more advanced XB-47 due mainly to the straight-wing design. The cluster of three J35 engines molded into each wing generated extra lift but also created excess drag. These nacelles allowed air to pass between the engines to provide cooling. Two prototypes were built, but when Boeing's B-47 was selected for production they were eventually scrapped. (Lewis)

227 The YB-60 was built in competition with the Boeing B-52 Stratofortress. It would have been cheaper to build than the B-52 because many of the parts were common with the Convair B-36 Peacemaker. The YB-60 had both swept wings and tail surfaces and was powered by eight Pratt & Whitney J57 engines mounted in pairs on pylons under the wings. Testing revealed that the YB-60 was 100 mph slower than the B-52 and demonstrated severe handling problems. When Boeing received a contract to build the YB-52 the two Convair YB-60s were eventually scrapped. (Lewis)

228 Muroc, California, was the name of a town located on Rogers Dry Lake in California. It was named by two settlers, Ralph and Clifford Corum, who spelled their surname backward in order to form the name Muroc. Due to the sparse population and natural characteristics of Rogers Dry Lake, it was the perfect site for testing experimental and military aircraft. Initially named Muroc Army Airfield, it became Muroc Air Force Base when the Air Force became a separate service in 1947 and was subsequently named in honor of Capt. Glen Edwards, who lost his life near the base while testing the Northrop YB-49 flying wing. (Lewis)

229 The single-engine two-seat Lockheed F-94C Starfire was the first operational U.S. Air Force jet fighter to be fitted with an afterburner. Although the AB provided a needed boost to takeoff performance, the straight-wing, tiptank-equipped jet remained subsonic. (Lewis)

Ultimate evolution of the original P-80 Shooting Star and T-33 trainer is Lockheed's F-94C Starfire interceptor.

230 It may seem like an amazing coincidence, but the price of a single tactical jet fighter has nearly equaled the cost of a front-line jet airliner of the same time period. For instance, in then-year-dollars, a four-engine Boeing 707 and Convair F-106A Delta Dart jet interceptor both cost $5 million in 1959, while an F-15C Eagle air-superiority fighter and DC-9 Super 80 twinjet, both built by McDonnell Douglas, cost $35 million each 20 years later. (Machat)

231 Convair's F-106 was the last of the first-generation Century series fighters and is always referred to as "the ultimate interceptor." Despite its inarguable success, the F-106 had the smallest production run of any Century series jet, with a total of 340 Delta Darts built. (Machat)

232 Speaking of the Century series, the first three members of that unique tribe were also the first three operational supersonic aircraft before the advent of Mach-2 jet aircraft. This dynamic trio consisted of the North American F-100C Super Sabre, McDonnell F-101A Voodoo, and Convair F-102A Delta Dagger. (Machat)

233 Oddly, the final three members of the Century series family were also the first three operational Mach-2 jets in the USAF

inventory, the Lockheed F-104A Starfighter, Republic F-105B Thunderchief, and Convair F-106. (Machat)

234 While the need for speed was paramount during the Cold War, stealth technology rendered defense radar all but useless, as was so aptly demonstrated by Lockheed's brilliant F-117 Nighthawk during Operation Desert Storm. Today, the latest generation of stealth fighter is not only invisible to radar, but supersonic as well. Lockheed Martin's F-35 Lightning II can reach a top speed of Mach 1.65. (Machat)

235 Aviation phraseology is carefully chosen for optimal identification and clarity when spoken and heard over a radio or intercom. For instance, the word "niner," adapted from Army usage, is used instead of "nine" which, on a static-filled frequency, can easily be confused with the number "five." (Machat)

236 Rapidity and brevity are also important factors when communicating on an aircraft radio, and to that end, pilots will use the term "balls" for numerical designations with multiple zeroes in them. For instance, the number 0003 would be referred to as "balls three," rather than saying "zero-zero-zero-three." Say those two phrases out loud and see which one takes longer. (Machat)

237 Under the heavy G-load of ACM (aerial combat maneuvering) in high-performance jet aircraft, clear radio terminology becomes essential, if not critical, in maintaining effective communication. For instance, the term "Fight's on! Fight's on!" is used to begin a practice engagement, while "Knock it off! Knock it off!" is used to terminate the encounter. Even under the grunting of heavy Gs, those terms are easily understandable over the radio. (Machat)

238 Last in our facts on military radio communication is the coded phraseology for firing live ordnance from an aircraft in combat. "Fox One" is for a radar-guided missile, such as a Falcon or Sparrow, being fired. "Fox Two," a heat-seeking missile such as a Sidewinder, and "Fox Three," a fire-and-forget missile such as an AMRAAM or

Grumman F 14 Tomcal fires a Phoenix missile at an unsuspecting adversary lurking more than 100 miles away.

Phoenix. The term "Fox Four" is both unique and obsolete. That stood for a Boeing B-52 bomber firing its tail guns. (Lewis)

239 Topeka Army Air Field was renamed Forbes Air Force Base, Kansas, in memory of Maj. Daniel H. Forbes, who was killed 5 June 1948 while testing the Northrop XB-49 Flying Wing jet bomber near the Muroc USAAF Flight Test Center. (Lewis)

240 When a South African Air Force Douglas Dakota (C-47) was struck by a Soviet SAM-7 missile while in flight, the tail surfaces of the aircraft received severe damage. The pilot, Captain Colin Green, brought the aircraft under control and then positioned his VIP passengers about the cabin to keep the aircraft in balance. He then adjusted engine power and flap settings to maintain control so a successful landing could be accomplished. Capt. Green was awarded a commendation for his actions. (Lewis)

241 The youngest person ever credited with a MiG kill was an 18-year-old tail gunner in a B-52D, Air Force Airman First Class (E-4) Albert Moore, who shot down a MiG-21 over

North Vietnam during Linebacker II in December 1972. He was the last tail gunner in history to shoot down an enemy aircraft. (Machat)

242 Lockheed's needle-nose F-104 Starfighter interceptor (named with the phrase "the Missile with a Man in It" for promotional purposes in the 1950s) was the first manned jet-powered aircraft to reach Mach 2, or twice the speed of sound, approximately 1,500 mph. (Lewis)

The first high-performance Unmanned Aerial Vehicle (UAV) was the Mach-2 North American X-10 prototype for the Navaho cruise missile in 1953.

243 North American Aviation developed the unmanned X-10 to test the feasibility of a surface-to-surface cruise missile. Powered by two Westinghouse J40 turbojet engines that were fitted with afterburners, the X-10 became the first air-breathing vehicle to reach Mach 2 and altitudes of 51,000 feet in 1953. The X-10 was configured with a delta wing, canard horizontal stabilizers, and conventional tricycle landing gear to allow for takeoffs and landings on Rogers Dry Lake adjacent to Edwards Air Force Base. The X-10 also tested the concept of on-board computers, inertial guidance systems, and autopilots. (Lewis)

244 Nicknames and callsigns have been part of military aviation from the beginning and are generally "awarded" to pilots based on three factors: name, physical appearance, or something that happened during their careers that they likely would rather forget. (Machat)

245 Examples of callsigns bestowed to pilots based on their names would be those such as Capt. Bill "Bartman" Simpson, Maj. Jim "Cary" Grant, 2nd Lt. Phil "Duke" Wayne, and Lt. Col. George "Lucky" Penny. (Machat)

246 Examples of callsigns based on personal "experiences" include an Air Force F-105 pilot whose M61 gatling gun jammed in the firing position during fighter lead-in training, nearly destroying the nose of the aircraft ("Trigger"), and an F-15 pilot who clipped the wing of another F-15 during a night rejoin, smashing the navigation lights on both jets ("Tips"). A Navy F/A-18 pilot who experienced an inflight emergency and had to fly her Hornet fighter from a carrier at sea to a land base with gear and flaps extended was forever thereafter known as "Dirty" (for the aircraft being in a "dirty" configuration). (Machat)

247 Full-Authority Digital Electronic Control (FADEC) is a product of the digital age that revolutionized aircraft flight control systems. In a dramatic and life-saving demonstration of FADEC's capabilities, after a midair collision on a training flight, an Israeli McDonnell Douglas F-15B Eagle landed with its entire right wing missing with help from the FADEC system installed in the aircraft. (Lewis)

248 McDonnell Douglas submitted the winning design for the F-15 air superiority fighter competition in the early 1970s to produce a truly legendary modern tactical aircraft still in use all over the world in both air-to-air and air-to-ground roles today. The F-15 was the world's first jet-powered aircraft to possess a thrust-to-weight ratio of more than 1:1, allowing the jet to accelerate in a completely vertical climb. (Machat)

Stripped of all unnecessary weight, the McDonnell Douglas F-15 Streak Eagle *set several time-to-climb records.*

249 In January 1975, a specially outfitted F-15 named the *Streak Eagle* set several time-to-climb absolute speed records, including a takeoff-to-82,000-feet climb in only 2 minutes and 41 seconds. This broke the previous record set by a Soviet Mig-25. Stripped of all exterior paint as well as 1,800 pounds of internal weight by eliminating the gun, flaps, speed brake, and associated actuators, the *Streak Eagle* also carried a reduced fuel load with only enough fuel to reach the record altitude in full afterburner and return safely for a landing. Ultimate altitude reached in this series of records was 98,250 feet. (Machat)

250 An abundance of impressive time-to-climb records have been set over the years, and most of those records in recent times were set by twin-engine jet fighters. However, the fastest time-to-climb records flown in a single-engine aircraft were set in April 1989 by a Lockheed U-2 Dragon Lady high-altitude surveillance aircraft. Flown from Edwards AFB, the U-2 shattered six existing records by climbing to nearly 74,000 feet in less than half the time of the previous records. (Machat)

251 When cans of beer arrived at tropical bases where North American F-86D Sabre jets were based they would lower the rocket pod below the fuselage, remove the 2.75-inch folding fin aerial rockets, insert the beer cans using a broom handle, and then climb to altitude in afterburner until the beer was cold then return to landing with a fresh supply of cold beer. (Lewis)

252 Not usually considered for long-distance flying records, the modern helicopter has had its share. Most notable was the first nonstop transatlantic crossing, which was accomplished by crews of the U.S. Air Force on 31 May and 1 June 1967. Flying in two Sikorsky HH-3E "Jolly Green Giant" rescue helicopters, Majors Zehnder and Maurras battled weather day and night for nearly 31 hours, landing in Paris, France, during the annual air show at Le Bourget airfield. The aircraft were refueled no fewer than nine times enroute, and at one point ice had forced the flight of three aircraft (including their tanker/pathfinder HC-130P Hercules) down to a scant 50 feet above the wave tops! (Kodera)

253 The five fastest single-engine jet-powered U.S. Air Force aircraft are the Convair F-106 Delta Dart (Mach 2.41), Lockheed F-104 Starfighter (Mach 2.2), North American F-107A "Ultra Sabre" prototype (2.12), Republic F-105D Thunderchief (Mach 2.08), and Lockheed Martin F-16 Fighting Falcon (Mach 2.0). It is interesting to note that all these aircraft made their first flights before 1960, except for the F-16, which first flew in 1974. (Machat)

254 The first U.S. jet aircraft to employ single-bogie bicycle landing gear (twin wheels fore and aft that retract up into an aircraft's fuselage) was the experimental prototype Martin XB-48, which first flew on 22 June 1947. Winner of the fly-off competition for a long-term jet bomber production contract was Boeing's B-47 Stratojet that made its first flight on 17 December 1947, the 44th anniversary of the Wright brothers' first flight made at Kitty Hawk, North Carolina. (Machat)

Representing the epitome of the large air-superiority fighter and small, lightweight fighter in the 1970s were the F-15 Eagle (top) and F-16 Fighting Falcon.

255 Rivalries between the armed services have been part of military culture since the beginning of time, but for the Air Force, friendly rivalries also exist between pilots of such aircraft types as fighters, bombers, and transports. Even more amazing are the rivalries between pilots of specific aircraft like the F-15 Eagle and F-16 Flying Falcon. To an F-16 pilot, the biggest advantage of an F-15 is

being able to play regulation tennis on top of the wing. To an F-15 pilot, the biggest advantage of the smaller F-16 is that two of them can be carried under the wings of an F-15! (Machat)

256 One aircraft in a flight of Convair F-106 Delta Darts engaged in air-to-air combat training went out of control, and the pilot was forced to eject when he was unable to recover from the subsequent spin. The change in aircraft CG after the ejection sequence inadvertently caused the jet to recover to normal flight. It gently landed, wings level and without a pilot, in a farmer's field with only minimal damage. The aircraft was recovered and placed back in service. Today the F-106 "Cornfield Bomber," as it became known, is on display at the National Museum of the U.S. Air Force in Dayton, Ohio. (Lewis)

257 The famed, if not cliché, Murphy's Law states: "Anything that can go wrong, will go wrong." Believe it or not, this was a phrase uttered by USAF Capt. Edward A. Murphy at his control console at Edwards AFB, California, for Project MX981, a rocket sled test with Col. John Paul Stapp's aeromedical research team measuring the effects of rapid deceleration on humans in 1949. When the sled's rockets wouldn't fire, Murphy uttered the phrase that would be forever linked to his name. (Machat)

258 The oldest surviving operational North American F-100 (S/N 52-5761) is the 14th Super Sabre built; it resides at the New England Air Museum at Bradley International Airport, Windsor Locks, Connecticut. That Hun was delivered to the 118th Fighter Squadron, 103rd Fighter Group in 1954 and spent her entire career with that unit. (Lewis)

259 Although that museum claimed its F-100A as "the oldest surviving F-100," believe it or not, there are two other F-100s that are older. YF-100A 52-5755 and 52-5760 are both at Edwards AFB, California. Sadly, ship "760" languishes out on the base bombing range, but "755" is the world speed record holder flown by Lt. Col. "Pete" Everest and is displayed proudly in the "Century Circle" at the base's West Gate. (Lewis)

260 During an operational reconnaissance mission, a Lockheed SR-71 Blackbird crew observed a Master Warning light and diverted to the nearest suitable airport, which was Bodø, Norway. They knew that landing an aircraft of this type at Bodø was going to cause quite a stir, but little did they know it was going to expand into an international incident when they learned that airfield had been the intended landing site for the ill-fated Lockheed U-2 piloted by Francis Gary Powers and shot down by the Russians on 1 May 1960. (Lewis)

Lockheed's Mach 3.3 SR-71 Blackbird is the world's highest-performance manned production jet-powered aircraft to this day.

261 Despite having been operational since 1964, there were still certain aspects of the Lockheed SR-71's performance envelope that remained classified until well after the aircraft was removed from service. With its top speed and service ceiling reportedly "Mach 3.2 at 80,000 feet" the Air Force's SR-71 and its A-12 predecessor used by the CIA were the highest-performance production aircraft ever built. The recently declassified top speed and service ceiling of the SR-71 are Mach 3.3 (2,530 mph) at 90,000 feet. (Machat)

262 The SR-71 is built primarily from titanium, a rare metal that was mined and produced in greatest quantity by the Soviet Union. To acquire that metal from sources within Russia during the Cold War, the CIA set up several "front" companies posing as Italian restaurants. The Soviets were told the titanium was for large pizza ovens being built throughout the United States. Little did they ever suspect that the materials they were only too happy to sell were being used to build an airplane that would spy on their country for the better part of three decades! (Machat)

263 With the previously mentioned performance data in mind, the Air Force was adamant about setting an SR-71 coast-to-coast record on what was then thought to be its final flight on 6 March 1990, a triplesonic cross-country dash from Palmdale, California, to Washington, D.C.'s Dulles International Airport, delivering the jet to the Smithsonian Institution's National Air & Space Museum. The record-shattering flight from a start gate over Ventura, California, to a finish gate over Salisbury, Maryland, took only 68 minutes at a cruise speed of Mach 3.2. At cruise, the aircraft covered 1 mile every 1.2 seconds. (Machat)

264 SR-71 designer and Skunk Works president Ben Rich had requested that the transcontinental speed record be set in less than 60 minutes to maximize the publicity value for the Air Force. Upon learning that, Lockheed engineers went to work evaluating the performance parameters required to accomplish that feat. A speed of Mach 3.5 would be necessary, but those engineers also discovered that should an engine "unstart" (flameout) occur at that speed, the aircraft would immediately pitch up and disintegrate with no hope of crew survival. Hence, the airplane was flown at a cruise speed of Mach 3.2. (Machat)

265 Upon returning to Plant 42 at Palmdale after the SR-71's coast-to-coast speed record, Lt. Col. Ed Yeilding and RSO Lt. Col. Joe "JT" Vida, the Blackbird's crew, were asked what the most difficult part of the flight was. Replied Yeilding, "Getting on a United 767 and taking six hours to get back to California!" (Machat)

266 *Toboggan* is the term used when it is necessary for a slower aerial tanker aircraft to descend at the same speed as a damaged or flamed-out fighter aircraft to match his descent rate during an in-flight emergency refueling. (Lewis)

267 The 509th Air Refueling Squadron, Pease AFB, New Hampshire, had a full-size neon Pegasus sign mounted on top of their operations building. They also painted Pegasus emblems on their Boeing KC-97 Stratotanker aircraft and wore a Pegasus patch on their flight suits. The famed "Flying Red Horse" was also, most appropriately, the logo for Mobilgas. In a passing of the torch, the new Boeing KC-46 tanker is named Pegasus. (Lewis)

268 For new jet pilots entering Air Force UPT, or undergraduate pilot training, learning numerical values takes on a whole new meaning. Field elevations, although indicated on aeronautical charts, are sometimes easily remembered by associating number pairings with significant dates, designations, or even aircraft. Such was the case at USAF Air Training Command's Reese AFB in El Paso, Texas, where the field elevation is 3,338 feet above sea level. Cadets could easily remember that number by associating two famous Air Force trainers: the Lockheed T-33 Shooting Star and supersonic Northrop T-38 Talon. (Kodera)

269 In 1955 the Goodyear Rubber Company designed and built a highly unusual aircraft called the Inflato-plane. Intended to rescue downed pilots and inflate like a life raft, it could be stored in a 44-cubic-foot container and transported by truck, Jeep, or airplane. It was powered by a two-cycle 40-horsepower engine and was designated XAO-3 during flight tests. The first flight occurred on 13 February 1956. (Frankel)

270 Tests of the Inflato-plane demonstrated that the airframe could be inflated with as little as 8 pounds-per-square-inch of pressure and it could carry a 240-pound load for a range of 390 miles at a cruise speed of 60 miles per hour. The rubber airplane could take off in 250 feet and land in 350 feet, had a rate of climb of

550 feet per minute, and had an estimated 10,000-foot service ceiling. After building 12 examples, the program was canceled when one Army official noted that a valid military use couldn't be found for an aircraft that could be brought down by a well-aimed bow and arrow. (Frankel)

Typical of jet aircraft design as World War II ended, North American's B-45 Tornado had straight wings and tailplanes like those on piston-powered aircraft.

271 The straight-wing, subsonic, four-engine North American Aviation B-45 Tornado was the U.S. Air Force's first operational jet bomber. The B-45 and German-British-Italian GR1/GR4 Tornado attack jet share the same name. (Lewis)

272 A Convair B-36 Peacemaker was used to ferry the Air Force's new B-58 Hustler aircraft from the factory in Ft. Worth, Texas, to Edwards AFB, California. In order to accomplish the trip they had to fly with the landing gear extended, plus engines number 3 and number 4 were not used and their propellers were removed to provide clearance for the B-58's fuselage. The nosewheel had to be lowered gently due to the limited clearance between the B-58's nose and runways. (Lewis)

273 The *Red Baron* was a highly modified Lockheed F-104 Starfighter that set an FAI Class C-1 Group III 3-km speed record of 1,590.45 kph (988.26 mph) in 1977, which stands to this day. The *Red Baron* was assembled by Darryl Greenamyer and sponsored by Ed Browning of the Red Baron Flying Service Idaho Falls, Idaho. The aircraft was destroyed in an accident in 1978. (Lewis)

274 The prototype XT-37 (SN 54-716) was built by Cessna in 1954. The aircraft, which was designed to be a primary trainer, used a very traditional configuration. It had a straight wing with a proven airfoil used on many Cessna private aircraft, and it employed generous tail surfaces. The XT-37 was expected to present no surprises. All engineering data, including extensive spin tunnel testing, predicted benign characteristics, but actual tests proved otherwise. Spins of more than one turn to the left were unrecoverable and the spin chute was deployed on four occasions. On the last deployment the chute pulled loose from the aircraft and the test pilot made the first successful ejection from a T-37. (Frankel)

275 Harry Clements, a young aerodynamicist who had graduated from college less than three years earlier, theorized that the side-by-side cockpit was the source of the T-37's spin difficulty. The wide fuselage actually generated lift during spin rotations. Clements suggested that 6-foot-long strakes be attached to the aircraft's nose to spoil the unwanted lift. The idea work brilliantly and spin recovery could be achieved within 1½ turns, meeting the Air Force specification. (Frankel)

276 On one test flight, Clements who was flying as a Flight Test Observer, took control of the aircraft and attempted a spin recovery. He recovered normally, but when the Air Force discovered that he had flown the prototype XT-37, his certification was immediately rescinded. Nevertheless he saved the T-37 program for Cessna and the Air Force and was recommended for an Air Force commendation. (Frankel)

277 When aircraft transponders were introduced into the military aviation world they were referred to as "Parrots" during radio communications. Phrases like Squawk Ident, Strangle your Parrot, Squawk Flash, Squawk 4730, or Squawk VFR were commonly used by controllers to obtain the required signals. Not all pilots were familiar with this new phraseology when transponders first started to appear on the scene. One pilot, who was unfamiliar with the new term, was asked to "Strangle your Parrot" responded by saying, "We don't have any parrots onboard, just engine parts." (Lewis)

278 On 27 February 1947, a North American F-82B Twin Mustang named "Betty-Jo" flew from Hawaii to New York, a distance of 5,051 miles, to make the longest nonstop flight ever flown by a piston-powered fighter aircraft. The two-man, twin-fuselage F-82 was equipped with four large external fuel tanks for the trip. (Lewis)

279 General Jeannie Leavitt graduated at the top of her class when she finished U.S. Air Force pilot training in 1992. After graduation she was initially assigned as a T-38 Talon instructor pilot. When combat assignments became available for female officers she trained in the McDonnell/Douglas F-15E Strike Eagle, becoming the first USAF female fighter pilot. She was also the first woman to command a fighter wing. (Lewis)

280 Although the Lockheed SR-71 is famous for high speed, one incredible story illustrates *how slowly* it could fly. While making a low demonstration pass over a British airbase the crew was having difficulty locating it in morning haze. As they searched for the site they failed to notice their airspeed had dropped to 172 knots! When the pilot realized his error he *slammed* both throttles full forward and into afterburner. As both burners lit, RAF cadets witnessed an incredible sight, an SR-71 at extremely low altitude and in a left bank with two massive flames shooting out of the engine exhausts. (Lewis)

A quantum leap forward, the Boeing KC-135 Stratotanker finally brought jet refueling speeds to Strategic Air Command bombers.

281 The first jet-powered KC-135 Stratotanker refueling aircraft rolled off the Boeing production line in Renton, Washington, directly behind the last piston-powered KC-97 to be built. (Lewis)

282 "Toxic Death" was the name given to Lockheed YF-117A Nighthawk aircraft number 781 after it was stripped of its classified equipment and stealth coating. With its radar absorbing paint removed and adorned with graffiti it was flown to Dayton, Ohio, to be added to the National Museum of the United States Air Force. This YF-117A prototype could not be modified into an operational aircraft so it was a perfect choice for display in the museum. (Lewis)

283 The Advanced Tanker-Cargo Aircraft program (ATCA) was designed to evaluate aircraft that would have a greater capacity than the Boeing KC-135 Stratotanker. The McDonnell/Douglas DC-10, Boeing 767, and Russian IL-76 were evaluated along with the Boeing 747 as possible candidates. Although the KC-10 Extender won that competition in 1982, and the Boeing KC-46A

Pegasus is currently under development to augment the KC-135, there is actually one KC-747 in operation with the Iranian Air Force. The KC-747 is the largest tanker aircraft in the world. (Lewis)

284 On 20 January 1974 Phil Oestricher, project test pilot for the F-16 program, was completing a series of high-speed taxi tests on the number one prototype prior to the first "official" flight scheduled in several days. He planned to accelerate to liftoff speed and "place some air under the wheels," a typical test technique used to check control authority by flying a foot or two above the runway. The YF-16 accelerated smartly and as Oestricher reached his target speed he reduced power, but a wiring problem prevented the engine exhaust nozzle from opening fully. More thrust was provided than expected, and the jet suddenly hopped into the air, technically making its "first flight." (Frankel)

285 Once the YF-16's wheels left the ground it was obvious that roll control was overly sensitive. Oestricher fought to stabilize the airplane, which rolled dramatically through several pilot-induced oscillations. At one point the right horizontal stabilizer scraped the runway. Concerned that he was about to lose the airplane, Oestricher applied power and climbed away in a very large left-hand pattern taking 6 minutes to return to the runway for a normal landing. An uneventful "official" first flight occurred two weeks later. (Frankel)

286 The first round-the-world nonstop flight of a jet aircraft was made by Boeing B-52 Stratofortresses. Maj Gen. Archie J. Old Jr. led the flight of three bombers, each powered by eight 10,000-pound-thrust Pratt & Whitney J57 engines. The global flight took 45 hours and 19 minutes, covering a distance of 24,325 miles at an average speed of 525 mph. The flight was completed at March AFB, California, on 18 January 1957. (Kodera)

287 America's first jet bomber was the Douglas XB-43 Jetmaster, first flying on 17 May 1946. Despite this accolade, the purely experimental airplane never entered production, essentially being a modification of the earlier Douglas XB-42 "Mixmaster" pusher propeller bomber prototype. (Kodera)

The Douglas XB-43 was technically the first jet-powered bomber in the United States, converted from its contra-rotating propeller XB-42 predecessor.

288 North American's B-45 Tornado, America's first jet bomber to enter service with the Air Force, was also the first jet bomber to drop a nuclear device. The RB-45C version (last of the series) was used extensively over critical areas of Korea and Manchuria, conducting sensitive reconnaissance in the hostile skies of the Korean War. Only 143 airframes of all marks were produced of this venerable airplane, starting in 1947. (Kodera)

289 The first jet-to-jet air combat dogfight in history was between a USAF Lockheed F-80 Shooting Star and two North Korean MiG-15s near the Yalu River during the then-new Korean War on 8 November 1950. U.S. Air Force 1st Lieutenant Russell Brown was the pilot. (Kodera)

290 The first jet-powered military transport was none other than the British de Havilland Comet 2 jetliner, militarized for the Royal Air Force. The airplane entered service on 7 July 1956 based at Lyneham, Wiltshire. These early Comets, enlarged and improved variants of the pioneering but flawed Comet 1, provided many years of safe and efficient service to the RAF. (Kodera)

291 The first time someone flew faster than 1,000 mph was 10 March 1956 in England. The pilot for the flight was Lieutenant Peter Twiss flying the exceedingly fast research aircraft the Fairey Delta 2. His official speed was 1,131 mph. Interestingly, the FD 2 later got a new, scaled-down wing design, which was the direct shape and cut of the BAC Concorde supersonic airliner. The new designator for the experimental aircraft was BAC 221 and it successfully yielded invaluable real-world aerodynamic test information during the development of the Anglo-French SST. (Kodera)

292 Chase Aircraft developed the largest glider in the United States with the XG-20. When the use of gliders was terminated after World War II, Chase used the design to make twin-engine C-123 Providers. The company also developed the XC-123A four-engine jet version that never reached production. That aircraft was converted into a Stroukoff YC-123D and used for boundary layer control testing. The YC-123E was also fitted with skis, and the YC-134 replaced Pratt & Whitney R-2800 engines with Wright R-3350s. (Lewis)

293 In 1944, the USAAF contracted Republic Aviation Corporation to design and build a long-range high-altitude reconnaissance aircraft capable of very high speed. Republic built

Perhaps the most aerodynamically advanced piston-powered aircraft ever flown, Republic's XR-12 was the work of design genius Alexander Kartveli.

two prototype aircraft designated XF-12 (later XR-12) that met or exceeded those requirements by selecting four R-4360 radial engines and installing them in an aerodynamically clean airframe. The aircraft could cruise at 400 mph at 40,000 feet for 4,000 miles. With the introduction of jet power after World War II, a production contract to build a fleet of XR-12s was never realized. One aircraft was lost at Eglin Air Force Base, Florida, following an engine fire and the other went to the Aberdeen Proving Grounds and was blown-up as a ground target. (Lewis)

294 Republic's elegant XR-12 prototype is to this day the world's fastest four-engine piston-powered aircraft, having attained a top speed of 462 mph at 40,000 feet during its initial Air Force flight trials. First flown on 7 February 1946, the aircraft was faster than most World War II fighters and contained its own photo darkroom to develop highly secret recon photos inflight. A 44-passenger airliner version named the RC-2 "Rainbow" was ordered by American Airlines and Pan Am, but never came to fruition because the Air Force contract was canceled. (Machat)

295 Another evolutionary design that fell victim to the coming Jet Age in 1947 was the Boeing B-54 "Ultra Fortress," the ultimate version of the B-50, itself an upgrade of Boeing's own B-29 Super Fortress. This aircraft was to be powered by the advanced Variable Discharge Turbine (VDT) version of Pratt & Whitney's mighty 28-cylinder R-4360 radial engine capable of producing more than 4,000 hp. With a fuselage length 10 feet greater than the B-50 and a wingspan extended 20 feet, large external fuel tanks and outrigger landing gear would have been necessary to carry the extended bulk of the airframe. Its additional 3,000-gallon fuel capacity would have given the B-54 a nonstop range of 9,300 miles. (Lewis)

296 Today, modified Boeing KC-135R Stratotanker aircraft are fitted with 22,000-pound-thrust GE/SNECMA CFM56 high-bypass turbofan engines that allow them to offload 50 percent more fuel, are 25 percent more fuel efficient, and reduce operating costs by an additional 25 percent. The operational range of the KC-135R is 60 percent greater, and it is also much quieter than previous models. (Lewis)

297 Bell Aircraft modified two P-63 King Cobra aircraft into "L-39s" by installing swept wings that incorporated both leading edge slats and trailing edge flaps. The wings were swept at 35 degrees. The conversion from a straight wing to a swept wing caused the center of lift to move aft, and the empennage needed to be enlarged and the fuselage lengthened to correct handling problems. NACA personnel at Langley studied the L-39 to gather data for building the X-2 research aircraft. (Lewis)

298 Aeromedical flight surgeon Col. John Paul Stapp is well known for his research in the effects of G forces on the human body. Col. Stapp did many of the rocket sled high-speed deceleration tests himself and withstood tremendous punishment during his career. Stapp's research showed that the human body could withstand more than 46 Gs while in a forward sitting position if properly restrained. He also reached a top speed of 632 mph on one test run at Hollo-man AFB, New Mexico, to become "the fastest man on earth." The name of his first rocket sled was the *G-Whiz*. (Lewis)

299 North American Aviation's F-100 Super Sabre's J57 engine could be started by either a ground power unit or an explosive cartridge installed in the fuselage to rotate the engine. When tran-sient crews told an F-100 pilot that they were unfamiliar with his aircraft, he informed them that if they pushed the jet down the taxi-way he would be able to "pop the clutch" and start the engine. They shoved him down a taxiway and when he was rolling fast enough, he tapped the brakes, compressing the nose gear strut, and simul-taneously hit the start button. As the engine came to life he calmly taxied to the runway for takeoff. (Lewis)

300 On 10 August 1961, a Republic F-105D Thunderchief lifted the largest load ever carried aloft by a single-engine aircraft when it carried a payload of more than 14,000 pounds (6,350.3

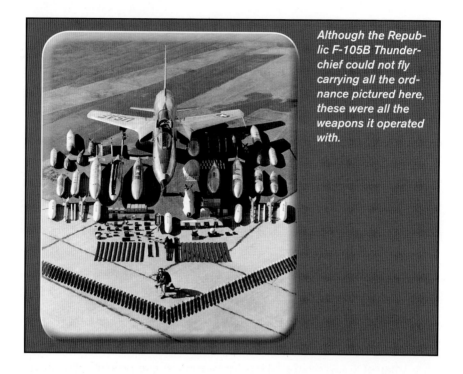

Although the Republic F-105B Thunderchief could not fly carrying all the ordnance pictured here, these were all the weapons it operated with.

kilograms) during a test at Eglin. The F-105 was the largest, heaviest, and most powerful single-engine, single-seat aircraft in the world at the time. (Machat)

301 In a classic example of sardonic military humor, a U-10 Helio Courier operating out of Bien Hoa Air Base, South Vietnam, flying Psy-War (Psychological Warfare) broadcasts recorded a pair of F-100 Super Sabre jets taking off in afterburner and played that sound over its huge loudspeakers during takeoff. The sound of a jet fighter in full afterburner turned heads whenever the little single-engine high-wing aircraft departed and climbed out of the pattern at 90 mph. (Lewis)

302 The need for a large long-range military transport aircraft in support of routes across both the Atlantic and Pacific oceans during World War II was met by Douglas Aircraft when the company designed and built the C-74 Globemaster. The four-engine aircraft didn't enter service until shortly before the end of the war, but it did fly during the Korean War and before that conflict as part of the Berlin Airlift. Of the 14 C-74s built, 11 flew in operational service. Aircraft number 5 was converted into the first C-124 Globemaster II. Due to the success of the design, C-124s were built and operated by the USAF for many years. (Lewis)

303 Ground effect is the cushion of air built up between the bottom of an aircraft and the ground at the approximate height of half the aircraft's wingspan. When a Boeing C-97 Stratofreighter experienced an engine failure over open water it was too heavy to sustain flight on the remaining three engines. To save the aircraft, a descent was made to just above wave top level so the aircraft could take advantage of ground effect and prevent ditching in the ocean. This cushion of air was enough to keep them airborne. As they flew along skimming the wave tops, the consumption of fuel lightened the aircraft enough so they could enjoy an increase in airspeed a few knots at a time until the crisis passed and they could sustain flight on three engines to a safe landing. (Lewis)

304 The Douglas C-124 Globemaster II was so large it had a crawlway system from the fuselage out to all four engines large enough for mechanics to enter the wing and reach the engine nacelles in flight. During an ocean crossing it became necessary to shut down an engine due to excessive oil consumption. Later in the flight a second engine failed, and since they couldn't sustain flight on two engines it was decided to start up the engine that had been shut down earlier and hand transfer oil from the second failed engine to keep the first one running. To do this, a hole was cut in the oil tank of the failed engine so oil could be drained from it and poured into the oil tank of the engine that had been shut down first. The mechanics managed to transfer enough oil to keep it running and were successful in saving the aircraft. (Lewis)

305 Fairchild modified a C-119 Boxcar to test the feasibility of operating an aircraft that could attach and detach cargo pods from below a specially designed fuselage. Designated the XC-120 Packplane, the aircraft underwent trials to see if the concept was feasible to use detachable pods that could be loaded or unloaded separate from the aircraft. To test the concept, a new four-wheel landing gear system had to be developed with the ability to raise and lower the fuselage when attaching the pods. Although tests proved the concept was feasible it was never adapted. (Lewis)

306 A Fairchild C-119 Flying Boxcar transport made the first aerial recovery of an object returning from Earth orbit when it captured film from a Douglas Thor–launched Corona orbital recon mission payload using a hook-and-cable system reeled out behind the aircraft. Once recovery was made of the nose cone payload, the cable was reeled into the back of the aircraft by a winch system. Later versions of this recovery method were performed using turboprop Lockheed C-130 Hercules transports. (Lewis)

307 A Boeing KC-135 Stratotanker towed a battle-damaged Republic F-105 Thunderchief out of North Vietnam and into friendly territory via its refueling boom. As the tanker was turning to roll out in front of him the F-105 pilot called that he had a flameout. Instead of doing a normal 15-degree angle of bank, the tanker rolled into a 30-degree bank, lowered its nose, and rushed in front of the fighter so the boom operator could hook him up. They dragged him out of enemy territory and dropped him off at the nearest base. (Lewis)

308 Avro Canada's CF-105 Arrow was intended to replace the CF-100 Canuck and serve as the primary interceptor aircraft for Canada. It incorporated twin turbojet engines, advanced electronics, and a delta-wing platform. Avro Canada anticipated that the CF-105 would be capable of Mach 2 speeds at altitudes above 50,000 feet. The first aircraft were fitted with Pratt & Whitney J75 engines because their Orenda Iroquois engines were still in development. The Arrow had excellent performance and handling and Avro Canada anticipated even better speeds and altitudes when the Iroquois engines were tested, but before they were ready the entire program was canceled. (Lewis)

309 Throughout aviation history, the design crossover from military aircraft to commercial airliners, and vice versa, has been used to great advantage. After World War II, there was the

Douglas DC-6A freighter, which became the Air Force C-118 transport, and Lockheed 1049 Super Constellation that became the Air Force C-121 and Navy WV-2 radar picket, early warning, and radar intercept transports. (Machat)

310 The inevitable design adaptation from commercial airliners to military transports of all types was quite apparent during the Jet Age, especially for the Air Force. The McDonnell Douglas DC-10-30CF tri-jet widebody convertible freighter won the ATCA Advanced Tanker competition in 1980 to become the KC-10 Extender aerial refueling transport. Since 1982, 60 KC-10s were built; 59 are still in service, with 1 aircraft having been lost in a ground fire accident. (Machat)

311 Many Boeing airliners were also adapted for Air Force roles starting with the 707-320B Intercontinental that became the radar dish–equipped E-3 AWACS early-warning and combat control aircraft; the 727-100 and -200 series that became the C-22A/B transports, and the 737-200, which became the T-43 navigational trainer. (Machat)

312 Lockheed Martin's F-22 Raptor is appropriately named for aggressive birds of prey, as well as the carnivorous dinosaurs known as velociraptors. However, fear and trembling in the camps of the politically correct felt that this name was inappropriate and not politically correct. Fortunately, the Air Force brass held its ground and the Raptor remained a bird of prey. (Caruso)

313 The official name of the Lockheed Martin F-16 is the Fighting Falcon. It was originally to be named simply the Falcon, after the Air Force Academy's mascot. However, Falcon was also the name of a French business jet and it certainly wouldn't do to have a U.S. fighter with the same name as a French commercial aircraft. Thus, "Falcon" became "Fighting Falcon" to avoid the embarrassment. F-16 pilots, however, wanted the aircraft to be named Viper, a request that was ignored. Nevertheless, the F-16 is mostly referred to today as Viper, and sometimes, derisively, as the Lawn Dart. (Caruso)

314 Speaking of aircraft names, there has been much confusion these last few decades about the names of aircraft manufacturers, resulting from the blitz of mergers that transpired after the end of the Cold War. Was there ever a Boeing P-51 Mustang, or Lockheed F-102 Delta Dart? No, but Boeing did acquire North American and Convair is now a legacy company for Lockheed Martin. Although these lines were a bit blurred immediately after those mergers, the rule today is that a company can lay claim to building an aircraft if it is still in production, or was indeed built by that company before production ended, hence the original McDonnell Douglas airplanes that became the Boeing C-17 Globemaster III, Boeing F-15E Strike Eagle, and Boeing F/A-18E/F Super Hornet. (Machat)

315 Today, the U.S. Air Force flies four different aircraft that all made their first flights in the 1950s and are literally irreplaceable by any newer aircraft. Those four are the Boeing B-52 (1952) Stratofortress; Lockheed C-130 Hercules (1954); Boeing KC-135 (1956); and Northrop T-38 Talon (1959). (Machat)

316 The Northrop T-38 is the only U.S. supersonic trainer flying today. However, it has another unique distinction: It is the only aircraft (and the very last aircraft) in the U.S. Air Force powered

Close "contact flying" is one of many maneuvers undergraduate pilot trainees must master in the T-38 before pinning on USAF Command Pilot wings.

by turbojet engines. All other USAF aircraft today are powered by turbofan engines. (Machat)

317 Speaking of geriatric jets, the mighty eight-engine Boeing B-52 has been flying in operational service since 1955, and there are now reports that grandchildren of original B-52H pilots (the last model still in USAF inventory) are flying the very same aircraft and signing the very same aircraft logbooks as their fathers and grandfathers! (Machat)

318 In one of the greatest examples of "beating swords into plowshares," aerospace technology for pilot survival in aircraft crashes was applied to saving lives in automobile accidents. In 1965 a New York state program contracted the Fairchild-Republic company on Long Island to design a "safety sedan" showing how this technology would work. Later developed into two working prototypes delivered to the Department of Transportation, the program resulted in more than 100 safety features found in cars today such as inertia-reel seat belts and shoulder harnesses, padded interiors, side-mounted fuel fillers, energy absorbing structure, side door beams, and air bags. (Machat)

319 The British Experimental Miles M.52 aircraft was developed to fly faster than the speed of sound. At some point prior to flight, the program was canceled and details of their design were given to the United States to help with plans to build an aircraft capable of exceeding the speed of sound. If the program hadn't been canceled the British might have been the first to break the sound barrier. A pilotless version of the M.52 did eventually exceed Mach 1, but well after the Bell X-1 flown by Capt. "Chuck" Yeager had already succeeded in flying faster than the speed of sound. (Lewis)

320 The world's fastest single-engine jet aircraft is the Convair F-106 Delta Dart. On 15 December 1959, an F-106A flown by Brig Gen. Joe Rogers flew a series of speed runs to establish a new world absolute straight-line speed record, which averages the two highest speeds flown consecutively on a high-altitude course. During one of these runs, the aircraft achieved a maximum speed of

Known as "the Ultimate Interceptor," Convair's F-106A Delta Dart set world records before serving with the Air Defense Command.

Mach 2.41, the highest speed ever flown by an operational single-engine jet aircraft to this day. (Machat)

321 The tri-service, multinational Joint Strike Fighter, the Lockheed Martin F-35 Lightning II, is misnamed on two counts. The concept demonstrator was designated the X-35, the "X" standing for Experimental. But in a gross miscarriage of naming etiquette, the "X" was exchanged for an "F." However, the next number available in the fighter designation sequence would have been F-24. Additionally, the name "Lightning II" is described as paying homage to the U.S. P-38 Lightning and the British BAC Lightning fighters. But that would make the F-35 the third aircraft with that name, the "Lightning III." (Caruso)

322 Did the Air Force ever fly a seaplane? Well, yes, in a manner of speaking; it was an amphibian used for air-sea rescue work during the Korean War and into the late 1950s for rescue use at coastal air bases around the world. The Grumman SA-16 (later designated HU-16) Albatross was a hard-working twin-engine sea and land aircraft that became the backbone of USAF fixed-wing SAR (Search and Rescue) missions at the dawn of the Jet Age. (Machat)

What's a flying boat doing in the desert? Grumman's SA-16 Albatross was used extensively for air-sea rescue work by the Air Force.

323 One of the names seriously considered for Boeing's C-17 transport aircraft was "Loadmaster." This name would recognize the invaluable contribution to air transport made by the crew members responsible for ensuring that all manners of cargo are loaded efficiently and safely. The Air Force responded by boldly selecting the name Globemaster III, which apparently required less out-of-the-box thinking. (Caruso)

324 The world's most powerful piston aircraft engine ever run was the Lycoming 7755 inline/radial engine of 1944, having attained 5,000 horsepower and being liquid cooled with overhead camshafts. The mammoth engine was designed to be used in the upcoming Convair B-36 long-range bomber, but it was replaced with the P&W R-4360 and canceled by the U.S. Army Air Forces in 1946. (Kodera)

325 The world's most powerful piston aircraft engine to enter production and actually fly on various airframe designs was the impressive Pratt & Whitney R-4360 from the late World War II period. More than 18,000 of these engines were produced, used on airplanes such as the Boeing Stratocruiser airliner and Boeing B-50 bomber. Six of the R-4360-51 VTD model were installed on the Convair B-36 and each with its two variable discharge turbines could achieve 4,300 hp apiece. (Kodera)

326 The first airplane to cross the Atlantic Ocean with more than 100 people onboard was the Douglas C-74 Globemaster I cargo aircraft with the U.S. Air Force. The date was 18 November 1949 and the route was from the airplane's home field at Mobile, Alabama (Brookely AFB), to Marham, England, with 103 passengers and crew aboard. The C-74 became the basis for the much-enlarged Douglas C-124 Globemaster II airplane. (Kodera)

327 Due to the enormous size of the B-36 bomber, communications with ground personnel was conducted by an inter-phone system plugged into the aircraft and fitted with a headset and microphone. During preflight, numerous calls were routinely passed to the pilots in reference to flight control checks, engine starts, opening and closing the bomb bay doors, etc. A problem that continuously caused irritation was when ground personnel unplugged their headsets without telling the pilots. This caused several delays because the flight crew were afraid to move the aircraft for fear they would hurt someone. (Lewis)

328 The FICON (fighter conveyor) program was conducted by the U.S. Air Force in the 1960s. The "Tip-Tow" aircraft (a neat play on words for "tiptoe") consisted of a specially modified Boeing ETB-29A Superfortress (serial number 44-62093) and two Republic EF-84D Thunderjet fighters. Modifications to the B-29 and F-84s allowed the F-84s to attach themselves to the B-29's wingtips. Unfortunately, the program was canceled after a spectacular fatal crash when the F-84s rolled inverted into the bomber while still attached. (Lewis)

329 Unique trapeze systems mounted in the bomb bay of Boeing B-29 and Convair B-36 bombers allowed both the McDonnell XF-85 Goblin and Republic YRF-84K Thunderflash to attach themselves in flight. A similar system mounted under the dirigible USS *Macon* allowed Curtiss F9C fighters to attach themselves, as well,

FICON stood for Fighter Conveyer, a unique method for the airborne carriage of their own fighter escorts by long-range bombers.

making these fighters "parasite" aircraft to escort and protect their motherships. (Lewis)

330 The first bomber to drop a British atomic bomb was the Vickers Valiant, WZ366 of the No. 49 Bomber Squadron. Squadron Leader E.J.G. Flavell was the aircraft commander who led his crew in the test drop over Maralinga, Australia. The flight was made on 11 October 1956. (Machat)

331 The General Dynamics F-111 swing-wing fighter-bomber never had an official nickname during its nearly 30-year operational career. Because of its long, low-slung nose, its crews referred to it as the Aardvark. On the day that the Air Force's F-111 was retired, 27 July 1996, the Air Force announced that it would officially be named the Aardvark. (Caruso)

332 Northrop Grumman's contender for the Advanced Tactical Fighter was the YF-23; it competed against the Lockheed Martin YF-22. Early on, the YF-23 had a red hourglass marking on its underside, leading to the jet being referred to as the Black Widow II. (The original Black Widow was Northrop's P-61 World War II night fighter.) This violated the protocol of the Air Force getting first crack at naming aircraft, so word came down that use of the name Black Widow was forbidden and the hourglass marking, prominently visible on the cover of an issue of *Aviation Week and Space Technology*, was to be removed. (Caruso)

A Boeing B-50 Super Fortress named Lucky Lady *became the world's first aircraft to fly around the world nonstop, using multiple inflight refuelings.*

333 Imagine flying an airplane nonstop around the entire earth. How could this be possible back in 1949? What made it finally work was the advent of aerial refueling on a practical basis, not just during stunts promoting endurance. The fledgling system was known as the grappled-line looped-hose technique and utilized the services of a modified B-29 bomber as the tanker aircraft. Applying the process in March of that year, the U.S. Air Force sent a Boeing B-50 bomber known as *Lucky Lady II* on a mission to circumnavigate the Earth without landing, being refueled by in-place KB-29s over the Azores, Saudi Arabia, the Philippines, and Hawaii. Two full crews were onboard the airplane for relief flying and the B-50 flew between 10,000 and 20,000 feet at an average speed of 249 mph. Total elapsed time was 94 hours, 1 minute round-trip from Carswell AFB, Texas. (Kodera)

334 On 23 January 1951, 1st Lt. Jacob Kratt of the 27th Fighter Escort Group performed the remarkable feat of downing two North Korean MiG-15s while flying his straight-wing Republic F-84G

Thunderjet. Three days later, he shot down a North Korean Yak-3, becoming the highest-scoring F-84 pilot of the Korean War. (Lewis)

335 During the Six Day War of June 1967, fighter aircraft of the Israeli Air Force amassed a string of aerial victories unseen in the Jet Age, destroying a staggering 452 enemy aircraft during that week of intense aerial action. A total of 338 Egyptian aircraft, as well as 61 Syrian, 29 Jordanian, 23 Iraqi, and 1 Lebanese aircraft were shot down. (Machat)

336 The first aircraft with a power-to-weight ratio high enough to achieve supersonic speed in vertical flight was the Northrop YF-17 Lightweight Fighter Prototype. Although the YF-17 lost out to General Dynamics' YF-16 in an Air Force fly-off competition, the design was resurrected by McDonnell Douglas to become the F-18 Hornet.

337 Everyone knows that the experimental Bell X-1 rocket plane flown by Chuck Yeager was the first aircraft to fly at supersonic speed, but the first jet aircraft to fly supersonic in level flight is thought to be North American's F-100 Super Sabre. The F-100 was indeed the

A unique inverse-tapered wing was flown on Republic's experimental XF-91 Thunderceptor, the first aircraft to fly Mach 1 in level flight.

world's first *operational* aircraft to fly supersonic, but the title "First Supersonic Jet in Level Flight" goes to the inverse-tapered-wing–equipped Republic XF-91 Thunderceptor, powered by a General Electric J47 turbojet and single-barrel XLR11 rocket motor. (Caruso)

338 The Lockheed F-104 Starfighter was capable of Mach 2 speeds but could go no faster due to two rather unusual limitations. The first was identified as the canopy Plexiglas fasteners that could fail if Mach 2 was exceeded. The other limitation had nothing to do with the aircraft itself but was a feature of the General Electric J79 engine: As the aircraft reached Mach 2 speeds, case pressure in the engine became critical. A red warning light on the instrument panel flashed "SLOW," warning the pilot when maximum speed was reached. (Lewis)

339 The Fairchild C-123 Provider was a production twin-engine Air Force transport that evolved from a series of unique aircraft beginning with the Stroukoff Avitruck prototype. In various versions, these aircraft were flown as a glider aero-towed into the air; a piston-powered transport; a jet-augmented piston-powered transport; an experimental pure jet (using the inboard nacelles and General Electric J47 turbojets from a B-47); a water ski–equipped amphibian; and even a contra-rotating tilt-wing turboprop as the one-of-a-kind experimental Hiller X-18. (Machat)

340 The first animal to be ejected at supersonic speed was a female bear named Yogi, on 21 March 1962. The sedated bear was strapped into an escape capsule designed by the Stanley Aircraft Corporation for the Convair B-58 Hustler. Yogi was ejected from a B-58 at 35,000 feet traveling 870 mph and parachuted safely to earth. Two weeks later, another bear, Big John, was successfully ejected at 45,000 feet and more than 1,000 mph, subsequently landing unharmed. (Caruso)

341 Over the years, Air Force jet aircraft have invariably been named for birds and animals. Examples include the F-89 Scorpion, General Dynamics F-111 Aardvark, McDonnell Douglas F-15 Eagle, Lockheed F-16 Fighting Falcon (or Viper), Republic A-10

Warthog, and F-22 Raptor. Turboprops would include the North American OV-10 Bronco, and Boeing V-22 Osprey, not to mention the Soviet Tupolev Tu-95 Bear. (Machat)

342 The Martin XB-51 Panther was a three-engine jet aircraft designed for close air support. It featured two J47 engines in pods below the forward fuselage and a third J47 mounted in the tail. It incorporated leading edge slats, full-span trailing edge slotted flaps and spoilers, plus a variable-incidence feature that allowed the swept wing to be rotated up and down to improve takeoff performance. Although the aircraft had excellent flight characteristics, it lacked the necessary range to satisfy mission requirements. The B-57 Canberra was selected over the XB-51 for production and was built under license by Martin. (Lewis)

343 The Navy's Grumman F9F Panther and Martin's tri-jet XB-51 shared the same name, as did Grumman's XF10F Jaguar and the SEPECAT Anglo-French jet attack fighter of the 1960s. (Lewis)

344 The first three enemy aircraft shot down over North Korea were brought down by North American P-82 (F-82) Twin Mustangs

After jettisoning its empty external fuel tanks, an F-82 Twin Mustang engages an enemy Yak fighter during the first aerial "kill" of the Korean War.

operated from bases in Japan. The first of these was a Yak-11 near Kimpo field. Planned as a long-range escort fighter, the F-82 didn't reach operational status until after the end of World War II. Often thought to be two P-51 Mustangs mated together, Twin Mustangs were able to use only 20 percent of P-51 parts in their construction. (Lewis)

345 Consolidated Aircraft was tasked by the USAAF to design and build a long-range bomber in conjunction with Boeing's B-29 in case the Stratofortress design was unsuccessful. The result was the four-engine B-32 Dominator heavy bomber that saw limited service in the Pacific theater during World War II. One feature of the B-32 was the installation of reversible pitch propellers on the inboard engines. There are no surviving B-32s, but a few gun turrets are on display in museums and a B-32 wing panel was erected near San Diego, California, in recognition of John J. Montgomery's early glider flights. (Lewis)

346 Where did all the numbers go? Since the beginning of military aviation, sequential numbering was used for aircraft designations from P-1 through P-82 for pursuit tactical fighters; B-1 through B-70 for strategic bombers; C-1 through C-141 for cargo transports; and T-1 through T-46 for trainers, all beginning after World War I and continuing well into the 1960s. (Machat)

347 In the Jet Age, it was no surprise when the Air Force named its Century series jets in accordance with the newly evolved triple digits. The F-100 through F-106 were operational jets, while the XF-103, F-107A, XF-108, and XF-109 became the "also rans." The F-110 (USAF version of the Navy F-4 Phantom) and swing-wing F-111 proudly continued and then abruptly ended that tradition. (Machat)

348 In 1962, Secretary of Defense Robert McNamara mandated that all branches of the service use the same aircraft designations, and then after the Vietnam War, numbering for most aircraft types or programs reverted back to the numeral "1." You had the Rockwell B-1B and Northrop B-2 bombers, Lockheed C-5 Galaxy, and Beechcraft T-1 Jayhawk trainer, but fighter numerology became rather scattershot and morphed ahead with the Grumman F-14, McDonnell Douglas F-15, General Dynamics F-16, Northrop YF-17, and McDonnell Douglas F-18. (Machat)

349 After leaving off with the F-111, the Air Force's new Lockheed F-117 Stealth Fighter arrived in 1981, but what happened to numbers 113 through 116? With the declassification of the Red Eagles program (Air Force pilots flying and evaluating captured Soviet fighters), it was revealed that the designations F-113, F-114, F-115, and F-116 were assigned to the MiG and Sukhoi jets being flown in super-secret operations at Tonopah, Nevada, in the 1980s. (Machat)

350 The wingspan of Northrop's futuristic XB-35 and jet-powered YB-49 Flying Wing in 1946 was exactly 172 feet, and the wingspan of the Northrop B-2 Stealth Bomber today is exactly 172 feet. (Machat)

351 The wonder and promise of the turbine-propeller engine, the turboprop, fostered many a successful and not so successful airplane following World War II. One of the most tantalizing and titillating was the futuristic-looking Republic XF-84H nicknamed *Thunderscreech* by all who heard it run. Mating an existing swept-wing F-84F fighter jet with an Allison T-40 turboprop engine and a T-tail, engineers created what to this day is the fastest ever propeller-driven airplane in the world. In flight trials during 1955 the aircraft reached a speed of 665 mph. Two were built and one can be seen today at the National Museum of the Air Force in Dayton, Ohio. (Kodera)

352 The world's first supersonic bomber was the delta-wing Convair B-58 Hustler. Designed to fly continuously at high altitudes above sonic speeds, 90-minute high-Mach missions were the norm. Unfortunately, Soviet anti-aircraft missile technology had advanced to the point where high-altitude penetration missions were now impossible, so Air Force planners moved the Hustler to lower altitudes, including on-the-deck profiles. While the airplane was adroit at such missions, the environment caused too high a fuel consumption and the airplane found itself unable to compete with the new

Delta-wing elegance is evident in this view of Convair's B-58 Hustler, the world's first Mach-2 bomber, which first flew in 1956.

F/FB-111, from the same parent company. The B-58 flew with the active Air Force only for a short 12 years, retiring in 1970. (Kodera)

353 On 21 January 1961, Air Force Maj. H. J. Deutschendorf set a world speed record flying a Convair B-58 Hustler over a 2,000-kilometer closed course at a speed of 808 mph. The major's son, John Deutschendorf, was a singer-songwriter whose first published song, "Leaving On A Jet Plane," became a hit for recording artists Peter, Paul, and Mary. John soon changed his last name to his favorite U.S. city, and became a successful recording artist in his own right two years later. Keeping the first letter "D" in his last name, he was better known as John Denver. (Machat)

354 The first successful ejection of a B-58 escape capsule with a human test subject was made on 28 February 1962 at Edwards AFB, California. Warrant Officer Edward J. Murray ejected from the bomber at 20,000 feet while flying 565 mph and was recorded

in free-fall for 26 seconds before the main parachute deployed. He landed safely on the ground 8 minutes later. (Machat)

355 Due to the large demand for transport aircraft during World War II the Budd Company was contracted to build RB-1 Conestoga aircraft for both the U.S. Army and Navy. Since there was a shortage of aluminum, Conestoga aircraft were made with stainless steel and the Budd Company was selected because it had experience working with this material building railroad cars. Subsequent availability of C-46 and C-47 aircraft caused the Army to cancel their contract for Budd C-93s and the Navy obtained only 17 examples. Leftover RB-1 aircraft were sold as surplus and some were used by cargo carrier Flying Tigers Airline. One example is displayed at the Pima museum. (Lewis)

356 Before the high-altitude Lockheed U-2 became operational as a recon aircraft, a number of North American Aviation F-100A Super Sabre jets were modified to fulfill the reconnaissance role. Designated the RF-100A and given the name *Slick Chick*, six aircraft were quickly modified and pressed into service. Fairings were installed on either side of the nose gear bay and the 20mm cannons were removed to make room for five cameras. Four external drop tanks were installed to provide the necessary range for the planned missions and 12-inch extensions were added to the wingtips to allow the aircraft to operate at altitudes as high as 53,000 feet. (Lewis)

357 Northrop's SM-62 Snark Cruise Missile was named for the contraction of the words "snake" and shark." Launched from fixed land bases, the Snark could reach nearly 600 mph on its way to pre-programmed targets up to 5,500 miles away, flying at an altitude of 50,000 feet. Upon re-entry, the entire forward fuselage containing the warhead would jettison from the engine, wing, and tail section, and glide in a ballistic arc to its intended destination. On a test flight from Cape Canaveral, Florida, in 1956, a Snark lost its inertial guidance system and wound up in the Amazon jungle in Brazil. Luckily, there was no live nuclear warhead onboard. (Machat)

The business end of a Northrop SM-62 Snark is depicted at the moment of launch as its two solid-fuel boosters blast the missile into the air.

358 By 1954 the Air Force was facing a looming problem with the arrival of Century series fighters. New pilots would be expected to transition from straight-wing, subsonic T-33s into swept-wing, supersonic fighters. Northrop and General Electric, working together, produced a remarkable result, the T-38 Talon, powered by two small afterburning J85 turbojets. Both manufacturers overcame numerous obstacles to meet the first flight deadline, and the Talon flew on 11 April 1969, completing its flight test program with no aerodynamic changes required. The T-38 entered service less than three years from its maiden flight, a remarkable achievement for a new supersonic aircraft system. The Talon is expected to serve beyond 2020, and grandchildren of pilots who trained in the T-38 are now earning their wings in the exact same airplanes! (Frankel)

359 Speaking of the Century series, a well-known photo of the new jets was taken in 1959 at Edwards AFB when numerous world records were being broken by these new aircraft. The view was looking straight down from a hovering helicopter and showed the North American F-100C, McDonnell F-101A, Convair F-102A, Lockheed F-104A, Republic F-105B, and Convair F-106A all parked in a circle pointing inward so their nose booms were almost touching. That famous photo was named "the Century Circle." (Machat)

360 In 1999, 40 years after the Century Circle photo was taken, a similar collection of Century jets were fully restored in famous unit markings, and then parked outside the west gate at Edwards around the cab of the original 1956 control tower that was replaced in the 1990s with a taller and more modern structure. Although originally planned to replicate the original photo, not enough land was made available for the project, so base personnel named it the "Century Semi-Circle." (Machat)

361 The first licensed pilot to serve as president of the United States was Dwight Eisenhower, the former army general. He was first but certainly not last: George H. W. Bush was sworn in 1988. The third pilot-president was his son George W. Bush in 2000. (Kodera)

362 You've certainly heard of the Air Force Thunderbirds, but did you know that in 1957 there was also an Air Force team called the "Thunderweasels"? Named for the aforementioned aerobatic team combined with the 774th Troop Carrier Squadron's Green Weasels, this four-ship team flew a most unlikely aircraft for their impressive (yet mild) formation aerobatics: the Lockheed C-130A Hercules! (Lewis)

363 Renamed "the Four Horsemen" as a more acceptable team moniker, the team made aerial demonstrations of their new turboprop Hercules transports as older, piston-powered Fairchild C-119 Flying Boxcars and C-123 Providers were being phased out of the inventory. Based at Ardmore AFB, Oklahoma, the Horsemen performed crowd-pleasing high-speed formation passes and other maneuvers for about a year before being phased-out by Air Force brass concerned about potential four-way midair collisions with their newest transport aircraft. (Lewis)

364 The four-engine Lockheed C-130 turboprop transport and eight-engine Hughes HK-1 Spruce Goose flying boat were both designed as large troop transports and had the same name, *Hercules*. (Lewis)

365 As good as Fairchild Republic's A-10 Thunderbolt II was as a tank-busting ground attack aircraft, an Air Force study resulted in a proposal for a single proof-of-concept test aircraft to be built as a two-seat night and all-weather version of the twin-engine attack jet. The one-of-a-kind N/AW A-10B was flight tested and evaluated at Edwards AFB in 1992, and although considered a successful aircraft in that role, the faster two-seat McDonnell Douglas F-15E Strike Eagle plus digital-age improvements to the original A-10 design made the N/AW A-10 concept unnecessary. (Machat)

366 The N/AW A-10B was converted from a single-seat A-10, but the modifications were too extensive to convert that airframe back to a single-seater. This one-of-a-kind test jet was stripped of all tactical and weapons systems, had its twin canopies painted black, and was then placed on permanent display parked in front of the Air Force Flight Test Center Museum at Edwards AFB, California. (Machat)

367 Major Rudolf Anderson Jr. was the only U.S. pilot killed during the Cuban Missile Crisis. He was one of the U-2 pilots who flew over Cuba to take reconnaissance photos of their Soviet missile

A Lockheed U-2C is shown over the North Base complex of Edwards AFB, from which the first Cuban Missile Crisis flight was launched in October 1962.

sites. Anderson was hit by surface-to-air SA-2 missiles that downed his aircraft. Shrapnel from one of the two SA-2s penetrated his cockpit and pressure suit, which most likely killed him instantly. (Lewis)

368 After World War II, the record year for most number of first flights of Air Force aircraft (actually, all types of aircraft) was 1956 when a total of 25 new or derivative aircraft types first flew. Such significant USAF airplanes as the Convair F-106 Delta Dart and B-58 Hustler were on that list, as were the Douglas C-133 Cargomaster, the "D" and two-seat "F" models of the North American F-100 Super Sabre, and the Boeing KC-135 Stratotanker. (Machat)

369 Lockheed's XF-90 was the first of their aircraft with afterburners and the first Lockheed aircraft to reach Mach 1, although it could only do so in a dive. Thrust from the twin J34 turbojets was far less than planned as engine technology lagged behind development of new airframes. Two XF-90s were built using new technology that made their airframes extremely strong, but they were 50 percent heavier than competitive designs. One of the XF-90s was tested to destruction and the other exposed to three nuclear blasts in Nevada. This second XF-90 is on display at the USAF museum. (Lewis)

370 Although head-up displays are used in everything from jet fighters to commercial airliners and even exotic sports cars, the first practical design of an optical device projecting visual information onto the inner windshield of an aircraft was the Republic XF-91 Thunderceptor in 1949. The center windshield was composed of two mitered vertical panes of glass that met at a 60-degree angle. Inside that structure was a single pane of glass that created a chamber inside the windshield filled with ambient air. Gunsight imagery was then projected onto that flat pane, mitigating the need for the pilot to take his eyes off the target ahead. (Machat)

371 The XF-91 exceeded Mach 1 in level flight aided by the supplemental thrust of an integral rocket engine, meaning a rocket powerplant built into the design of the aircraft. Three other experimental prototype jet fighters were built in Europe powered by single turbojet engines boosted with either ramjet or integral rocket motors. These supersonic aircraft were the French NORD Griffon II (Mach 2.19) and Trident III (Mach 1.6), and the British Saunders-Roe SR. 53 (Mach 1.6). (Machat)

With his Republic F-105D Thunderchief safely back on the ramp, Col. Jack Broughton debriefs his Crew Chief on another mission over North Vietnam.

372 Called "the greatest wing commander the Air Force ever had" by Brig Gen. Chuck Yeager, Col. Jack Broughton was a "fighter pilot's fighter pilot." Broughton flew in the Korean War and Vietnam War, and was the only pilot of captain rank to command the Thunderbirds Aerial Demonstration Team. He also has the distinction of flying every fighter aircraft built by the Republic Aviation Corporation from P-47 Thunderbolts over Berlin in 1946 to the F-105 Thunderchief over Vietnam in 1966. In between he operationally flew the F-84G Thunderjet and F-84F Thunderstreak and made flights in the RF-84F Thunderflash to complete the entire Republic set. (Machat)

373 Douglas AD (A-1E) Skyraider aircraft with the call sign Sandy were used to protect Sikorsky MH-53 Jolly Green search and rescue helicopters for the U.S. Air Force during the Vietnam War. The Sandys could loiter for long periods at low altitude and employ a variety of munitions to counter enemy activity while the helicopters completed rescue operations. They were nicknamed SPADs due to the use of older propeller-driven aircraft during the war where jet aircraft were more frequently employed. (Lewis)

374 After several months in service some Cessna T-37 trainers experienced random engine flameouts shortly after executing their break into the pattern for landing. After spending hours investigating inlet airflow under every conceivable condition, engineers failed to duplicate the condition. Finally it was noticed that the flameouts were occurring in the earliest-serial-number aircraft. This led to the discovery that, over time, engine mount grommets were softening from the hot environment of the engine bay. These softened grommets allowed the engines to shift slightly under G load, which in turn allowed throttle linkage to move to the "idle shut-off" position, causing fuel starvation. Stiffening the engine mount grommets kept the engines running under all conditions. (Frankel)

375 Both of Northrop's XB-35 and YB-49 flying wings were advanced bomber designs developed shortly after World War II. Turbojet engines were incorporated into two of the piston-powered XB-35s to test them using jet power. With the elimination of the fuselage the flying wings demonstrated excellent performance but they also had stability problems. The Convair B-36 was selected over the Northrop flying wings for production and Northrop's flying wing program was canceled. Instructions were then issued to destroy all the existing airframes. Years later the Northrop B-2 Spirit proved both the flying wing design and stealth characteristics. (Lewis)

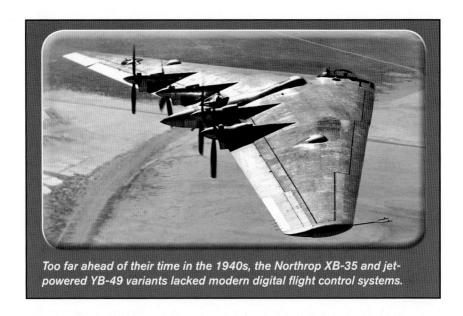

Too far ahead of their time in the 1940s, the Northrop XB-35 and jet-powered YB-49 variants lacked modern digital flight control systems.

376 The cutting-edge British Aircraft Corporation BAC TSR.2 (Tactical Strike and Reconnaissance) aircraft was developed in Britain after World War II. When the first prototype took to the air in late 1964, it was the most technically advanced aircraft in the world. Production of the TSR.2 placed the British aircraft industry as a world leader in aircraft design and development. Despite meeting every aspect of the government's requirement, and completing numerous test flight milestones, the project was abruptly canceled under political pressure. The airplane was powered by two of the newly developed Bristol Siddeley Olympus 320 turbojet engines, each producing more than 30,000 pounds of thrust in reheat (afterburner). These were among the most powerful engines in the world at that time. (Frankel)

377 On 22 February 1965, with Chief Test Pilot Roland Beaumont at the controls, the TSR.2 exceeded Mach 1 for the first time, in level flight along the Irish Sea, and with only one engine in afterburner. The jet easily accelerated away from its Lightning T.Mk 4 chase plane, which had both its engines in afterburner. Although the TSR.2's engine had numerous development problems, the follow-on variant of the Olympus went on to power the Concorde supersonic airliner for nearly three decades of steady reliable service. (Frankel)

378 Convair's chief pilot Beryl A. Erickson made the first flights of a number of significant Convair aircraft, including the six-engine B-36 Peacemaker and Mach-2 B-58 Hustler. Erickson also always claimed the distinction of being the first pilot in history to log 100 hours of supersonic flight time, all while flying the B-58. (Machat)

379 Erickson is also the first pilot to make an undetected low-level intrusion into "denied" airspace while proving the concept of low-level penetration for SAC bombers inbound to their targets deep within the Soviet Union. On 18 September 1959, Erickson piloted a B-58 from Carswell AFB, Texas, to Vandenberg AFB, California, and overflew the Edwards AFB runway essentially undetected on approach. He was never above 1,000 feet on the high-speed inbound leg but returned to Carswell at high altitude after making the Vandenberg turn point. No aerial refueling was required to make that flight! (Machat)

380 Beryl Erickson was one of many contractor test pilots who had no military experience before being hired by a manufacturer of military aircraft for flight testing advanced, high-performance aircraft of all types. Other such civilian pilots included Lockheed's Tony LeVier and Herman "Fish" Salmon, Douglas Aircraft's Gene May, and beloved Republic test pilot Carl Bellinger. (Machat)

381 One of several narrow escapes from death for test pilot Carl Bellinger came when he was landing an F-84 Thunderjet at Republic's Farmingdale, Long Island, plant in the late 1940s. The aircraft experienced complete brake failure, and after rolling off the end of the runway, the jet had slowed, but still jumped a drainage ditch, hit a chain link barbed-wire fence, and flipped upside-down into an employee parking lot. Thankfully, the inverted cockpit wound up hanging in the empty parking space of a company employee who had stayed home sick that day! (Machat)

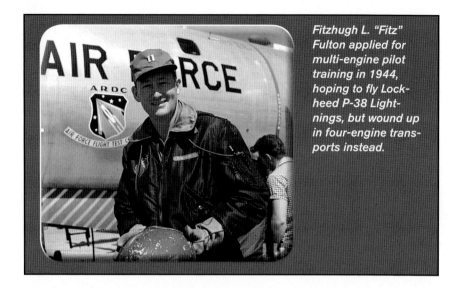

Fitzhugh L. "Fitz" Fulton applied for multi-engine pilot training in 1944, hoping to fly Lockheed P-38 Lightnings, but wound up in four-engine transports instead.

382 Fitzhugh "Fitz" Fulton's amazing test pilot career began when he was transferred from the East Coast to the dry climate at Edwards AFB because his daughter suffered from asthma. He went on to fly some of the most advanced and sophisticated aircraft in the inventory, including the North American Aviation XB-70 Valkyrie, Lockheed YF-12, B-58 Hustler, and the Boeing 747 SCA modified to carry the space shuttle. He also flew C-54 Skymasters during the Berlin Airlift and Boeing B-29, B-50, and B-52 launch aircraft to become known as "the Father of the Mother Ships." (Lewis)

383 Fitz Fulton made the last flight of the surviving North American XB-70 Valkyrie experimental bomber in 1969, delivering the six-engine triple-sonic aircraft to the Air Force Museum at Wright-Patterson AFB in Dayton, Ohio. (Ship 2 had been lost in an accident at Edwards AFB in June 1966.) The date of the XB-70's final flight that year was February 4. Fulton retired from his long and successful USAF and NASA career in 1986 and passed away in 2014 at a retirement community near Los Angeles after battling a long illness, at the age of 89. The date was February 4. (Machat)

384 The USAF and USN adopted officially the use of knot (slang for nautical-mile-per-hour) and nautical mile as standard aeronautical units of measure for speed and distance on 26 June 1946. A nautical mile is exactly 6,000 feet in length, which works perfectly mathematically when dealing with a 60-minute/second clock and timing situation. Its whole number is also easier to work with than the statute mile of 5,280 feet. (Kodera)

385 In 1934, Robert Switzer and his brother, Joseph, experimented with organic compounds from their father's drug store that displayed a natural florescence, blending these compounds with shellac in the family bathtub to arrive at the first florescent paint. "Glowing paint" was initially used for entertainment purposes, but it generated interest among industrial users, so Switzer marketed the paint under the name Day-Glo, and during World War II it was used on large fabric panels to identify friendly troops to Allied dive bombers. (Frankel)

386 By the late 1950s Day-Glo paint was also applied to non-tactical military and civilian aircraft for collision avoidance. The CAA considered a proposal that civilian aircraft should carry large areas of Day-Glo. Unfortunately, florescent paints proved fragile and rapidly faded from continued exposure to sunlight. By the late 1960s non-florescent red and orange paints had replaced Day-Glo. (Frankel)

387 The old ways are often the best ways, but even the U.S. Army Signal Corps finally had to bow to the march of technological progress when, on 4 December 1956, it officially discontinued the use of carrier pigeons in military combat environments. (Kodera)

388 Sadly, among the many operational and/or prototype Air Force aircraft that were either lost in accidents or scrapped at the end of their careers are the Convair XB-46 and YB-60, and Martin XB-48 and XB-51 bombers, all of which competed unsuccessfully for lucrative production contracts in the early years of the Cold War. Not one of these airplanes survived to be exhibited in museums today. (Lewis)

389 Additional Air Force aircraft considered ahead of their time when they first flew in the years immediately following World War II were three experimental prototypes from three novel and innovative U.S. aircraft manufacturers: the Northrop XB-35 and YB-49 flying wings, and the Hughes XF-11 and Republic XR-12 high-performance photo reconnaissance aircraft. None survive today. (Machat)

U.S. NAVY

390 First jet fighter in the United States to exceed 1,000 mph was the Chance Vought F8U-1 Crusader naval fleet defense interceptor. The pilot for the day's record was CDR R. W. Windsor, who reached a top speed of 1,015 mph over a closed course. (Kodera)

391 Although the aircraft carrier HMS *Arc Royal* had been mothballed, the British Royal Navy incorporated several innovative features adapted by U.S. Navy aircraft carriers that greatly improved both safety and operational efficiency. These included angled decks to allow both takeoffs and landings to be conducted simultaneously without fear of collision; steam catapults to allow the launch of larger, more powerful, and heavier aircraft; mirror landing systems to enhance the ability to fly a more precision glide path to landing; and ski jump ramps for launching Harrier VTOL jump jets. (Lewis)

392 North American's FJ-1 Fury was the first operational jet aircraft in the U.S. Navy. It first flew on 11 September 1946. The aircraft was developed using similar tail, wings, and canopy as the P-51D Mustang. It was a transitional design with straight wings, and only 30 aircraft were completed and delivered. (Lewis)

393 The FJ-1 also made the first operational landing of a Navy airplane aboard an aircraft carrier on 10 March 1948. Although the Fury could take off without the use of a catapult, it required the full length of the carrier deck to become airborne. Because it didn't have folding wings, North American installed a unique nose wheel that allowed the aircraft to kneel so they could load more planes into the limited space on aircraft carrier decks. (Lewis)

394 The "Battle of Palmdale" involved an attempt by U.S. Air Force F-89 Scorpion aircraft to intercept a Grumman QF6F Hellcat drone that the U.S. Navy had launched from Pt. Mugu Naval Air Station on a test flight. When contact with the drone was lost F-89s were scrambled from Oxnard Air Force Base to intercept and shoot down the drone. The F-89 Scorpions were armed with rockets for air defense and contained no guns, making them ill-suited for the task. Although several attempts to bring down the drone were made, they were unsuccessful and started several large brush fires in the process. The drone eventually ran out of fuel and crashed in an unpopulated area of the desert. (Lewis)

395 When a U.S. Navy F-4 Phantom aircraft attempted a gear-up landing at DaNang Air Base, Vietnam, the tailhook failed when the pilot engaged the barrier cable, so as the aircraft was sliding down the runway the pilot selected afterburners then rotated the aircraft off its belly so he could fly out over the gulf to allow himself and his RIO to eject, which they did successfully. Everything went well until the rescue helicopter attempted to hoist the RIO (back seater) up but managed to injure him in the rescue process. (Lewis)

396 LTJG William T. Patton from Navy's VA-176 squadron shot down a MiG-17 over Vietnam on 9 October 1966. This was the second victory scored by a propeller-driven piston-powered Doug-las Skyraider against a NVAF MiG. (Lewis)

397 The height of the hangar decks on British aircraft carriers made it necessary to modify their Corsairs so they would fit below decks. Wingtips of the aircraft were cut down by 8 inches to allow them to be stored in the hangar decks. The wingtips of the British Corsairs had a noticeable flat appearance compared to the round wingtips on U.S. F4Us. (Lewis)

398 Although the Blue Angels are America's oldest military precision aerobatic demonstration team, the world's oldest aerobatic team is France's *Patrouille Acrobatique de France* (French Acrobatic Patrol), also known as the *Patrouille de France* or PAF. This aerobatic demonstration team of the French Air Force originated in 1931; it is not only the world's oldest, but one of the most skilled aerial demonstration teams ever formed. Its pilots currently fly the Dassault/Dornier Alpha Jet. (Lewis)

Martin's magnificent XP6M-1 Seamaster was the world's only four-engine jet flying boat and was capable of near-sonic speeds.

399 The Glenn L. Martin Company designed and built the P6M SeaMaster four-engine jet flying boat. The U.S. Navy lacked an aircraft that could deliver nuclear weapons and wanted to find ways to correct the problem. The P6Ms were initially powered by J71 engines but were later fitted with J75s and could sustain Mach 0.9 in level flight at low altitude. Two prototype aircraft were built and both were lost due to pitch control failures. An additional 10 aircraft were built but the P6M never went into full production. The program was canceled and the remaining P6Ms were scrapped. (Lewis)

400 It was the twin-engine Douglas F3D Skyknight that became, surprisingly, the first specific U.S. Navy aircraft to shoot down more enemy airplanes in Korea than any other single Navy type.

The stubby subsonic jet carried a crew of two in a side-by-side cockpit: the pilot and a radar intercept operator (RIO). (Kodera)

401 On 17 September 1958, the Navy's new super carrier USS *Forrestal* (CVA-59) arrived on station in the Mediterranean on its first deployment. Onboard was a complement of contemporary naval aircraft, including the new supersonic F8U-1 Crusader. In a unique happenstance, all the other aircraft in Carrier Air Wing 10 that cruise were built by the Douglas Company in El Segundo and Torrance, California. These were the A3D Skywarrior, A4D Skyhawk, F4D Skyray, and three versions of the venerable AD Skyraider: the AD-5N, AD-5W, and AD-6. This was the only cruise in naval history to have every Douglas type aboard. (Machat)

402 Grumman's S2F Tracker was a conventional twin-engine design built for the U.S. Navy as an anti-submarine aircraft. The S2F designation was often pronounced "STOOF" by Navy personnel. Grumman used the basic airframe to develop a later-model E-1 Tracer that had a radome mounted on top of the airframe. Tracers were dubbed STOOF with a ROOF. One woman, who had never seen an E-1 before, called a nearby Navy base and excitedly told them, "A flying saucer has stolen one of your aircraft." Many S2s have found a new life converted with turboprop engines as high-performance fire bombers. (Lewis)

403 Grumman also produced the C-1 Trader COD (Carrier Onboard Delivery) version of the S2F to shuttle men and supplies to and from aircraft carriers. These piston-powered workhorses were replaced by another Grumman aircraft, the turboprop C-2 Greyhound, which was also converted from a carrier-based radar patrol aircraft, the E-2C Hawkeye. (Lewis)

404 Lieutenant Royce Williams, U.S. Navy Grumman F9F-5 Panther pilot, shot down three MiG 15 fighters while flying a Combat Air Patrol (CAP) mission off the aircraft carrier USS *Oriskany*. His flight leader developed mechanical problems and returned to the ship with his wingman flying chase. Shortly after they left,

Williams and his wingman encountered seven MiG 15s. During the dogfight that ensued, he managed to shoot down three of the MiGs even though his F9F had been hit by enemy fire. Williams coaxed his F9F back to the *Oriskany* and landed safely. (Lewis)

405 The first incidence of a successful nighttime radar interception of a jet aircraft by another jet aircraft occurred on 2 November 1952 when an F3D Skyknight from VMF(N)-513 downed a Soviet-built North Korean Yakovlev Yak-15 fighter during the Korean War. (Kodera)

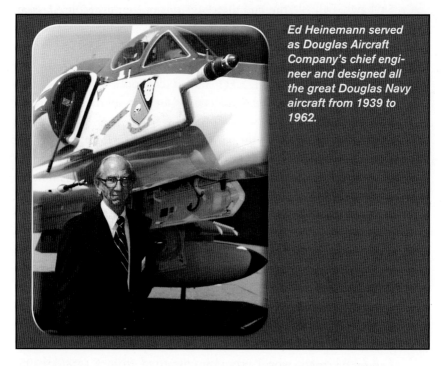

Ed Heinemann served as Douglas Aircraft Company's chief engineer and designed all the great Douglas Navy aircraft from 1939 to 1962.

406 Legendary designer Ed Heinemann, chief engineer of the Douglas Aircraft Company and "father of the naval aviation greats" such as the AD Skyraider, A3D Skywarrior, A4R Skyhawk, F4D Skyray, and D-558-2 Skyrocket, always strove for simplicity and weight reduction wherever possible in his aircraft designs. His famous phrase uttered many times to members of his design team was, "Add lightness and simplificate!" (Machat)

407 First U.S. Navy jet fighter designed to be supersonic in-service was the enigmatic Douglas F4D Skyray, the delta-wing interceptor from designer Ed Heinemann and his El Segundo, California, design team. The airplane first flew in January 1951 and was the first Navy jet fighter to exceed Mach 1 in level flight. For his pioneering work on the airplane, Heinemann received the Collier Trophy for a significant aviation contribution. Second on the naval supersonic chronology list was the Grumman F11F Tiger from Calverton, New York. (Kodera)

408 By late 1953 the Douglas F4D-1 had established itself as an exceptionally promising airplane, but it was apparent that its basic aerodynamics, developed in the late 1940s, were dated. Douglas had little difficulty in convincing the Navy to authorize work on an improved Skyray, which became known as the F5D-1 Skylancer. The new airframe was lengthened by 8 feet, retained the same wing planform but the wing was thinned by 30 percent. Its inlet ducts were flattened, and a new V-shaped windshield was designed. The new 17,200-pound-thrust engine planned for production Skylancers was not available during flight test so the prototypes flew on the same 16,000-pound-thrust J57 engine that powered the Skyray. However, the sleeker Skylancer reached a speed of Mach 1.63, more than 60 percent faster than the Mach 1.1 Skyray. A stunning example of what a little aerodynamic improvement can do. (Frankel)

409 Naval carrier aircraft are typically burdened with arresting gear, folding wing structure, and reinforced landing gear, which hinder performance. So it was unusual when the Navy's XF4D-1, prototype of a soon-to-be batwing carrier-based interceptor, broke the world's absolute speed record on 3 October 1953 averaging 753.4 mph over a 3-km course. (Frankel)

410 One month later the Air Force flew its new North American YF-100 to 757 mph over the same course. However, the official rules of the Federation Aeronautique International require an increase of at least 1 percent. Thus 760.9 mph would be required to achieve a new record. The Air Force, relying on a little-known technicality, re-flew the record attempt over a 15-km course. This flight produced an average speed of 754.98 mph, 2.02 mph slower than the earlier attempt, but it was still faster than the Skyray. The FAI ruled that 15-km flight was no longer subject to the 1-percent rule, so the Skyray became the world's fastest airplane for only one month. (Frankel)

411 In yet another example of Navy and Air Force interaction, McDonnell Douglas offered the U.S. Navy a carrier-based version of their F-15 dubbed the F-15N Sea Eagle as a substitute for the Grumman F-14 Tomcat that had been experiencing problems with their Pratt & Whitney TF30 engines. Although the Sea Eagle would have both Sparrow and Sidewinder missiles as well as a gun, it lacked the long-range AIM-54 Phoenix missiles used by the Tomcat. (Lewis)

412 Navy jets flew from aircraft carriers in the early days of jet operations with their canopies open for takeoff and landing. This was to expedite safe egress from the cockpit in the event of water landings after catapult launch or arresting gear accidents, which were all too common at the time. (Caruso)

413 Phantom Phacts: The McDonnell (and McDonnell Douglas after 1967) F-4 Phantom was the world's first tactical jet fighter to reach a production total of 5,000 aircraft built. Literally defining the relatively new concept of a "multirole" aircraft, F-4s were flown by U.S. Navy, Air Force, and Marine Corps, as well as the air arms of 11 foreign countries, both land and aircraft carrier–based. (Machat)

414 During the Vietnam War era, notable Navy aircraft types were brought into the Air Force inventory: the Douglas AD Skyraider, which became the A-1E and A-1H models; and the McDonnell F-4 Phantom II that retained its Navy designation but was modified for USAF roles as a gunfighter (F-4E), Wild Weasel ECM aircraft (F-4G), and photo-recon jet (RF-4C). The third Navy jet to become an Air Force aircraft was the Vought A-7 Corsair II. (Machat)

415 The U.S. Navy contracted with Convair to design and build three variants of the Tradewind flying boat. The P5Y design

The Navy's largest turboprop was the Convair R3Y-2 Tradewind, designed as an airborne troop transport and adapted as an aerial tanker.

could carry bombs, mines, depth charges, and torpedoes, and was armed with five pairs of 20mm cannons. The R3Y-1 variant was designed to be used as a troop transport, or cargo or air refueling aircraft; and the R3Y-2 was fitted with a hinged nose for heavy transport delivery and landing-ship service. Tradewind aircraft suffered problems with their Allison T40 turboprop engines throughout the program, and these problems were never completely resolved, leading to early retirement of the aircraft. (Lewis)

416 The world's first nuclear-powered aircraft carrier was the U.S. Navy's CVN-65 *Enterprise*. The ship was commissioned in 1961 and inactivated in 2012, making her the longest serving aircraft carrier in Navy history. Almost four football fields long, *Enterprise* could carry 4,600 crew and 100 aircraft. Longest warship ever built at the time, the *Enterprise* name will live on as CVN-80 in the new Gerald R. Ford class of carriers. (Kodera)

417 The ill-fated McDonnell Douglas A-12 Avenger II was to be the Navy's first stealthy combat aircraft. Its tailless triangular flying wing shape led to it being called the "Flying Dorito." Because this was a top-secret development, program personnel were afraid to put out the triangular corn chips at social events for fear that classified information might slip out. (Caruso)

418 The A-12 should perhaps have been designated the A-13, since there had already been an A-12: the Lockheed reconnaissance precursor to the famed Blackbird family. Had the Navy's aircraft been designated the A-13, the number might have led to more scrutiny of the design's development; instead, the unlucky program was canceled in January 1991. (Caruso)

419 Three U.S. aircraft have been named "Cobra." The Bell Aircraft AH-1 Cobra helicopter, Northrop Corporation ground attack YA-9A Cobra, and supersonic YF-17 Cobra. The A-9 lost out to the Fairchild A-10 Thunderbolt II (Warthog) during a fly-off competition and the YF-17 lost out to the General Dynamics F-16 Falcon but went on to be produced for the U.S. Navy as the F/A-18A, B, C, and D Hornet; the F/A-18E, F, Super Hornet; and F-18G Growler ECM aircraft. (Lewis)

420 The first 18-cylinder piston aircraft engine in the United States was the Pratt & Whitney R-2800 Double Wasp of 1939. By combining two rows of piston cylinders the Pratt engine was capable of 2,000 horsepower in its first iteration, leaping in later development all the way up to 2,800 hp. This is perhaps the classic engine of all reciprocating powerplants in aviation history. It found application in World War II aircraft from the Vought F4U Corsair to the Grumman F6F Hellcat and countless other successful military combat aircraft. (Lewis)

421 Lockheed Corporation designed and built the R6V Constitution aircraft in response to a request from the U.S. Navy to provide a replacement for existing flying boats currently in operation. Pan American was also interested in the design as a possible large-capacity airliner for their routes. Only two prototype aircraft were built and both entered service with the U.S. Navy. The aircraft were found to be both underpowered and the engines prone to overheating. It was deemed too large for practical use by Pan Am as an airliner. The two Constitutions were sold as surplus and have subsequently been scrapped. (Lewis)

422 Largest flying boat ever to fly was the Hughes HK-1 Hercules, also known derisively as the Spruce Goose, due to its all-wood construction. The Hughes/Kaiser design flew only once. The largest flying boat ever to become operational was the Martin JM3 Mars, of which 21 were ordered but 5 built. They served the United States Navy until 1956 and, following retirement, 2 went on to fly as water bombers in Canada. (Kodera)

Convair's delta-wing XF2Y-1 SeaDart was the world's fastest seaplane, but the concept of high-speed operations on water proved impractical.

423 They first water-based aircraft to exceed the speed of sound (Mach 1) was the intriguing Convair XF2Y-1 SeaDart turbo-jet-powered seaplane. This event occurred on 3 August 1954 at San Diego, California, the manufacturer's home city. (Lewis)

424 The *Essex* class carrier USS *Franklin D. Roosevelt* (CVB-42), commissioned on 27 October 1945, was the first U.S. aircraft carrier to be named after a person. Until that time, carriers were generally named after battles in which the United States had been involved or named for historic U.S. warships. (Caruso)

425 The first purely jet-powered aircraft to land aboard an aircraft carrier was a de Havilland Vampire piloted by Royal Navy Lieutenant Commander F. M. Brown on 3 December 1945. The specially modified Vampire landed aboard the Royal Navy's HMS *Ocean*. (Caruso)

426 The first purely jet-powered aircraft to operate from a U.S. aircraft carrier was the McDonnell XFH-1 Phantom. On 21 July 1946 LCDR James Davidson, USN, made a series of takeoffs and landings aboard the USS *Franklin D. Roosevelt*. (Caruso)

427 With post–World War II funding limitations in effect, successive designs from a given manufacturer often shared the same numerical designation, despite being an almost completely new aircraft. For Grumman's famed Navy "cats," the straight-wing F9F-1 through F9F-5 was the Panther; its swept-wing cousin with uprated engine was the F9F-6 through F9F-8 Cougar; and the much-improved, and much more powerful supersonic version was to be the F9F-9 Tiger. The Navy realized the significance of the latter design and the Tiger was properly redesignated F11F. (Machat)

428 None of the U.S. Navy's fastest single-engine jet-powered aircraft are in service today because, since 1958, the Navy rightfully insists on having two engines for safety and reliability for their carrier-based jets. The two operational supersonic single-engine Navy jets were the Vought F8U-1 Crusader (Mach 1.86) and Grumman F11F-1F Tiger (Mach 1.1). Two other fast Navy aircraft that never entered production were the Vought XF8U-3 Super Crusader (Mach 2.39) and Douglas XF5D-1 Skylancer (Mach 1.48). It is interesting to note that all these aircraft made their first flights before 1960. An exception is the Lockheed Martin F-35B. (Machat)

429 The reason the island on an aircraft carrier is placed on the starboard side is apocryphal. The gyroscopic effect of the rotary engines on early airplanes pitched the nose up on a left turn, down on a right turn, so pilots preferred to turn left in the event of a go-around. Or, it may have been simply arbitrary, as one of the ship's designers later claimed. When later carriers did have an island, placing it on the starboard side became the norm. (Caruso)

430 Throughout aviation history design cross-over from military aircraft to commercial airliners, and vice versa, has been used to great advantage, and Navy aircraft were no exception. The Douglas twinjet DC-9-30 airliner became the C-9B Skytrain II (named after the C-47 of World War II), while Lockheed's pioneering turboprop L-188 Electra became the P-3 Orion anti-submarine, patrol, and ELINT aircraft, which only recently was replaced by the Boeing P-8 Poseidon, a military conversion of the long-produced 737-800 jetliner. (Machat)

431 The U.S. Navy was concerned about failure of the wing sweep on their F-14 Tomcat during flight operations. Could the F-14 continue to operate effectively if one of the wings failed to move to the selected position? The Navy asked Grumman to run tests to see if the Tomcat was controllable with asymmetrical wing positions. Grumman's Chief Test Pilot, Chuck Sewell, flew the aircraft with one wing locked forward and the opposite wing positioned at 35, 50, 60, and 68 degrees sweep. Sewell found that he could maintain control and land with one wing at 20 degrees and the other in a 60-degree position. (Lewis)

432 While Grumman's F-14 Tomcat is considered one of, if not the most successful carrier-based fleet defense interceptors ever built, its success was largely a result of exemplary engineering using data derived from a predecessor aircraft whose performance was considered underwhelming at best. The first of two Grumman XF10F Jaguars was flown in May 1952 as a proof-of-concept prototype to demonstrate the feasibility of variable-sweep wings on a Navy fighter. Although underpowered with its Westinghouse J40 turbojet, the Jaguar proved the viability of the articulated wing pivot mechanism essentially used in the F-14. (Machat)

433 Three years before he was selected as a NASA Mercury Astronaut, Marine Col John Glenn became the first pilot to make a supersonic coast-to-coast flight across the United States on 16 July 1957. Making the record run for Project Bullet in a new Vought F8U-1P Crusader, Glenn accomplished the flight from NAS Los Alamitos, California, to New York's Floyd Bennett Field in 3 hours and 23 minutes, refueling from three North American AJ Savage tankers along the way. (Machat)

Before John Glenn was a Mercury Astronaut, he made the first U.S. supersonic coast-to-coast flight in this Vought F8U-1P Crusader.

434 The day after setting the cross-country speed record, Glenn flew his photo-recon Crusader from Floyd Bennett Field out over neighboring New York Harbor, making a south-to-north "on the deck," photo pass of the Statue of Liberty, taking a picture of the iconic structure with his belly camera. To accomplish this, Glenn flew the jet in "knife-edge" flight (wings perpendicular to the water) with his right wingtip low enough to kick-up spray. (Machat)

435 The largest aircraft ever flown from an aircraft carrier was a Lockheed C-130 Hercules (USMC KC-130F), which made a successful series of landings and takeoffs from the USS *Forrestal* (CVA-59) in 1963. The Marine test aircraft became the largest and heaviest aircraft to ever land on, and takeoff from, a carrier with its 98-foot length, 133-foot wingspan, and 155,000 pounds maximum gross takeoff weight (MGTOW). (Machat)

436 To test the feasibility of operating Lockheed U-2s from aircraft carriers at sea in remote parts of the world, a flight test U-2 was flown from the USS *America* (CVA-66) in 1966 making 29 touch-and-go landings, 21 takeoffs from the flight deck (non-catapult), and 21 landings to a full stop. The U-2's wingspan of 103 feet barely cleared the carrier's island structure. (Machat)

437 The largest and heaviest *operational* Navy aircraft flown routinely from an aircraft carrier is the Douglas A3D Skywarrior series, affectionately nicknamed "the Whale." With a length of 76 feet 4 inches, a wingspan of 72 feet 6 inches, and a MGTOW of 82,000 pounds, the Skywarrior won that title handily. (Machat)

438 Naval aviation enthusiasts may argue that other larger and more modern aircraft beat the Skywarrior's claim as larger or heavier, but here are the facts: North American's piston-powered A2J Savage was 70 feet long, had a 72-foot span, and weighed 61,200 pounds at launch. That company's A3J Vigilante was 76 feet 6 inches long, had a span of 53 feet, and weighed 62,950 pounds at launch, while the Grumman F-14 Tomcat had a 63-foot length, a 64-foot wingspan (wings fully extended), and weighed 74,350 pounds MGTOW. (Machat)

439 Unfortunately, many operational and/or prototype aircraft built for the U.S. Navy were either lost in accidents or scrapped at the end of their careers with not even one example left anywhere in the world. Paramount among these aircraft types would be the Lockheed R6V-1 Constitution transport, Convair R3Y Tradewind flying boat, and Vought XF8U-3 Super Crusader. (Lewis)

Formation aerobatics reached new heights when the Navy's Blue Angels flew their supersonic Grumman F11F-1F Tigers.

440 Of all the great aircraft flown by the U.S. Navy Aerial Demonstration Team, the perennial favorite in the 1950s was the Grumman F-11F-1F Tiger. This single-seat single-engine jet was the Blue Angels' first supersonic aircraft, although it was never intentionally flown supersonic at an air show due to the potential damage caused by the pressure wave of a sonic boom at low altitude. (Machat)

441 Just for comparison, the top five fastest single-engine jet-powered foreign aircraft are the former-Soviet Mikoyan Ye-166
(modified MiG-21) at Mach 2.3, the Chinese Chengdu J-10 (Mach
2.2), the French Dassault Mirage III (Mach 2.1), Swedish SAAB J37
Viggen (Mach 2.1), and Israeli Aircraft Industries Kfir (Mach 2.0).
(Machat)

U.S. ARMY

442 The Cessna 185 (L-19/O-1 Birddog), Cessna 310 (U-3 Blue
Canoe), Cessna 337 Skymaster (O-2 Skymaster), Helio Courier (UA-10), and de Havilland Beaver (L-20) were all civilian aircraft adapted for military use as utility and liaison aircraft for the
U.S. Army and Air Force from the 1950s through the Vietnam War
era. (Machat)

443 The Army's Grumman OV-1 Mohawk and Air Force North
American OV-10 Bronco twin-turboprops were pure military
designs from the start, intended for down and dirty interdiction
work and forward air control roles in Southeast Asia. However,
both these aircraft were adapted for civilian use with the U.S. Forest Service as lead-in and spotter aircraft for larger fire bombers.
(Machat)

444 With camera drones being all the rage today, it's sometimes
hard to realize that the first operational camera-carrying
aircraft controlled by radio was developed for the U.S. Army in
the mid-1950s. The 12-foot-long RP-71 took off with a jet-assist
booster and could climb at 3,000 feet per minute to reach altitudes
as high as 25,000 feet. With a top speed of 225 mph, the RP-71
could take either still or movie footage of strategic targets and other
military points of interest before being brought back to its launch
point by a ground operator. The engine would then be shut down
and the drone would parachute back to Earth with its photos ready
for developing and analysis by field commanders. (Machat)

445 In the cat-and-mouse adventure known as the Cold War, the Soviet Communist empire was pursued by Western democracies, and vice versa. In this high-stakes game of intrigue, few shocks were felt as deeply as the orbiting of the world's first artificial satellite, Sputnik. On 4 October 1957 the Soviet Union placed in orbit a 24-inch globe that carried instrumentation to verify and assess Earth's upper atmosphere, but it may as well have been laden with atomic bombs, the implications to world peace being that acute and dangerous. This single event changed the nature of the nascent space exploration program in the West, especially in the United States, and a new term was instantly coined: the *Space Race*. (Kodera)

Chapter 3

Experimental Research Aircraft

Experimental aircraft have been developed since the beginning of flight, but the rare X-Planes flown at the fabled test site originally known as Muroc, and then Edwards, were truly one-of-a-kind. Contributing reams of data to engineers probing the untested frontiers of flight, these "flying test tubes" paved the way to the stars. From the world's first supersonic flight in 1947 to the first flight outside the Earth's atmosphere in 1956, these machines did it all. Mach 2 fell in 1953, then Mach 3 in 1956, and Mach 4, 5, and 6 all in 1961. Altitudes well above 300,000 feet were reached by 1963. Triumph and tragedy often accompanied these flights, but the contributions of the famed experimental wonders of flight test cannot be denied.

THE JET AGE

446 For variable-geometry wings in the Jet Age, the Germans designed the Messerschmitt P.1101 with wings that could be placed in either full sweep or low-speed configuration on the ground only prior to flight. This aircraft was captured by Allied forces at the end of World War II and was studied extensively by Bell Aircraft Company in Buffalo, New York, which modified the design with moving/articulating wings and a larger airframe, yielding the X-5 research aircraft. (Kodera)

Bursting out of the bright desert sun are all the legendary X-Planes from the Golden Age of flight test.

Graphic comparison of the World War II German P.1101 (top) and 1950s Bell X-5, first experimental testbeds for variable-sweep wings.

447 The first experimental tactical fighter, first carrier-based variable-geometry-wing (VGW) aircraft, and first operational Navy VGW jet were all built on knowledge gleaned from the Bell X-5, utilized by Grumman and General Dynamics to produce a series of fighter aircraft in the 1950s, 1960s, and 1970s (XF10F Jaguar, F-111B, and F-14 Tomcat), and even the Boeing Company for their entry into the still-born SST supersonic transport competition of 1967. French and Soviet VGW designs have also been flying successfully for decades. (Kodera)

448 Both the Convair XFY-1 Salmon and Lockheed XFV-1 Pogo aircraft were experimental vertical takeoff and landing (VTOL) designs built for convoy protection and intended to takeoff and land on platforms installed on ships. These test aircraft were powered by Allison YT40-A-6 turboprop engines driving twin three-blade contra-rotating propellers. (Lewis)

449 The Lockheed XFV-1 was only tested in horizontal flight using a cage-like fixed landing gear while Convair's XFY-1 Pogo was first tested using a tether to keep the aircraft vertical during initial flights. Subsequent testing of the Pogo, including full transition from vertical to high-speed level flight and back to vertical for landing was demonstrated successfully. Although both aircrfaft flew, neither advanced beyond the test phase due to the difficulties of pilot visibility during landings and the reliability of the ill-fated T40 engine. (Lewis)

450 The British Whittle engine's circular airflow design did not allow it to flameout, as was the case with U.S. axial airflow jet engines. To demonstrate the reliability of the Whittle engine, a de Havilland Vampire jet powered by the Whittle was the first jet to traverse the Atlantic, from the United Kingdom to the United States. (Keeshen)

451 The Northrop X-4 Bantam was designed as a proof-of-concept aircraft to determine if the horizontal tail interfered

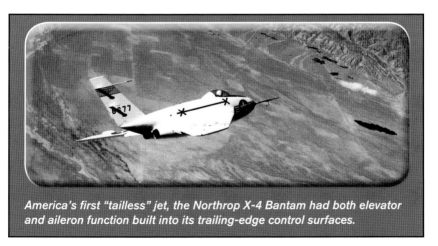

America's first "tailless" jet, the Northrop X-4 Bantam had both elevator and aileron function built into its trailing-edge control surfaces.

with airflow at supersonic speeds. It was believed that the horizontal tail interrupted the supersonic shock wave coming from the wings, causing stability and handling problems. The configuration was known as "semi-tailless" and it was prone to porpoising as it approached supersonic speeds. Only two X-4s were built. (Veronico)

452 Known as the X-6, this massive bomber aircraft was to be powered with a nuclear reactor. To prove part of the concept, Convair B-36H 51-5712 was fitted with a 3-megawatt air-cooled nuclear reactor, which did not power the aircraft but was to determine the effects of the reactor on the aircraft's other systems. The converted B-36 Peacemaker was scrapped in 1958, but the program continued until it was canceled by President John F. Kennedy in 1961 after nearly 15 years of development and more than a $1 billion investment. (Veronico)

453 Bell's X-14 was an ungainly looking aircraft designed to demonstrate the controls required for the forthcoming proof-of-concept aircraft that would become the Harrier vertical takeoff and landing (VTOL) fighter. The X-14 was assembled from existing aircraft parts: a Beechcraft Bonanza wing group and landing gear as well as a Beech T-34 Mentor tail group. As the airframe underwent different modifications, its designation changed from X-14 to X-14A and X-14B. The aircraft also served as a lunar lander trainer (X-14A) and was later fitted with General Electric J85 engines (X-14B). The aircraft was retired in 1981 and is now part of the Ropkey Armor Museum in Crawfordsville, Indiana. (Veronico)

454 Hiller Aircraft Corporation's X-18 Propello-plane was a tilt-wing, vertical/short takeoff and landing (VSTOL) aircraft. Work on this technology demonstrator began in 1955. To save money and bring the aircraft to flight sooner, it used the fuselage of a Chase YC-122C cargo plane, a pair of Allison T-40-A-14 turboprop engines from the "tail-sitter" vertical takeoff fighter prototype program (Convair XFY-1 Pogo and Lockheed XFV-1), and ducted exhaust from the engines for pitch control. The wing and engines rotated from horizontal to nearly 90 degrees. Lessons learned from the X-18 were carried over to the XC-142A VSTOL cargo transport. (Veronico)

America's first delta-wing jet, the Convair XF-92, was flown by contractor, Air Force, and NACA pilots, including Scott Crossfield.

455 In the 1950s, only deceased pilots had streets on Edwards AFB named in their honor, but Scott Crossfield became the first man alive who had a street, Crossfield Boulevard, named after him at Edwards. While on a test flight in the Convair XF-92A he made a forced landing on Rogers Dry Lake and subsequently experienced brake failure, forcing him to steer his crippled aircraft down a narrow dirt path at the edge of the lakebed. His efforts were successful and he managed to keep the aircraft on solid ground until it rolled to a stop. (Lewis)

SUPERSONIC FLIGHT

456 The U.S. Air Force and NACA selected Bell Aircraft to develop a test aircraft that could exceed the speeds and altitudes of previous "X" designs. Two aircraft, designated the X-2 and named "Starbuster," were built. One was lost during a captive engine test

flight, killing Bell pilot Skip Ziegler. The second aircraft probed the "thermal thicket" at speeds up to Mach 3, conducting research on thermal heating caused by friction at high Mach numbers. On the X-2's 13th powered flight, Capt. Mel Apt reached Mach 3.2 but the aircraft experienced inertia coupling and tumbled out of control. Mel Apt and the remaining X-2 were lost. (Lewis)

Looking dapper in his tweed suit, Douglas Test Pilot Johnny Martin poses with the D-558-2 Skyrocket. Martin was Donald Douglas' personal pilot.

457 The Douglas D-558-2 Skyrocket, built for an experimental Navy program, was first flown on 4 February 1948 piloted by Douglas Chief Pilot Johnny Martin who was also Donald Douglas's personal pilot for corporate trips in the company Super DC-3. Martin accumulated 2.5 hours of time conducting taxi tests before taking the jet-powered Ship 1 airborne and made a total of 15 flights in that airplane. (Machat)

458 Skyrocket number two made its first flight on 2 November 1948 piloted by company test pilot Gene May, who made a total of 39 Skyrocket flights. He also piloted the first flight of Ship 3 on 27 April 1949. (Machat)

459 Without a doubt, the most popular and well-known Douglas test pilot, whose name became a household word in the early 1950s, was Bill Bridgeman. Although a former naval aviator in the Pacific in World War II, he became one of the few civilian test pilots to set world records testing experimental rocket planes with speed marks of Mach 1.72 and 1.88 (1,245 mph) and an altitude record of 79,494 feet, all in 1951. Bridgeman had the most Skyrocket flights of any Douglas pilot with 76 total. (Machat)

460 Other high-time Skyrocket pilots were U.S. Marine Corps Col Marion Carl (5 flights), NACA's Jack McKay (29 flights), NACA pilot Scott Crossfield (89 flights), and NACA pilot Joe Walker (5 flights). Air Force pilots Lt. Col. Frank K. "Pete" Everest and Air Force Test Center Commander Brig Gen. Al Boyd also made rocket familiarization flights in the D-558-2. (Machat)

461 The Douglas Skyrocket flew in three different power-plant configurations: a pure jet, hybrid jet/rocket, and

The turbojet-powered Skyrocket making a JATO takeoff from the dry lakebed at Muroc.

air-launched pure rocket. The hybrid model could take off using the jet engine to climb to high altitude where the rocket engine would then be ignited to test supersonic speeds. The jet/rocket model didn't allow for reaching the full potential of the aircraft, however, and was eventually abandoned for the pure rocket design that was air-launched from a mothership at 35,000 feet where maximum speeds of the test aircraft could be then realized. NACA Test Pilot A. Scott Crossfield made numerous flights in the Skyrocket and became the first man to reach Mach 2 in this aircraft. (Lewis)

462 Brig Gen. Pete Everest was known as "the fastest man alive," which was also the title of his autobiography published in 1957. As Chief Air Force Project Pilot on the Bell X-2 program, Everest set a new speed record of Mach 2.87 (2,185 mph) on 27 July 1956,

"Fastest man alive," Lieutenant Colonel Frank K. "Pete" Everest in the cockpit of the Bell X-2 that he flew to a world speed record in 1956.

becoming the fastest man in the world. On 27 September 1956, his successor in the airplane, Capt. "Mel" Apt, exceeded Everest's record by becoming the first man to fly Mach 3, but he was killed after the X-2 tumbled out of control, thereby retaining Everest's title as "the fastest man alive." (Machat)

463 Although the Bell X-2 rightly deserves the distinction of being the first "aircraft" to fly three times the speed of sound, the first aerial vehicle to achieve that speed was Germany's lethal "Vengeance Weapon" designated as the V-2, a short-range ballistic missile that rained death and destruction on London and reached a velocity of Mach 3 upon re-entry of the Earth's lower atmosphere on its descent to the target. (Machat)

464 Much like the American folklore comparisons of the Lincoln and Kennedy assassinations, the experimental Republic XR-12 and North American XB-70 shared a number of odd, if not startling, facts. For instance, both aircraft represented a new level of performance for their respective photo-recon and strategic bomber roles, but both programs were canceled when the aircraft were replaced by new jets for the XR-12, and Intercontinental Ballistic Missiles for the XB-70. In both cases, the two prototypes built were kept on flight status as experimental research aircraft. (Machat)

465 Taking the almost bizarre XR-12/XB-70 comparison even further, both aircraft were the largest ever built by their manufacturers and both were the fastest ever flown for their size, a four-engine piston-powered aircraft (the XR-12 at 462 mph) and six-engine delta-wing jet bomber (the XB-70 at Mach 3, or 2,300 mph). The second and more advanced examples of each type were lost in accidents with the XR-12 crashing at Eglin AFB, Florida, in November 1948, and the XB-70 crashing after a midair collision with an F-104 chase plane in June 1966, minutes after the photo on the next page was taken. (Machat)

Republic's XR-12 Rainbow (top) and North American's XB-70 Valkyrie, the largest and fastest multi-engine aircraft built by those companies.

466 The XR-12/XB-70 story continues with the number of fatalities involved in each crash: two. For the XR-12, which crashed into the Gulf of Mexico after an inflight explosion due to a fuel leak in the number two engine nacelle, one crewman perished after he was unable to bail out of the rapidly diving airplane, and a second crewman survived the bailout but drowned in the Gulf of Mexico when high winds dragged his parachute through the water. NASA Chief Pilot Joe Walker was killed when his F-104 collided with the

XB-70, and USAF Capt. Carl Cross, making his first flight in the airplane, perished when he was unable to eject from the flat-spinning bomber. (Machat)

467 The only difference in the stories of the XR-12 and XB-70 is the ending for the surviving Ship 1 airplanes. The first XB-70 continued in its flight test role at Edwards until 1969 when it was flown to Dayton, Ohio, to be enshrined in the Air Force Museum at Wright-Patterson AFB (known today as the National Museum of the U.S. Air Force). Republic's first XR-12 remained in the flight test role at Eglin until 1952 when it was flown to the Aberdeen Proving Grounds and blown up as a ground target! (Machat)

468 Called "God's gift to flight test" by former X-15 test pilot and NASA Astronaut Maj. Gen. Joe Engle, Rogers Dry Lake offers a total of 13 miles of runway surface for airplanes in distress that can make safe emergency landings literally in any direction required. Aircraft from other bases around the United States have flown to Edwards to use the lakebed for emergency landings as well. (Machat)

469 Lakebed Runway 18 at Edwards was at one time divided into three parallel runways: one for wheeled turbojet and piston-powered aircraft, one for wheeled Lifting Body experimental aircraft, and a dedicated runway for the exclusive use of the North American X-15 rocket plane. That was necessitated by the X-15's steel main landing gear skids that ate into the hardpack lakebed surface at the aircraft's 200-mph touchdown speed. (Machat)

470 Although technically part of the hallowed first generation family of exotic experimental "X Planes," the turbojet Douglas D-558-I Skystreak and rocket-powered D-558-2 Skyrocket were not formally designated as such because they were U.S. Navy programs. Hence, these two experimental "greats" are often not included in the pantheon of pioneering X-Plane research aircraft. Had they been, the line-up would have been the subsonic Skystreak, Bell X-1 (Mach 1), Skyrocket (Mach 2), Bell X-2 (Mach 3), and X-15 (Mach 4, 5, and 6.) (Machat)

Douglas Test Pilot Gene "The Flying Grandfather" May flew most of the contractor flights of the Douglas D-558-1 Skystreak,

471 From 1984 to 1992, NASA tested the Grumman X-29 forward-swept wing fighter. Developed from a request for proposals from the Defense Advanced Research Projects Agency (DARPA) and the U.S. Air Force Flight Dynamics Laboratory, Wright-Patterson AFB, Ohio, the first of two prototypes flew on 14 December 1984, followed by the second five months later on 23 May 1989. In addition to forward-swept wings fitted with flaperons (combination flaps and ailerons), the X-29s had canards in place of a horizontal tail and elevators, and a triple-redundant digital flight control system. The X-29 also investigated high angles of attack of up to 67 degrees. Both X-29s were preserved, one at the National Museum of the U.S. Air Force in Dayton, Ohio, and the second at NASA Armstrong Flight Research Center, Edwards AFB, California. (Veronico)

472 Although the special runway constructed for space shuttle landings at the Kennedy Space Center at Cape Canaveral, Florida, is claimed to be "the longest concrete runway in the world" at 15,000 and 1 foot long, that extra foot in length was to wrest the crown from Edwards AFB, California, which boasts a 15,000-foot-long by 300-foot-wide main runway. In actuality, the Edwards Runway 22/04 is 299 feet wide, the extra foot of concrete having been

surreptitiously relocated to build a swimming pool for the base commander's residence in the original "P" housing area south of main base. (Machat)

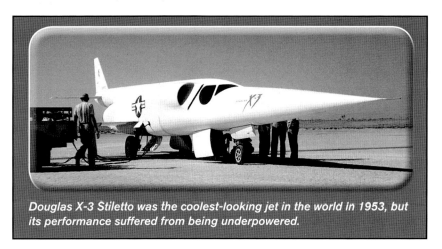

Douglas X-3 Stiletto was the coolest-looking jet in the world in 1953, but its performance suffered from being underpowered.

473 The Douglas X-3 Stiletto was one of the most futuristic aircraft ever built and was flown by Douglas, NACA, and Air Force pilots on 51 research flights from 1952 to 1956. Underpowered due to the lack of suitable Westinghouse J46 engines it was designed for, the Stiletto required a ground run of more than 3 miles across Rogers Dry Lake for takeoff. A new set of tires had to be used on every flight. (Machat)

474 The Douglas X-3 always seems to get a bad rap in the aviation press, but it was a pioneering aircraft in many regards. While its performance was underwhelming to say the least, the X-3 was the first airplane with an air-conditioned cockpit. It was also the first manned aircraft to use a trapezoidal wing (later used successfully on the F-104 and X-15), and the first aircraft to employ titanium structure (the jet's exhaust rings and lower tail section were built using that alloy). (Machat)

475 Many exotic and experimental aircraft (and helicopters) took off and landed at the Hughes Airport in Culver City, California, home of the Hughes Aircraft Corporation. From the giant XH-17

Against a bank of summer thunderstorms, Howard Hughes pilots the second XF-11 photo-recon prototype from his flying field in Culver City, California.

cargo helicopter to the twin-tailboom XF-11 photo-recon prototype shown above and many others in between, the once grass strip hosted many amazing experimental aircraft. The fastest airplane to land and take off from the Hughes field was a Mach-2 Convair B-58 Hustler named *Snoopy*, sent to Culver City from Edwards AFB to test the new Hughes AN/ASG-18 fire control system for the Lockheed YF-12 Interceptor. (Machat)

THE EDGE OF SPACE

476 Capt. Iven Carl Kincheloe Jr. became a jet ace during the Korean War and went on to be a test pilot at Edwards AFB, California. He later joined the Bell X-2 rocket program where he flew the aircraft to a speed of 2,000 mph and an altitude of 126,200 feet, causing him to be called "America's No. 1 Spaceman." Kincheloe was selected to be chief Air Force program pilot for the upcoming North American Aviation X-15 program. Sadly, he lost his life while flying a Lockheed F-104 Starfighter in 1958, and was replaced in the X-15 program by his best friend, Major Robert M. White. (Lewis)

Captain Iven Kincheloe poses next to the Bell X-2 rocket plane that carried him to the edge of space in September 1956.

477 In the early days of flight, terminology was simple: the "largest" and "fastest" airplanes, or the airplane that flew the farthest. Today, by comparison, there is a much greater need for specifics in describing aviation's superlatives. For instance, the X-15 was the world's fastest aircraft when it flew to Mach 6.7 in October 1967. Today, it is the world's fastest "manned" aircraft since high-speed

unmanned aerial vehicles like the X-51 Waverider have attained speeds as high as Mach 10. Another difference is that the X-15's pilot landed that aircraft to be flown over and over again. The X-51 returned valuable hypersonic data before crashing into the Pacific Ocean. (Machat)

478 Former USAF test pilot and NASA astronaut Joe H. Engle was only 32 years old when he flew the North American X-15 to 280,600 feet on 29 June 1965, making him the youngest pilot ever to qualify for Astronaut Wings. Engle and Neil Armstrong were the two youngest pilots to fly that aircraft. (Machat)

479 Joe Engle was not only one of the youngest pilots to fly the X-15, but also the oldest pilot to fly the space shuttle at the time. Joe also became the first man in the world to fly a "used space

Joe H. Engle flew the X-15 before being assigned as an Apollo Astronaut. He later piloted the second orbital flight of the space shuttle.

ship," i.e., a spacecraft that had been flown in space previously, when he commanded STS-2, the second orbital mission of Space Shuttle *Columbia*, which landed on Rogers Dry Lake at Edwards AFB on 14 November 1981. (Machat)

480 As mentioned, another famous X-15 pilot who went on to greater heights was Neil Armstrong, the only X-15 pilot to become both a Gemini and Apollo astronaut for NASA. Of his historic accomplishment of being the first human to set foot on the lunar surface during the Apollo 11 mission in July 1969, Armstrong was quoted as saying, "I'd much rather be remembered as the first pilot to land on the Moon instead of the first man to walk on it!" (Machat)

481 NASA used a converted Lockheed C-141A Starlifter named the Gerard P. Kuiper Airborne Observatory (KAO) to make astronomical discoveries from 1974 to 1995. KAO made 1,424 research flights during its 21-year lifetime. The modified C-141A was fitted with a 36-inch-diameter infrared telescope that was installed ahead of the wing, behind a door that opened to the atmosphere at altitude. Observers onboard KAO discovered the rings of Uranus, water in Jupiter's atmosphere, early evidence of a black hole at the center of our galaxy, and much more. (Veronico)

482 One of the first dedicated airborne astronomy platforms was NASA's LearJet Observatory, known as the "LJO." Fitted with an 11.8-inch (30-cm) unpressurized telescope port open to the atmosphere, the LJO began observations in October 1968 and was the first airborne telescope fitted with a chopping secondary mirror for subtracting sky brightness from signal. Researchers onboard the LJO found evidence of concentrated sulfuric acid as the major aerosol in Venus' clouds, and determined the luminosities of star-forming molecular clouds. (Veronico)

483 The Boeing YAL-1 Airborne Laser Test Bed was a 747-400 freighter jam-packed with the infrastructure to initiate and fire a 1-megawatt chemical oxygen iodine laser (referred to as COIL). The directed energy–equipped airborne laser proof-of-concept turned science fiction into science fact on the evening of 2 February 2010, when a solid fuel rocket was destroyed and again on 11 February 2010, when a sea-launched, liquid-fueled, ballistic missile was tracked and destroyed by the high-flying YAL-1. Both successful tests took place off the Southern California coast. (Veronico)

484 NASA's space shuttle program required a way to transport orbiters across country. Each orbiter had a length of 122.17 feet and a wingspan of 78.06 feet, too wide for transport by road or rail. The solution was to modify two Boeing 747s to carry the orbiters piggyback style. Known as Shuttle Carrier Aircraft (SCA), the aircraft were acquired from the commercial market and modified to carry the 172,000-pound (empty) spacecraft. SCA N905NA was purchased from Boeing and delivered to American Airlines on 29 October 1970 and registered N9668 (747-123, manufacturer's serial number 20107, line number 86). NASA acquired N905NA on 18 July 1974. N911NA was originally delivered to Japan Airlines as a 747-SR46 (manufacturer's serial number 20781, line number 221) on 26 September 1973 with the registration JA8117. N911NA was acquired by NASA on 27 October 1988. (Veronico)

The ultimate in aerial delivery, NASA's Boeing 747 Shuttle Carrier Aircraft (SCA) transporting shuttle orbiter Columbia to the Kennedy Space Center.

485 When NASA bought its first used Boeing 747 from American Airlines, it left the airplane in its original bare-metal delivery color scheme since American's red-white-and-blue window stripes tied in nicely with the patriotic aspect of NASA's proud new program. The word "American" was removed from above the windows on the forward fuselage, but oxidation of the bare metal fuselage during its four years of airline service lightened the color of the metal and the area protected by the painted logotype was slightly darker and slightly brighter than the surrounding finish. As a result, the word "American" appeared as a ghost-like image on the airplane for the duration of its service life in that color scheme. (Machat)

486 The second 747 SCA acquired, from Japan Airlines, was delivered to NASA in original JAL colors, and was thus repainted during its SCA conversion process. NASA wanted a simple and cost-effective color-scheme, so Boeing complied by using the design and colors of its first 747 customer. Flying with a white upper fuselage and simple thin royal blue window line, the airplane employed the color scheme (sans lettering and airline logo) of Pan American World Airways! (Machat)

487 Both SCAs were declared surplus after the end of the Space Shuttle program, with N905NA transferred to Space Center Houston, the official visitor center for NASA Johnson Space Center, south of Houston, Texas. Here the SCA will be displayed with a full-scale, highly detailed mock-up of a Space Shuttle mounted on top. N911NA was flown to the Dryden Aircraft Operations Facility in Palmdale, California, home of NASA's SOFIA program. Here, maintenance technicians removed several internal parts that were added to SOFIA's spares inventory. The aircraft, in display condition, was towed to the nearby Joe Davies Heritage Airpark at the Palmdale Airport. (Veronico)

488 NASA's Stratospheric Observatory for Infrared Astronomy (SOFIA) is the world's largest flying telescope. SOFIA is a converted Boeing 747SP (N534PA former Pan Am *Clipper Lindbergh*, ex–United Air Lines N134NA) fitted with a 100-inch-diameter

telescope. The observatory has a suite of seven instruments that make astronomical observations at mid- and far-infrared wavelengths (30 to 240 microns). The observatory became fully operational in 2014 and has a 20-year lifespan. (Veronico)

489 Cape Canaveral, Florida, became an iconic name in America's Space Program, for this was the hallowed ground from which every major U.S. missile type and every U.S. manned space flight was launched. Although the complex itself was renamed the Kennedy Space Center in the mid-1960s, the geographical location and adjoining town is still called Cape Canaveral. Residents are justifiably proud of their telephone area code, which is "3-2-1." (Machat)

490 It is somewhat unbelievable that many of the iconic X-Planes and experimental prototypes tested and flown at Edwards AFB were either lost in accidents or scrapped at the end of their careers with no example left today. Paramount among these aircraft would be the Mach-3 Bell X-2, Hiller X-18 tilt-wing VTOL aircraft, and Convair X-6 variant of the B-36 that was the world's first aircraft ever fitted with an onboard nuclear reactor. (Lewis)

Commercial Aviation

In post–World War II America, well-dressed passengers flew on a luxurious four-engine double-deck airliner called the Stratocruiser, but it was actually Boeing's B-29 (and more powerful B-50) that were the progenitors of that aircraft. On the other hand, the workhorse Douglas C-47 Skytrain military transport originated from the legendary DC-3 airliner. Airliners have come far since then, and little could anyone have imagined that a U.S. transcontinental flight taking 12 hours in 1950 would take half that time by jetliner less than 10 years later, or that twin-engine airliners would be capable of carrying 350 passengers and flying at 600 mph non-stop between any two cities in the world today!

BEFORE THE WAR

491 The continental United States is a large expanse of territory, and crossing it by airplane with paying passengers aboard, well . . . one might as well have said fly to the moon. Undeterred by the rudimentary flying machines of 1929, Transcontinental Air Transport, TAT, began one-carrier air service linking Los Angeles to New York on 7 July 1929. The trip required more than just air conveyance, both the Rocky Mountains as well as the lack of lighted airways being huge impediments to flying; passengers also rode a

Formally dressed passengers deplane from a TWA Lockheed Super-G Constellation in this staged promo shot taken at Kansas City.

corresponding train, which was intermittently used for difficult sections of the route. Fares traveled by Ford Trimotors in the daytime and on the train overnight. Total elapsed time for the trip was 48 hours, ultimately faster than surface transportation. (Kodera)

492 TAT was one of several progenitor airlines, which when later amalgamated became Transcontinental and Western Airlines, otherwise popularly known as the world-beating TWA. (Kodera)

The tower atop the Empire State Building used by King Kong to swat down attacking biplanes was originally a mooring mast for Zeppelins.

493 The classic art deco architecture of the Empire State Building in New York, once the world's tallest skyscraper, was intended to be functional. Completed in 1931, the building itself tops out at

the 86th floor, but the pointed structure above that extending up to 102 stories was to be the mooring mast for German passenger-carrying Zeppelins. Although a good idea in theory for traveling directly from Europe to the heart of midtown Manhattan, the problems of mooring the mammoth airships so that passengers could safely exit into the building through passageways built into the Zeppelin's nose were insurmountable, especially in high wind conditions. What was to be the airline terminal is now the 102nd-floor observatory for tourists. (Machat)

494 As technology marched onward and airlines tried making a business of flying, certain additions to the system became true necessities. Early among these was two-way radio communications between the ground and the airplane. America's first airport to install and utilize radio was Cleveland's Municipal, inaugurating the capability on 15 May 1930. Following the Ohio airport's lead, over the next five years 20 additional airports gained the ability to talk to airplanes. (Kodera)

495 Striving to take a load off the very busy pilot of an airliner, especially in the early days of air transport, the admirable folks at Sperry Gyroscope developed the first autopilot for use in an airliner. Known as a "mechanical copilot," the device was first operated aboard an Eastern Airlines Curtiss Condor on 10 November 1931 flying from New York to Washington, D.C. (Kodera)

496 When beloved New York City Mayor Fiorello LaGuardia flew home from a meeting in Chicago, his Ford Trimotor landed at the largest commercial airport in the New York metropolitan area, which happened to be directly across the Hudson River in Newark, New Jersey. Incensed that he had to deplane in New Jersey, LaGuardia simply refused to get off the airplane, saying he'd bought a ticket to "New York," and by gosh, he was going to New York! The airplane took him to Floyd Bennett Field in Brooklyn, but years later a sandy landfill on the north shore of the borough of Queens, named North Beach, became what is now LaGuardia Airport. (Machat)

Modern new terminals in the 1960s obliterated LaGuardia Airport's original elegant art deco terminal built in 1939.

497 How to keep passengers occupied on a long flight? Serve food. The first time meals were cooked onboard an airliner was 1 May 1927 on an Imperial Airways flight from London, England, to Paris, France. The equipment used that day was an Armstrong Whitworth Argosy, and 18 lucky people were in the passenger cabin to enjoy the repast. (Kodera)

498 Pan American World Airways was renowned for its pioneering work spanning the globe's oceans with commercial flying boats, starting in the late 1920s. Airline service eventually covered both the Pacific and Atlantic oceans as well as the Caribbean Sea. These were luxurious, golden days for international air transport and Pan American became a household name denoting American exceptionalism and daring. Other than ocean liners, the only way to cross the great oceans of the world was via Pan Am flying boat. (Kodera)

499 Pan Am is widely known for its pioneering transatlantic flights, but which European carrier has spanned the ocean with scheduled service for the longest period of time? KLM Royal Dutch Airlines. On 21 May 1946, one of its DC-4s, PH-TAR, christened *Rotterdam,* spanned the North Atlantic from Amsterdam to New York with intermediate stops at Glasgow, Scotland, and Gander, Newfoundland. The carrier still operates that route today, giving it the distinction of having done so for more than 70 years. (Proctor)

500 The CEO of an early airline to employ female cabin attendants, TWA's President Jack Frye insisted upon calling them hostesses, when the young ladies began serving on Douglas DC-2 fights. He felt that "stewardess" was too impersonal, and the women were acting on behalf of the airline as hosts, just as they would treat guests in their own homes. When some of the company's DC-2s were sold to Braniff Airways, Frye also granted the buyer use of the hostess name, which reportedly had been trademarked. Although airlines like Eastern initially employed men exclusively and called them "stewards," the various titles later disappeared with widespread employment of males, and "cabin attendant" or "flight attendant" became the new norm. (Proctor)

501 From 18 to 20 June 1937 a Russian Tupolov ANT-25 single-engine monoplane piloted by Valery Chkalov and Georgy Gromov with A. Belyakov as navigator flew nonstop from Moscow across the North Pole to a landing in Vancouver. When they

The Russians loved giant airplanes, and a truly mammoth aircraft for its time was the Antonov ANT-2 in 1937.

touched down at Pearson field they had been airborne for 63 hours and 25 minutes, covering 5,670 miles. (Lewis)

502 When Transcontinental & Western Air (TWA) suffered the loss of one of its Fokker F.10 aircraft it looked to replace them with aircraft having metal construction. The only aircraft available was the Boeing 247 but these were built by Boeing for United Airlines. When TWA requested bids for a three-engine aircraft to replace its F.10s Douglas Aircraft offered a counter-proposal. The result was the twin-engine DC-1 prototype, which demonstrated it could operate successfully on TWA routes. Although only one DC-1 was built, it quickly evolved into the DC-2 and later the legendary DC-3. The DC-1 crashed in Malaga, Spain. (Lewis)

503 The 1934 MacRobertson Air Race from London, England, to Melbourne, Australia, was significant in that the second- and third-place winners were airliners, and in both cases, U.S.-made types. In second was a Douglas DC-2 owned by KLM Royal Dutch Airlines and in third place, a Boeing 247, archrival to the Douglas Company's transport in the twin-engine airliner marketplace. The winner? A small, single-place purpose-built design from de Havilland, the DH 88 Comet racer, name progenitor to Britain's famed jet airliner. (Kodera)

Douglas Aircraft's first four-engine airliner, the DC-4E, was essentially "twice a DC-3" and did not go into production.

504 The Douglas DC-4E was developed to replace the DC-3 with the intent to double passenger capacity and add modern innovations such as boosted controls, air conditioning, pressurization, and a modern electrical system, and it was the first large aircraft to incorporate a nosewheel. Four major airlines provided funds for development, but because the cost rose significantly, two of them opted to switch to the pressurized Boeing 307. The three-section tail was chosen instead of a single unit to allow use of existing hangars. The aircraft never entered production and was sold to Japan where many of the DC-4E features were incorporated into their Nakajima G5N World War II bomber. (Lewis)

505 The DC-5 was a Douglas aircraft design that is not well known. It was meant to operate on routes not well suited for either the DC-3 or DC-4. The high-wing design with a tricycle landing gear was a configuration adapted by many manufacturers of turbo-prop commuter aircraft in later years. Two variants of the DC-5 were the C-110 and the R3D used by the U.S. Navy and Marine Corps. One DC-5 was purchased by William Boeing for his personal use. DC-5s were used by KLM and Australian National Airlines. The last surviving DC-5 ended up in Israel. (Lewis)

506 With KLM's order for the DC-5, that prestigious airline became the world's only commercial airline to fly every single production Douglas Aircraft Company and McDonnell Douglas Corporation airliner type ever built. This included the DC-2, DC-3, DC-4, DC-5, DC-6, DC-6B, DC-7C, DC-8-30, DC-8-55, DC-8-61 and -63, DC-9-10 and DC-9-30, DC-10-30, and MD-11. (Machat)

507 KLM stands for *Koninklijke Luchtvaart Maatschappij*, although the full name is seldom uttered and just KLM Royal Dutch Airlines (The Flying Hollander) is used instead. KLM was established in 1919, and its first flight was on 17 May 1920 between Amsterdam and London, which makes KLM the oldest airline still in service. (Lewis)

508 Construction of the Bristol Brabazon was a massive undertaking, and its failure was largely attributed to the British aircraft industry's poor understanding of postwar market conditions. Although it offered many advanced design features, the vision for the Brabazon was to provide the elegant luxury of a 1930s ocean liner. The Brabazon design could accommodate 100 passengers in a cabin similar in size to a Boeing 747, which could hold more than 300. In the end, no airlines were interested in purchasing the aircraft and the one flying example was scrapped while the second example was never completed. (Lewis)

509 When Boeing produced the then-mighty Model 307 Stratoliner for TWA and Pan Am in 1940, it was generally acknowledged as the first U.S.-built four-engine land plane for commercial use. But was it? Ten years earlier, Dutch-born Anthony Fokker's U.S.-based Atlantic Aircraft Corporation delivered two Fokker F-32s to Western Air Express for use between Los Angeles (Alhambra) and San Francisco (Alameda). In the end, neither the F-32 nor the Stratoliner proved financially successful. Only 2 F-32s and 10 Stratoliners were built. But for their time, both were attention-getters that paved the way for future four-engine commercial aircraft following World War II. (Proctor)

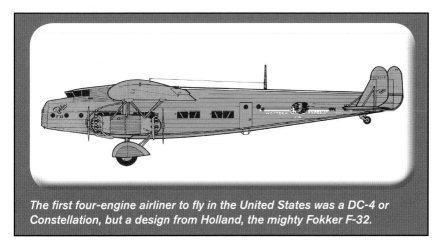

The first four-engine airliner to fly in the United States was a DC-4 or Constellation, but a design from Holland, the mighty Fokker F-32.

510 The first in-flight movie was shown by *Deutsche Luft Hansa* on 6 April 1925. Passengers were treated to single-reel films, which weighed less than full-length features. Fortunately, the films were silent, since the noisy environment inside the airliner would have made it just about impossible to hear a sound track. (Caruso)

511 Although male "stewards" and "pursers" were part of airliner crews from early on, the first "stewardess" was Ellen Church. She was a registered nurse who sold Boeing Air Transport (later part of United Air Lines) on the concept by stressing the necessity of having a trained healthcare attendant available to the often sick and incapacitated passengers aboard the early air transports. The year was 1930 and a huge trend was begun. (Kodera)

512 The immortal Douglas DC-3 came to be because of the insistence of one man. American Airlines' boss C. R. Smith entreated Donald Douglas at length to build him his dream airplane. As a matter of fact, Smith made one of the most expensive phone calls in history when, in 1935, he spoke to the aircraft manufacturer long distance, discussing the design of the airplane for more than two hours. The final bill from the phone company? $325. In today's inflated currency value that is equivalent to approximately $7,500 in charges. Looking back, that was a small price to pay to change the entirety of aviation history. (Kodera)

513 Why did the Douglas DC-4 *follow* the Douglas DC-5? Actually, it did not. The original DC-4, a one-of-a-kind airliner designed for a consortium of U.S. airlines and later designated DC-4E, came one year prior to the -5 in 1938. The later production DC-4 followed in 1942. World War II delayed the commercial entry of the airplane and so separated it from its smaller but higher-numbered cousin by several years; hence the confusion. (Kodera)

514 Train service in the United States was the primary means of transportation well into the 1950s and early 1960s. How farsighted then in April of 1946 when the New York Yankees signed a contract with United Airlines to fly the team to all game cities for the upcoming season. This was the first exclusive use of airplanes to move ball teams around the country. Later, in the 1950s, several teams bought dedicated surplus airliners and placed their names on the aircraft. (Kodera)

515 The first airliner to include a pressurized cabin was the Renard R-35 from Belgium. Built in 1938, the tri-motor, low-wing monoplane had seating for 20 passengers who could cruise in habitable altitude comfort as high as 29,500 feet, thanks to its pressurization. The aircraft's first and last flight was on 1 April 1938, having crashed shortly after takeoff. The company was unable to continue manufacturing following loss of the airplane. (Kodera)

Boeing's sleek Model 307 was essentially a B-17 bomber with a bullet nose and a pressurized cabin for its 32 passengers.

516 In the United States, Douglas Aircraft in Santa Monica, California, built the DC-4E prototype airliner in mid-1938, an airliner featuring pressurization for its cabin. Too large and complex for the airlines, a smaller and less complex unpressurized airplane was produced starting in 1942. In the meantime, Boeing Airplane Company of Seattle, Washington, constructed what would become the first pressurized commercial airliner to see production. The airplane was known as the 307 Stratoliner and was based on the company's B-17 bomber, but with a passenger fuselage. It entered service with Pan American World Airways and Transcontinental and Western Airlines (TWA) in 1940. (Kodera)

517 The word "mayday," used by pilots in an emergency, comes from the French word *m'aidez*. Translation: "help me."

518 Many great and successful aircraft types built before World War II were either lost in accidents or scrapped at the end of their careers with not even one example left anywhere in the world today. Paramount among these aircraft types are the legendary Pan American flying boats that ruled the transoceanic skies for nearly

two decades, including all the Sikorsky S-42, Martin M-130, and Boeing B314 Clippers. (Lewis)

THE GREAT PROPLINERS

519 Commercial aviation changed dramatically following World War II. It became possible to fly the same long-range routes as the flying boats using large new four-engine land planes that took off and landed at regular airports. The beautiful and unique flying boat was doomed to recede to a smaller role in various spots around the world. The last Pan American Clipper services were flown over the Pacific and Atlantic in January and May of 1946, respectively. (Kodera)

520 Technically, the world's first aviation distance record was 120 feet, the length of the Wright brother's first flight at Kitty Hawk, North Carolina, on 17 December 1903. In airliner ads of the 1950s, that historic flight was superimposed across the 129-foot wingspan of a Lockheed Constellation to show man's progress in aviation. Today, that same flight could be made down the aisle in the economy coach section of an Airbus A380. (Machat)

521 Pan American World Airways established transpacific service using four-engine Martin M-130 flying boats. Three M-130s were built for Pan American and a fourth, with greater wingspan and twin rudders, for the Soviet Union. M-130s were used in support of Pacific routes until Pan Am converted to larger, longer-range Boeing 314 Clippers. All the M-130s were lost in separate accidents: one between Guam and Manila; another survived an air attack at Wake Island but crashed near Ukiah, California, during U.S. Navy operations; and the last one broke up and sank in Trinidad. (Lewis)

522 Pan American Airways System contracted with Boeing Aircraft to build B-314 Clipper long-range flying boats for use on both their Atlantic and Pacific routes. Boeing incorporated the wing from their XB-15 bomber to obtain the necessary range. After the attack on Pearl Harbor, Boeing 314s were conscripted into the U.S.

Navy and were operated by them and BOAC during World War II. The introduction of long-range land-based aircraft rendered flying boats obsolete. The Douglas DC-4/C-54 and Lockheed L-749/C-69 aircraft were more economical and airfields constructed during the war made their use possible. Of the 12 Boeing 314s built not one survives. (Lewis)

523 After World War II, the record year for most first flights of all types of aircraft was 1956 when a total of 25 new or derivative airplanes first flew. Among these were the airliners that, in every sense of the word, represented the absolute zenith of piston-powered transport, the Douglas DC-7C on 22 February and the Lockheed 1649 Starliner on 11 October. These two aircraft offered true airborne luxury and comfort on routes that linked all major continents by air, but in a cruel bit of irony, they were used in front-line service for only four years, replaced by first-generation jetliners in the early 1960s. (Machat)

524 Early commercial "polar" flights between the U.S. West Coast and Europe were actually flown over the northern polar regions rather than over the North Pole, a popular misconception. Among the earliest operators was Scandinavian Airlines System (SAS), which accomplished the feat with the delivery flight of its first Douglas DC-6B. Departing from Santa Monica on 19 November 1952, OY-KME *Arild Viking* stopped at Edmonton, Alberta, and Thule, Greenland, enroute to Copenhagen. (Proctor)

525 However, regularly scheduled polar service did not begin until 15 November 1954, between Copenhagen and Los Angeles. Nonstop (eastbound) service on SAS became possible with the DC-7C, following deliveries starting in 1956. In addition, Copenhagen-Tokyo flights became a reality, truly crossing the North Pole and stopping at Anchorage. (Proctor)

526 Douglas Aircraft Company launched the ultra-long-range DC-7C *Seven Seas* following a joint order from Pan Am and SAS. In addition to nonstop trans-Atlantic capability in both directions, the type could operate U.S. West Coast–Europe and other extended-range flights. An outgrowth of the popular DC-7 series, it featured upgraded engines and additional fuel capacity; 121 were built. (Proctor)

The classic lines of the original triple-tail 049 Constellation of the mid-1940s still looks elegant today.

527 A common misconception exists that Howard Hughes "designed" the graceful, triple-tailed Lockheed Constellation. Indeed, the eccentric, controlling shareholder of Trans World Airlines submitted specifications for a 44-passenger pressurized airliner able to cross the country in eight hours. But it was the manufacturer's design team (Kelly Johnson and Hal Hibbard) that became responsible for what emerged as the Model 49. (Proctor)

528 Lockheed's 1649A Starliner, competitor to the DC-7C, was the final version of the graceful Constellation design. Although not quite as fast as the Douglas, its range exceeded that of the DC-7C by 600 miles. Only TWA placed a large order, for 25 airframes (named *Jetstreams* by that airline), and just 44 were built. Both the Starliner and DC-7C were made redundant by jets, with most of the survivors being converted into long-range freighters. (Proctor)

529 While Douglas Aircraft reigned supreme for piston-powered airliner manufacturing from the end of World War II through the beginning of the Jet Age, it may be surprising to learn the actual production numbers of each type. Only 1 DC-1 prototype (1933) and 12 DC-5 twin-engine transports (1939) were built, but 704 of the "thoroughbred" DC-6 series (1948) were built. The larger, faster DC-7 series (1953) was less than half that number at 338, but the largest production run of a Douglas airliner was 989 for the DC-3, first flown in 1935. (Machat)

530 Several sources claim that 10,000 DC-3s were built by Douglas, but that is simply not accurate. As mentioned, there were 989 actual DC-3 airliners with fully outfitted passenger interiors and fold-down airstair doors. The remaining 9,000-plus airframes were Army C-47 series transports with uprated engines, spartan troop and freight carrying military interiors, and double clamshell cargo doors. (Machat)

531 The first 18-cylinder piston aircraft engine in the United States was the Pratt & Whitney R-2800 Double Wasp of 1939. Combining two rows of piston cylinders with the Pratt engine, it was capable of 2,000 hp in its first iteration, leaping in later development all the way to 2,800 hp. This is perhaps the classic engine of all reciprocating powerplants in aviation history. After World War II it found application in the Convair-Liner series and Douglas DC-6/-6B commercial aircraft where its economic prowess and reliability was proven daily in large profits for the airlines. (Kodera)

532 While many postwar military aircraft augmented their takeoff performance by using JATO (Jet Assisted Take Off) or RATO (Rocket Assisted Take Off), solid rockets affixed inside the fuselage or externally in bottles that could be dropped or jettisoned after takeoff, several commercial jet airliners were fitted with JATO for operations at hot, high airports such as Denver, Colorado, in the United States, or Mexico City in Mexico. One such airliner was the Douglas DC-4 operated by Braniff International Airlines for flights out of Mexico City. Three airliner types that used JATO were the Douglas DC-9-30 flown by Overseas National Airlines (ONA), the de Havilland DH 121 Trident, and the Douglas DC-4 operated by Braniff International Airlines. (Machat)

The fastest operational four-engine piston-powered airliner ever flown is the Douglas DC-7, which cruised at 360 mph at 25,000 feet.

533 Today, U.S. transcontinental nonstop flights are scheduled for little more than 5 hours, but for the most part less than 6. Near the end of 1953, a piston-powered Douglas DC-7 on its delivery flight from Santa Monica, California, to Miami, Florida, accomplished a sub-six-hour feat. The 2,353-mile stretch was covered in 5 hours, 50 minutes. Favorable winds resulted in an average speed of 403 mph for the trip. (Proctor)

534 As piston-engine airplanes became more and more complex, there arose the need for a dedicated crew position to tend to the workings of all the airplane's systems. Originally called "flight mechanic" as the position was inaugurated on the large flying boats of the 1930s, the Sikorsky S-42, Martin M-130, and the Boeing 314, the title changed when in Germany the Dornier DO-X began flying in commercial service. The new name "flight engineer" stuck, and has been with the aviation community ever since, requiring special certification different and specific from that of a pilot. (Kodera)

535 Designed as a DC-3 replacement, the 36-passenger Martin 202 competed with the Convair 240 and saw only limited sales. Plagued by accidents, it was unable to generate follow-up orders and only 43 were built, including 12 Martin 202As. The follow-on Martin 404 was only slightly more successful with 101 civil versions produced, plus 2 for the U.S. Coast Guard. (Proctor)

536 When new, modern Douglas DC-6s began flying in airline service offering pressurized cabins for high-altitude comfort, many supplemental operators, then known as "non-skeds," along with a few other airlines such as Capital and PSA, began painting square outlines around the oval passenger windows on their slower, unpressurized DC-4s, no doubt to trick customers into thinking they were flying on Sixes. (Proctor)

537 Most people know that the first dedicated airplane used for presidential travel was a Douglas C-54 Skymaster named "the Sacred Cow" used by Franklin Roosevelt. However, there were other airplanes in which a president flew. His cousin Teddy Roosevelt was the first president to fly in an airplane, a *Wright Flyer*, in October 1910. Franklin Roosevelt, utilizing then-new technology, flew to his nominating convention in 1932 aboard a Ford Trimotor, and in 1943 when he traveled as president to Casablanca for the D-Day planning conference he was aboard a Pan American Boeing 314 Clipper. (Kodera)

538 Terminology was much simpler in the early days of commercial aviation, when the inaugural service of a new airliner was introduced on a specific date. Today, specificity is needed to describe airliner firsts, such as "first scheduled service," "first revenue service," and "first operational (or charter) nonstop service."

For instance, the first twin-engine jet airliner to make a transatlantic crossing was the French SE.210 Caravelle. Operated by Sterling on a scheduled charter flight on 23 June 1970, the jetliner flew from Copenhagen, Denmark, to Omaha, Nebraska, with stops in Keflavik, Iceland, and Gander, Newfoundland. (Machat)

Douglas promotional illustration shows a gleaming new Hawaiian Airlines DC-9 Super 80 jetliner with Honolulu in the background.

539 Airline safety has come a long way in recent decades, but there is one airline that has never suffered a fatal injury to a passenger nor lost an airframe to an accident. That airline is Hawaiian Airlines, which has been in continuous operation since 1929. This makes it the oldest U.S. carrier to maintain this perfect record. (Kodera)

540 China National Aviation Corporation (CNAC) operated a fleet of Douglas DC-2 and DC-3 aircraft. One of their DC-3s, while on the ground in China, was attacked by Japanese aircraft and the right wing was severely damaged. Lacking a replacement DC-3 wing they improvised with the use of a DC-2 wing brought to China strapped to the belly of another CNAC aircraft. After attaching the wing to the crippled DC-3 they tested it to see if it was airworthy. Although the right wing was 5 feet shorter than the left and extra rudder and aileron trim was needed, it flew quite well. The resultant aircraft was dubbed the "DC-2½." (Lewis)

541 A Frontier Airlines DC-3 experienced severe weather, wind shear, and downdraft conditions during flight several miles north of Phoenix, Arizona. All efforts to climb out of the downdraft were unsuccessful, and when they hit a mountain crest it sheared off 9 feet of the left wing. They were able to keep the aircraft flying and managed a landing at Phoenix without injuring any of the 26 people on board. (Lewis)

A true miracle. This United Air Lines Convair 340 landed gear-up in a field after both engines quit on a flight from Fresno to LAX.

542 On 30 December 1964, a United Air Lines Convair 340 experienced double engine failure while flying from Fresno to Los Angeles. While IFR south of Tehachapi, the propliner lost both engines due to a fuel system problem, broke out of the clouds at 5,000 feet over what is now Six Flags Magic Mountain, and made a perfect dead-stick belly landing in a muddy beet field in Newhall. All 47 souls on board walked away without a scratch. (Machat)

543 Originally thought to be damaged enough that it would have to be trucked back to San Francisco for repair, that United Convair was instead raised up and put back on its gear, repaired with new engines and props, and flown out of the field to San Francisco less than a month later. Converted to a turboprop Convair 580 in the 1970s, the stalwart airframe is still flying today as an avionics systems testbed for the Honeywell Corporation. (Machat)

544 If you were to bet a friend on which propeller-driven airliner was in production the longest at the Douglas Aircraft Company, the DC-6 or DC-7, the obvious answer would lose him or her the bet. It seems that the Douglas assembly line at Santa Monica, California, rendered the last DC-6B some 13 days after the final DC-7C, on 17 November 1958. (Kodera)

545 It is sobering and hard to believe that many operational and/ or prototype airliners built in the United States and abroad were either lost in accidents or scrapped at the end of their careers with not one airplane surviving for us to see today. Paramount among these aircraft types are the Douglas DC-5, Bristol Brabazon, Saunders-Roe SR. 45 Princess flying boat, and the Fairey Rotodyne hybrid VTOL/turboprop airliner. (Lewis)

THE JET AGE

546 In 1941, the first Whittle jet engine produced all of 3,000 pounds of thrust. The new General Electric GE90-115B high-bypass geared turbofan used on the Boeing 777-300ER set a world record by producing 127,900 pounds of thrust (111,000 hp) for 60 continuous hours in test stand conditions. The price for the GE90-115B today is $24 million, the same price as five Boeing 707 jetliners in 1958 dollars! (Lewis)

547 The world's first jetliner with aft-mounted engines and the incumbent clean wing was the Sud Est SE.210 Caravelle first flown in 1955. This design philosophy was copied worldwide for years to come in both commercial airliner and business jet

United was the only U.S. airline to operate the French Sud SE.210 Caravelle. The sleek twinjet was exceedingly popular with passengers. (Courtesy of Ion Proctor)

applications. The Caravelle was a truly elegant design and stood as the epitome of French aesthetics for decades, superseded years later by a supersonic transport that began life as the "Super Caravelle" when the concept first came on the scene in 1962. That airplane flew in 1969, renamed as "Concorde." (Kodera)

548 It is a little-known fact that a small group of Boeing engineers served as advisors assisting de Havilland on the design of the S-duct for their revolutionary DH.121 Trident three-engine jetliner, which entered service in 1962. One year later, Boeing's own three-engine jet, the incomparable 727 complete with S-duct for its center engine, took to the air and eventually became the world's most successful airliner of that era and the first jetliner to exceed more than 1,000 units produced. (Machat)

549 In stark contrast to today's digital-age airliners with only a pilot and co-pilot in command of 600-passenger intercontinental "Super Jumbo" Airbus A380s, the first Boeing 707s to cross the Atlantic carried a cockpit crew of five men (no women were flying as airline captains in 1959). Manning the flight deck of Pan American 707s flying from the United States to Europe were the captain, first officer (co-pilot), flight engineer, navigator, and radio operator. (Machat)

550 When the new Boeing 737 MAX goes into service, it will be built with essentially the same exact windshield structure as its pioneering predecessor, the Model 367-80, or "Dash 80" prototype jet transport that first flew in July 1954, more than 60 years ago! The only difference will be the absence of the four smaller "eyebrow windows" above the main windshield panes that were originally designed to give the pilots more visibility in turns to identify and avoid traffic at lower altitudes. Modern TCAS collision avoidance systems have eliminated the need for those small upper windows. (Machat)

551 Although the aforementioned windshield design of the Boeing 707, 727, and 737 is quite functional, pilots of the early 707s complained they were always cold on the outboard sides of their body while flying at stratospheric cruise altitudes where outside air temperatures can drop to -70 degrees F. It was rumored that flight crews at American Airlines bought heavy sweaters and then cut them in half to combat this chilling aspect of jet pilotage. At altitude, the captain would wear the left half of the sweater while the co-pilot wore the right half. (Kodera)

552 JetBlue Airlines has a penchant for naming their individual A320 and Embraer E-190 aircraft using the word *blue*. Examples include *Blue Suede Shoes*, *Song Sung Blue*, and in a subtle slap at competitor Southwest Airlines, *Canyon Blue* (that airline's official color). JetBlue also had a novel policy of allowing employees who had suggested those names to accompany the new A320s on their delivery flights from the Airbus factory in Toulouse, France, to the airline's headquarters city of New York. (Machat)

553 Perhaps the most novel use of the word *blue* in a JetBlue Airbus name came from an event broadcast live on national television. An A320 bound from Burbank, California, to New York had a problem with its nose landing gear after takeoff, when the twin wheels turned 90 degrees after a locking pin became dislodged from the nose strut. The aircraft circled over Los Angeles burning off fuel before making a textbook emergency landing at LAX during which the nose tires blew out and the wheels were ground down to their hubs in a shower of sparks, again, all broadcast live on national TV. That A320 was repaired and appropriately renamed *Blue My Tires*. (Machat)

This is the third of nine factory color scheme variations on Eastern Air Lines DC-8s.

554 Airline color schemes are modified many times over the lifespan of an airliner, but the record for most number of revisions in the shortest time has to go to Eastern Airlines, which at first simplified then completely redesigned the markings of their Douglas DC-8-21 jetliners continuously from first delivery in 1960 through the introduction of the "Whisperliner" era with its distinctive two-tone "hockey stick" motif in 1965. No fewer than nine modifications or designs were used within that five-year period. (Machat)

555 Speaking of color schemes, the names of many legendary designers and even contemporary fine artists have been associated with airliner markings since the art deco period of the 1930s. Perhaps the most famous designer at the beginning of the Jet Age was Raymond Loewy who devised numerous clean, modern-looking

schemes that included Pan American, TWA, United, and Eastern for new Boeing 707s, Douglas DC-8s, and Convair 880s. (Machat)

556 The titles above the windows of Eastern's new Lockheed L-188 Electras were different on each side of the airplane. On the right-hand side it read, "FLY EASTERN'S PROPJET ELECTRA." On the left it read, "FLY EASTERN'S ELECTRA PROPJET." Why? So the lettering wouldn't get lost when the aft passenger boarding door was open. Those designers thought of everything back in those days, but now it doesn't matter; passengers just go to the airline's website. (Machat)

557 Everyone knows that a jumbo jet can carry a lot of passengers (just count them all at the baggage claim area), but this next statistic takes the cake and the world's record. The greatest number of passengers ever carried by a single commercial airliner is 1,088 by an El Al Airlines Boeing 747 during Operation Solomon, which involved the evacuation of Ethiopian Jews from Addis Ababa, Ethiopia, landing in Tel Aviv, Israel. It started on 24 May 1991 and 2 of those passengers include two live births, which took place in-flight. (Kodera)

558 SNECMA, known today as Safran Aircraft Engines, is the name and acronym of a highly successful European aircraft engine manufacturer: Société Nationale d'études et de Construction de Moteurs d'aviation, which translated into English means National Company for the Design and Construction of Aviation Engines. Their hallmark engine, the CMF56, is a highly successful powerplant used on several models of Boeing, McDonnell Douglas, and Airbus jet aircraft in both civilian and military applications. (Lewis)

559 The first turbine-powered commercial airliner to carry passengers across the Atlantic was the British Bristol Britannia. A BOAC Britannia 312 made that scheduled revenue flight from London's Heathrow Airport to New York's Idlewild on 19 December 1957. The Britannia was referred to as "the Whispering Giant." (Machat)

560 First-generation four-engine jetliners were produced by the hundreds, with the Boeing 707 being first to reach the one thousand mark after many years. Considering this fact, today's order lists for twin-engine jetliners, which carry more passengers on longer-range routes and with one less flight crew member in the cockpit (computers having replaced the flight engineer), are graphic testimony to aviation progress. For the narrow body twin-jets, order books as of this writing show 4,477 Airbus A320 family jetliners on order, besting Boeing's 2,965 for their new advanced 737 MAX. (Machat)

561 The first jet airliner to fly around the world in revenue passenger service was a Pan American World Airways Boeing 707-320 Intercontinental, which made the flight in October 1959, just one year after Pan Am inaugurated transatlantic jet service. The aircraft was named *Jet Clipper Windward*. (Machat)

562 While the world's first generation of long-range jet airliners were powered by four engines for both necessary thrust, safety, and redundancy, especially over long stretches of ocean, modern airliners now require only two engines, saving considerable cost in both fuel and maintenance. A single General Electric GE90 high-bypass-ratio turbofan produces nearly 100,000 pounds of static thrust, the equivalent of 111,526 hp. (Machat)

563 The first German jetliner ever built was the Baade 152, also known as Dresden 152, VL-DDR 152, or simply "the 152." Springing from the old Junkers factory and design bureau, this ungainly aircraft had high-mounted wings with anhedral, two tandem double-wheel main landing gear mounted along the fuselage centerline, and outrigger wheels at the wingtips. The first flight was in March 1958 and three prototypes aircraft were completed while 20 other examples were on the assembly line. Eventually, since this was Soviet-controlled East Germany, Mother Russia shut down the airplane and its development in 1960, preferring their own Tupolev Tu-124 jetliner to replace the 152. The first prototype 152 crashed, and all the rest were scrapped. (Kodera)

564 While the elegant de Havilland Comet will forever be acknowledged as the world's first jet airliner, having entered service in
1952, the world's first commercial airliner to fly solely on turbine
power was an AVRO Lancastrian I, modified as an airborne testbed and fitted with two 5,000-pound-thrust Nene turbojet engines
mounted in the aircraft's outboard nacelles. (Inboard engines were
the standard Rolls-Royce Merlins.) That aircraft transitioned to
turbine power in-flight on 8 August 1946. (Machat)

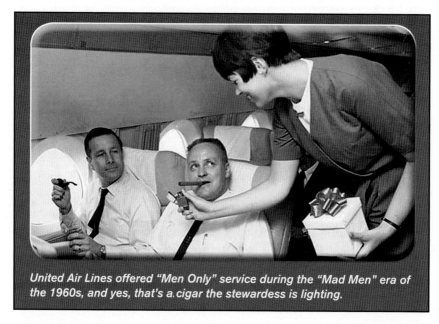

*United Air Lines offered "Men Only" service during the "Mad Men" era of
the 1960s, and yes, that's a cigar the stewardess is lighting.*

565 In the 1960s, every Monday through Friday at 9:00 am and 5:00
pm at Chicago's O'Hare and New York's Idlewild airports, a
United Air Lines Caravelle boarded businessmen carrying leather
briefcases, but no women were allowed. United's famous "Men
Only" executive service was perceived as a special perk for successful
businessmen well before the age of women airline captains, astronauts, and fighter pilots. Cigars were not only permitted on these
flights, but were eagerly provided to passengers by the stewardesses
themselves, the only two women on the aircraft. These flights ended
in 1970 when United was sued by the National Organization of
Women (NOW), bringing the famed service to an end. (Machat)

566 Most airliner designations are based on being part of a series of notable commercial aircraft built by a manufacturer, such as the famed Douglas "DC" series, or Boeing 700-series jetliners. In 1959, Convair's 880 first flew, followed by the 990 later that same year. The 880 was named for the number of feet it traveled in one second at cruise speed, while the 990 (originally named the 600 and Coronado) was re-designated as such to have a higher and even more impressive number. No more than 65 of either type were built, ending Convair's reign as a prime builder of airliners. (Proctor)

567 When the first Boeing 747 "Jumbo Jets" entered revenue passenger service in 1970 they were the largest commercial airliners ever flown. The cockpit crew of pilot, co-pilot, and flight engineer sat 35 feet above the ground with a total of 365 switches on the various instrument and overhead control panels. (Machat)

568 Largest aircraft in the world at the time of publication is the new Airlander 10, developed by Hybrid Air Vehicles (HAV) in the United Kingdom. At a total length of 302 feet, this combination airship-airplane-helicopter can carry 48 passengers. Originally developed for the U.S. Army, new applications are being sought now that the original contracting party has terminated their involvement with the aircraft. (Kodera)

569 The overall largest *airplane* in the world is the Antonov AN-225 Mriya from the Ukraine. Designed as the airplane to carry the Russian Buran space shuttle, much like the Boeing 747, which carries the U.S. space shuttle, the An-225 is the largest plane in operational service. The only airplane to exceed the wingspan of the Mriya is the one-off Hughes HK-1 Hercules or "Spruce Goose," which flew just once, in November 1947. (Kodera)

570 In 1966, three airline industry legends retired from their long-standing careers at the helm of three major U.S domestic and international airlines. They were Howard Hughes (TWA), W. A. "Pat" Patterson (United), and Eddie Rickenbacker (Eastern). Each of these airline titans shepherded their companies from the post–World War II Golden Age of propliners into the Jet Age with the Boeing 707 (TWA), Douglas DC-8 (United and Eastern), and Convair 880 (TWA).

571 Although the Anglo-French Concorde was the world's first supersonic airliner, Russia's Tupolev Tu-144 was the first SST to fly. Tupolev's design team promised their jet would fly in 1968, and that aircraft made its inaugural flight at 4:30 in the afternoon on 31 December 1968. Concorde's first flight was made two months later on 2 March 1969. Being first isn't always best, however. The Tu-144 suffered serious technical problems and was grounded, while Concorde flew in service from 1976 to 2003. (Machat)

572 Flying faster than sound was an extremely important goal, the military implications being obvious. Applying the same aerodynamic principles to commercial air transport would also yield significant advantage to the world and its commerce. The race was on in the 1960s with the French/British, Americans, and Russians all vying to finish first. Indeed, the first supersonic airliner to fly was developed by the Russian design bureau Tupolev as their Tu-144. Fulfilling a promise to fly an SST in 1968 by becoming airborne late in the afternoon on 31 December that year, the Soviets had cloaked the airplane in their typical secrecy. Aerodynamically inferior to the European Concorde or the U.S. Boeing 2707 concept, the Tupolev had several crashes and saw limited service, initially as an airliner and then a cargo-hauler before being retired in 1983. (Kodera)

573 The first ever supersonic passenger services were begun by the Anglo-French Concorde on 21 January 1976. Both airlines using the airplane, British Airways (BA) and Air France (AF), simultaneously flew that day. BA inaugurated service between London and Bahrain, while AF chose service from Paris to Rio de Janeiro. Routes to New York and eventually Washington, D.C., commenced in 1977 and were the only scheduled BA and AF routes remaining in the latter days of the airplane. Final flights took place in 2003. (Kodera)

574 On 7 February 1996, the world record for the fastest passenger flight in history was set between London Heathrow and New York's JFK by British Airways Concorde G-BOAD. Veteran BA Captain Leslie Scott, together with First Officer Tim Orchard, commanded the record-breaking flight in 2 hours, 52 minutes, 59 seconds. Concorde "Alpha-Delta" is also the highest-time aircraft of the SST fleet, having logged 23,397 hours of flight time. (Machat)

575 Concorde was never allowed to fly at supersonic speed over any land mass to avoid exposing people or animals to the concussive effects of its sonic boom. For flights to and from the United States, or on legs of special round-the-world charter flights from New York to Miami, the SST could be no closer than 30 miles to the U.S. coast when flying above Mach 1. (Machat)

576 Supersonic passengers could claim the honor of having landed before they took off. Flying Concorde westbound to the United States from Paris or London, the airliner would leave Europe in the early afternoon and land in New York or Washington, D.C., late morning local time, having outraced the sun on the 3½-hour transatlantic flight. (Machat)

577 If someone told you that the world's first operational supersonic airliner had a tail wheel, as odd as that sounds, they would

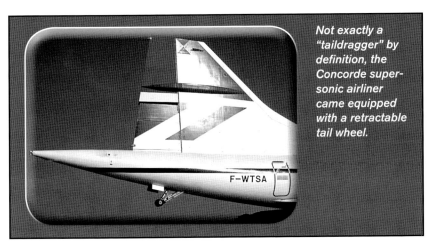

Not exactly a "taildragger" by definition, the Concorde supersonic airliner came equipped with a retractable tail wheel.

F-WTSA

be telling the truth. While not "taildraggers" in the literal sense, Concordes were indeed fitted with a dual retractable tail wheel landing gear to guard against tail strikes at the extremely high angles of attack the aircraft flew during takeoff and landing. (Machat)

578 There are many stories of how Concorde was used to close multi-billion-dollar business deals, or shuttle Sheiks and oil barons between Europe and the Mideast. Perhaps the most unique use of the airplane was when a rock music superstar had his hair cut in New York the morning of his concert at Madison Square Garden, but was dissatisfied with the results. He then had his personal barber flown over from London on Concorde to re-do the job before he went on stage that night. That singer was Rod Stewart. (Machat)

579 Speaking of legendary rock stars, famed singer, songwriter, and drummer Phil Collins, formerly of Genesis, used Concorde to commute from New York's Kennedy International Airport to London's Heathrow Airport to perform in back-to-back "Live Aid" concerts the same day.

580 Concorde G-BOAD Alpha Delta was also the only Concorde to have flown in scheduled service wearing another airline's color scheme when operated jointly with Singapore Airlines in 1980. Only the left side of the aircraft was painted in Singapore's colors, however, as the right side remained in British Airways markings. (Machat)

581 In a stunning bit of marketing bravado, both Air France and British Airways flew Concordes in interline service with Braniff International Airlines, but those aircraft were never painted in Braniff colors despite airbrushed photos showing the orange Braniff color scheme on the jet. Air speed over land was limited to Mach .99 to avoid producing a sonic boom, but full first-class service was given to passengers. Unbelievably, the one-way airfare was only $79. (Machat)

582 Concorde was also used in a unique one-of-a-kind promotion for Pepsi-Cola and was painted in a garish, but highly noticeable, red and blue color scheme. Due to the aerodynamic heating of the aircraft's external skins in supersonic flight, the speed of this jet was limited to Mach 1. (Machat)

583 On 15 July 1968, the first scheduled airline flights between the Soviet Union and the United States of America became reality, despite the tensions of the Cold War.

584 First negotiated by President Kennedy, Pan American and Aeroflot entered into a joint agreement to fly reciprocal service linking New York and Moscow using Boeing 707-320B and Ilyushin Il-62 aircraft. (Machat)

585 Pan American's eastbound flight to Moscow took 10 hours and 35 minutes, including ground time in Copenhagen, while the return flight took 11 hours and 45 minutes. First-class round-trip airfare was $1,100 and an economy ticket cost $730. It is interesting to note that Aeroflot had been operating nonstop flights between Moscow and Havana, Cuba, since the late 1950s using giant Tupolev Tu-114 turboprops and continued that long-range service despite having new jets on the Moscow–New York route. (Machat)

586 Few people realize that to meet American Airlines' requirements for a 250-passenger twin-aisle aircraft capable of operating from New York's smaller LaGuardia Airport to Chicago (plus Los Angeles-Chicago for United), McDonnell Douglas designed a twin-engine wide-body airliner. When airlines realized they should really use the jet coast-to-coast, the fuselage was stretched, a third engine was added at the base of the vertical stabilizer, and the DC-10 was born. (Machat)

587 DAC intended to build the twin-engine version from the start, including mock-ups, large-scale models, airport studies, and airbrushed renderings in the markings of every airline imaginable. Parent company McDonnell did not approve the program. (Machat)

Original design requirements for a jumbo jet capable of operating from LaGuardia Airport called for a twin-engine aircraft.

588 The Douglas DC-9 was originally intended to have a clamshell integral airstair door like its DC-3 ancestor, but future DC-9 customer Scandinavian Airline System brought a simple fact to the attention of Douglas engineers: In their winter operating environment, if it was snowing at time of boarding, a pile of accumulated snow on the stairs would then be dumped on the heads of first-class passengers when the door was closed. Hence, DC-9s to this day are equipped with self-contained articulated folding stairs that retract below the forward boarding door before takeoff. (Machat)

589 As was realized over time at Long Beach, only derivatives (DC-9-40, DC-9-50, DC-9-65 [Super 80/MD-80] MD-87, MD-90, MD-95 [717], and MD-11) were approved by parent company McDonnell from 1970 to 1997 when Boeing finally acquired the company. (Machat)

590 In a graphic example of how the advent of jet airliners impacted the traveling public, as of 1982, the entire worldwide fleet of Douglas jetliners, including all versions of the DC-8, DC-9, DC-10, and MD-80 series aircraft, had carried 2.5 billion passengers, the equivalent of more than half the population of the earth. Distance traveled while carrying those passengers was more than 22 billion miles. (Machat)

591 Thankfully, airline travel is as safe as it's ever been, although with any airliner accident, there can be major loss of life. Many of the rules and regulations that address and govern passenger and crew safety are the direct result of lessons learned in earlier accidents. For instance, opening the curtains between first class and coach for takeoff or landing is the result of an accident in the early 1960s in which first-class passengers lost their lives trying to get to the forward boarding door, not knowing the closer over-wing emergency exits were right behind the closed curtain. (Machat)

592 Those 3-inch-wide stripes that surround doors and over-wing emergency exit hatches were legislated into existence as the result of an airliner crash landing that occurred at night and in bad weather. Although the crash itself was survivable, passengers' lives were lost in the ensuing fire when rescue crews could not easily see the doors and exits to initiate emergency rescue. (Machat)

593 The 250-knot "speed limit" for aircraft flying at altitudes below 10,000 feet is a direct result of a tragic midair collision in December 1960 in which a four-engine jetliner missed a procedure turn while descending for landing at New York's Idlewild Airport and overran a smaller and slower piston-powered Lockheed Constellation on approach to nearby LaGuardia with the loss of 128 passengers and crew, and 6 people on the ground. The jetliner was descending at 3,600 feet per minute and flying at more than 400 knots. (Machat)

594 Sometimes with new technology, old habits die hard. As the first generation of U.S jetliners began taking shape on the drawing boards at Boeing, Douglas, and Convair, the idea of converting piston-powered airliners to turboprops (essentially a jet engine driving a propeller) was seriously studied. Douglas envisioned a turboprop "DC-7D" while Lockheed test flew an "L-1249" Constellation fitted with Allison 501 turboprops. In the end, Douglas opted for the pure-jet DC-8, while Lockheed applied those same engines to its new L-188 Electra. (Machat)

595 The world's most successful airliner, in terms of numbers built, has to be the Boeing 737 series, with more than 10,000 airframes ordered to date. Astoundingly, the jetliner was nearly canceled early in its production life as the battle with the Douglas DC-9 took its toll on orders for the pudgy Boeing. Enter Ed Colodny, then president of Allegheny Airlines, soon to be USAir, who worked with the Seattle manufacturer to lengthen and re-engine the airplane to produce the -300, -400, and -500 series. This reinventing of the type led to the ensuing renaissance and enshrinement of Boeing as the world's premier airliner manufacturer. (Kodera)

Supplemental engine-carrying installation for Lockheed's TriStar was used on the long-range L-1011-500 variant only. (Andy Cardadeiro via Jon Proctor)

596 Although modern airliner powerplants were exceedingly reliable in the jumbo jet era, occasionally the need arose to transport a spare or replacement engine to an airplane halfway around the world. What if there were no outsize cargo transports readily available for that task? The answer was to attach the extra engine to a supplemental pylon inboard of wing-mounted engines closest to the aircraft's fuselage. These types of installations began with the

first Boeing 707s as well as the Vickers Super VC-10, but the Boeing 747, Douglas DC-10, and L-1011-500 pictured on the previous page all served as spare engine carrier aircraft. (Proctor)

597 The world's first jet airliner to reach 1,000 units produced was the Boeing 727. Total production for this "DC-3 of the Jet Age" was 1,832 airplanes built for hundreds of airline, government, and executive operators worldwide. (Machat)

598 Painting large airliners requires large automated facilities to apply as much as 500 pounds of paint per airplane for an airliner like the Boeing 747-8. The colors are all digitally matched, and for the McDonnell Douglas DC-10, 39 different shades of white were used for various customer airlines depending on the aircraft's specific color scheme. (Machat)

599 Eastern Air Lines inaugurated its novel "Boston-Washington Shuttle" service from New York's LaGuardia Airport in 1961, with hourly flights to those two cities. Much like a commuter train, there were no reservations, no seat assignments, and tickets could be purchased onboard. The airline also proudly announced that "no passenger would be left behind," and to emphasize that point, when the Lockheed "Super-G" Constellation making the first Boston flight left the gate, one extra passenger was left. Eastern rolled out a twin-engine Martin 404 Silver Falcon and flew the lone lucky passenger to Boston. (Machat)

600 It has often been quoted that the wingspan of the 747 is longer than the distance of the Wright brothers' first flight, which was just more than 120 feet. But more interesting, on takeoff, the engines of a 747 displace enough air to fill the Goodyear Blimp in 7 seconds. (Keeshen)

601 Airline pilots never eat the same meal while flying. This is a precaution so that in the rare event one pilot suffers food poisoning, the other pilot should be able to continue the flight or divert to an emergency location, if needed. For this same reason, the president and vice president of the United States do not fly on the same airplane. Prince Charles and Prince William also do not fly together. (Lewis)

602 With the advent of jet airliners in the late 1950s, airports were redesigned to adapt to the Jet Age. New York's Idlewild Airport (now JFK) was the first in the nation to be designed in a circular cluster of free-standing buildings dedicated to individual airlines, with each terminal featuring its own distinctive architecture. Known as "Terminal City," this unique arrangement surrounded reflecting pools, fountains, and greenways with the International Arrivals Building (IAB) and 13-story control tower at the apex. Today, only the preserved and restored TWA terminal remains, built in 1962 and converted into a hotel/museum today. (Machat)

603 A most significant statistic was recorded as the close of 1958. Ironically, that was the year BOAC and Pan American both inaugurated transatlantic jet service, but as of 31 December, official tallies revealed that for the first time in history the total number of passengers carried by air exceeded the total number of passengers carried by sea in transatlantic service. The writing was on the wall for steamship travel between New York and Europe, which lasted only another decade before most modern ocean liners were docked forever or scrapped. (Machat)

604 Braniff International Airlines launched a brilliant marketing campaign in 1965 called "the end of the plain plane." With a complete redesign of every aspect of the airline's visual presence from crew uniforms to ground equipment and the aircraft themselves, Braniff created one of the most distinctive and innovative marketing efforts ever seen in commercial aviation. The fuselages of all aircraft were painted a solid vibrant color with the wings, engines, and tailplanes painted white. In addition to the primary colors of red, yellow, and blue, shades such as lime green, purple, and yellow ochre were used, creating the inevitable label given the look: the "jelly bean" scheme. (Machat)

605 13 May 1982 was an unlucky day for Braniff International Airlines. Their entire fleet sat grounded one day after the airline became the first U.S. carrier to file for bankruptcy as a direct result of airline deregulation enacted in 1978. When the order to cease operations was sent out to all airborne Braniff aircraft, Flight 501, the legendary bright orange Braniff 747 named *The Great Pumpkin*, was just crossing the coastline of Southern California on its way from Dallas to Hawaii. The captain refused to divert to Los Angeles International and delivered his 350 passengers to their Hawaiian vacations as promised. The jetliner returned to DFW in Dallas the next day as the last scheduled Braniff flight ever made. (Machat)

The legend begins as "Dan Cooper" bails out of a Northwest Airlines Boeing 727-100 on Thanksgiving Eve 1971.

606 The legend of D. B. Cooper began on the dark and stormy night of 24 November 1971 when mysterious passenger "Dan Cooper" (at least that was the name on his ticket) flew from Spokane to Seattle and hijacked the Northwest Orient Airlines Boeing 727-100 demanding $200,000 in $20 bills and four military-style parachutes, leading authorities to believe he would take a hostage with him when he bailed out of the jet with the ransom. (Machat)

607 After releasing everyone onboard except the jetliner's crew, Cooper demanded that the aircraft be refueled for a flight to Mexico, stipulating the exact route of flight on a specific Victor Airway to another refueling point in Reno, Nevada. The airplane was depressurized and configured with landing gear extended, flaps 30 degrees, and flying at an indicated airspeed of 160 knots at an altitude of 10,000 feet. These were the same exact parameters used by the CIA for inserting agents into denied territory in Southeast Asia at night from a Boeing 727-100. (Machat)

608 Cooper bailed out over the Washington-Oregon border and disappeared without a trace. The day after the hijacking, all 15 CIA 727 flight crew members were given lie detector tests (all 15 passed with flying colors). Although several of the $20 bills were found many years later dredged from the bottom of the Columbia River, despite massive manhunts, no trace of D. B. Cooper was ever found, and the FBI only recently closed the case unsolved. To prevent copycat hijackers from bailing out of rear airstairs, an external blade-like device was invented to thwart the door from being opened in flight. That device was named "the Cooper vane." (Machat)

609 When a letter or package absolutely positively had to be there the next morning, businesses worldwide had no hope of delivering those items if the destination was more than a few hours away. All that changed on 17 April 1971 when an enterprising Yale graduate and former Marine named Fred Smith started an air freight business by carrying 18 packages in a Dassult Falcon 20 bizjet converted with a cargo door. Using an aerial hub in Memphis, Tennessee, to process overnight packages, Smith's business grew into an industry giant today called Federal Express. (Machat)

610 At the end of World War II, there were five U.S. manufacturers building airliners: Boeing, Convair, Douglas, Lockheed, and Martin. By 1970, there were only three: Boeing, McDonnell Douglas, and Lockheed. In 1972, a new consortium composed of

five European nations (France, Germany, England, Spain, and the Netherlands) was formed. This industrial coalition was named Airbus Industrie and produced only one aircraft type: the Airbus A300 widebody twinjet. (Machat)

611 In a rather dramatic "sea change," in 1982 the airliner "Big Three" shifted from Boeing, McDonnell Douglas, and Lockheed to Boeing, Airbus, and McDonnell Douglas, as the A300 gained both traction and momentum in the world's airliner sales market. In 1997, the industrial sands shifted once again with Boeing acquiring McDonnell Douglas to become the sole U.S. aircraft manufacturer building airliners. (Machat)

612 Although the double-deck Airbus A380 Super Jumbo is billed as the first airliner to carry more than 500 passengers, that title could be modified as the world's first airliner "originally designed" to carry more than 500 passengers. In 1980, Japan Air Lines ordered seven special "high-density" Boeing 747SRs (for short range) as the ultimate in airborne commuting. The inaugural flight on 5 October 1982 took off from Tokyo carrying a full load of 550 passengers and landed a short time later in Okinawa. (Machat)

613 Because of the need for air traffic controllers to be able to view the runway at all times, the windows of the tower are set at precisely 15 degrees to block reflections and glare. (Proctor)

614 The iconic pagoda control tower and adjacent futuristic terminal building at Dulles International Airport in Washington, D.C., was designed by the brilliant Finnish architect Ero Saarinen. Built in 1962 and billed as the "Airport of the Future," Dulles was truly an architectural and operational expression of the burgeoning Jet Age. To avoid large blocks of aircraft clogging gate areas, passengers were transported to airliners parked a mile away on vast remote ramps by "mobile lounges" that elevated them to the jetliners' boarding doors. Arriving aircraft used this procedure in reverse as passengers were transported back to the main terminal by mobile lounge. (Machat)

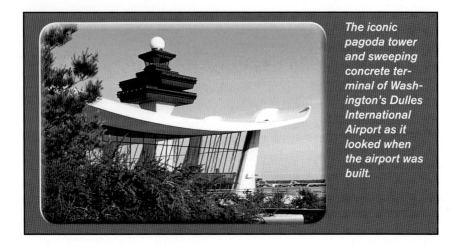

The iconic pagoda tower and sweeping concrete terminal of Washington's Dulles International Airport as it looked when the airport was built.

615 The average lifespan of an airliner is 20 to 25 years, but the calendar is not the ultimate determination. The number of times an aircraft is pressurized, roughly about 75,000 times, is what eventually leads to metal fatigue. (Proctor)

616 While flying, the body loses water; it varies depending upon the person, but averages about 2 cups per hour. This dehydration can lead to potentially fatal blood clots for passengers, especially on extremely long nonstop flights. (Proctor)

617 So along those lines, the world's largest purchaser of champagne used to be British Airways. Their passengers consumed a minimum of 90,000 cases yearly. However, Singapore Airlines is the second largest buyer of Dom Perignon champagne in the world, with Emirates purchasing the most bottles of bubbly. (Proctor)

618 Rick "the Human Fly" Rojatt was a stunt man who attached himself to the top of the fuselage of a Douglas DC-8 four-engine jet airliner and flew at speeds up to 280 mph and an altitude of 5,000 feet. A rain shower was encountered during the flight and he was pelted with raindrops at 300 mph, causing him to black out. He needed six weeks in the hospital to recover from this stunt but went on to do many more during his career. The DC-8 was flown by United captain and air racing pilot Clay Lacy. (Lewis)

619 During flight, cabin air pressurization numbs our taste buds, causing changes in the taste of food and drinks. For this reason, airliner food is heavily salted and spiced. (Proctor)

620 On 12 January 1991, the first Boeing 727 ever built ended airline service after flying 64,492 hours in 48,057 flights. After delivery to United Air Lines in 1963, the 727-100 flew 3 million passengers and generated $300 million for United, which paid $4.4 million for the airplane. Repainted in its delivery color scheme, Boeing 727 N7001U is now on permanent display in its final home at the Museum of Flight on Boeing Field in Seattle, Washington. (Machat)

621 About 100 people die onboard airliners in-flight every year. Cabin crews are trained in first aid and must complete yearly exams to remain qualified. (Proctor)

622 In case of an emergency, the lights may go out in an aircraft. Studies have shown that it is better to see in the dark if your eyes are accustomed to the dark. Therefore, lights are turned off during takeoff and landing so that your eyes can adjust to these lower levels of light. If there is an accident you are ready to see your way out quickly and safely. (Keeshen)

623 American Airlines began accepting delivery of McDonnell Douglas MD-80s in May 1983. With acceptance of its 200th aircraft in 1990, it became the first airline to accumulate a fleet of that size, one that would reach 260 two years later. American's acquisition of a substantial portion of TWA's MD-80s pushed the number well over 300. However, the claim has since been well surpassed by Southwest Airlines, which counts its Boeing 737 fleet size at more than 700. (Proctor)

624 The first scheduled flight of a jet airliner across the Atlantic carrying revenue passengers took place on Saturday, 4 October 1958. The aircraft was a BOAC de Havilland Comet 4, which just that morning had received its official FAA certification for the route from London's Heathrow Airport to New York's Idlewild Airport.

Wanting to take full advantage of being able to beat rival Pan American with transatlantic jet service, BOAC personnel took a planeload of passengers boarding a turboprop Bristol Britannia bound for New York, and placed them hurriedly on the Comet. (Machat)

625 When Juan Trippe learned of the BOAC surprise, he immediately arranged to have a not-yet-in-service Boeing 707 that was conducting route-proving flights on the East Coast land at Idlewild, making sure the gleaming new aircraft was not only at the airport when the Comet landed, but parked right next to it at the adjoining gate of the International Arrivals Building. The Comet, splendid in its regal BOAC colors and highly polished lower fuselage, looked comparatively small next to the mighty Boeing, a subtle but effective marketing coup for Pan Am's Trippe. (Machat)

After being beaten by the British Comet, Pan American launched Boeing 707 flights from New York to Paris in October 1958.

626 Pan American inaugurated its first transatlantic jet service on 25 October 1958, flying eastbound from Idlewild to Paris, essentially retracing Charles Lindbergh's epic solo nonstop flight of May 1927. Lindbergh departed Long Island's Roosevelt Field some 15 miles east of Idlewild and arrived in Paris 33½ hours later. Pan Am's 707, carrying 120 passengers, made the same trip in just under 6 hours. (Machat)

627 Often referred to as a Jetway, so named by its manufacturer, a loading bridge is loosely defined as a device that bridges the distance from the second story of an air terminal building to an airliner boarding door. Some earlier devices on ramp level protected passengers as they walked from the terminal building to aircraft boarding steps, but United Air Lines holds the distinction of using the first "Aero-Gangplank," on a trial basis, at Chicago's O'Hare Airport in 1958, a follow-up to its earlier proposed and more complicated "Air-Dock" design. With the advent of jet airliners utilizing two boarding doors, dual-loading bridges began appearing at some airports, but nose-in parking later dictated single air bridges. (Proctor)

628 Showing why aviation historians often have gray hair, the delivery ceremony for the "2,000th Douglas-built jet transport" was held at the McDonnell Douglas Long Beach facility on 15 September 1982. The aircraft was a United Airlines DC-10-10CF, "CF" standing for "Convertible Freighter," and this was the first new jetliner built specifically for use by the U.S. Air Force Civil Reserve Air Fleet. Only problem was that according to production line numbers, that DC-10 was actually the 2,001st Douglas jet transport. The 2,000th airplane was an Alitalia DC-9-80, but the company wanted to use the United DC-10 for a better public affairs impact, a prudent choice considering the Air Force angle. (Machat)

629 As with military aircraft, there has been much confusion over the last few decades about the names of aircraft manufacturers, resulting from the spate of post–Cold War corporate mergers. Was there ever a Boeing DC-3 or Bombardier Twin-Otter? No, but Boeing did acquire McDonnell Douglas, and de Havilland of Canada is now a legacy company for Bombardier. Although these lines were a bit blurred immediately after those mergers, the rule today is that a company can lay claim to building an aircraft if it is still in production, or was indeed built by that company before production ended; hence, the original McDonnell Douglas MD-95 (final iteration of the Douglas DC-9 first flown in 1965) became the Boeing 717 before going out of production. (Machat)

630 The largest passenger aircraft overall is the four-engine double-deck Airbus A380-800 assembled at Toulouse, France, with major structural components shipped by sea, land, and air from all points in Europe. Although slightly less in passenger capacity, the latest version of Boeing's classic 747 Jumbo Jet, the 747-800, is slightly longer by 3 feet. (Kodera)

631 On 25 October 1991, the first Airbus A340 took flight at the manufacturer's final assembly plant in Toulouse, France. More than just the next member of the Airbus airliner family, the A340 and its twin-engine twin, the A330, represented a new paradigm in airliner design by becoming the first standardized airframe that could be ordered as either a two-engine or four-engine aircraft. These high-capacity long-range fly-by-wire aircraft formed the backbone of many new international low-cost airlines and are still in frontline service today. (Machat)

632 The heaviest airplane in the world is the Antonov AN-225 Mriya, weighing more than 640 tons. The -225 is the first of the "million pound airplanes," a rather extreme distinction. (Kodera)

633 First commercial jet airliner to be painted all white was the Delta Air Lines "Golden Crown" Convair 880, named in Delta

Called the "Aristocrat of the Jets" by Delta Air Lines, Convair's 880 jetliner looked magnificent in this regal all-white color scheme introduced in 1960.

ads in the early 1960s as the "Aristocrat of the Jets." The aircraft was designated for the 880-feet per second it traveled at cruising speed. (Machat)

634 Sister ship to the 880 was the world's fastest first-generation jetliner, the Convair 990. Fitted with Whitcomb "speed pods," the 990 flew at Mach .96, or 615 mph. Jetliner was called the "Maserati of the jets" by its pilots, all of whom loved flying the airplane. (Machat)

635 Both the Convair 880 and Convair 990 were quickly outsold by the medium-range Boeing 720 and follow-on orders for the Boeing 707. Only 65 880s found their way to commercial service, mainly with TWA and Delta Air Lines, while just 37 Convair 990s were built, with 20 going to American Airlines. These short runs marked the end of commercial aircraft production for Convair. (Proctor)

636 Developed as a direct competitor to the 880 and 990, the 720 helped to keep its established airline customers from defecting to Convair jets. All but a handful of the 154 turbojet-powered Boeing 720s and turbofan-powered 720Bs were sold to existing 707 operators. (Proctor)

637 Boeing introduced a short-body version of its successful 747, the 747SP, increasing range to accommodate long segments such as New York–Tokyo and Sydney–Los Angeles. The type entered service with Pan Am on 25 April 1976. Although it built only 45 "SPs," relatively low design costs and the ability to keep customers in the Boeing family made the effort well worthwhile. (Proctor)

638 American Airlines began the first pure-jet airliner service across the United States on 25 January 1959. While American had planned to be the first to introduce jets on the domestic market, National Airlines renegade president Ted Baker stole the show by leasing Boeing 707s from Pan American and beginning seasonal jet flights between New York and Miami on 10 December 1958. A unique arrangement allowed National to leave New York in the morning and return the same afternoon, then return the 707 to Pan Am for its evening departure to Europe. (Proctor)

639 A year later, Northeast Airlines (then flying piston-powered DC-3 and DC-6Bs, plus turboprop Viscounts) entered into a similar agreement with TWA for the winter months, allowing Northeast passengers to escape the chilly New England winter by jetting off to Miami on a leased TWA Boeing 707 jet. (Proctor)

640 The ultimate in deception occurred when all-cargo Boeing 707s arrived with windows painted on the fuselages. Perhaps airline managers didn't want customers who were contemplating a flight to think their company was flying windowless airplanes. One example was Trans World Airlines (TWA), which took delivery of a few non-convertible 707-331Cs in this manner. Later, bold "CargoJet" markings seemed a better alternative and the "windows" were eliminated during the scheduled next repaint, thus saving the considerable expense of masking each window in the process. (Proctor)

641 Pan American flight 843 lost 25 feet of the right wing of its Boeing 707-320B when engine number 4 suffered a catastrophic turbine failure. The emergency occurred at an altitude of only 800 feet just after departing San Francisco International Airport. The aircraft lost both the outer portion of its right wing and the entire number-4 engine when a reserve fuel tank exploded following the engine turbine failure. The crew extinguished the fire and made an emergency landing with no injuries to passengers or crew, and miraculously to no one on the ground where the engine landed. (Lewis)

642 As technically impressive as the Fairey Rotodyne was as a commuter aircraft concept, the big machine was just too far ahead of its time. The ultimate demise of the Rotodyne was the result of unfavorable economic factors plus the fact that it produced an inordinate amount of ear-splitting noise on the ground. The Rotodyne's tip jets produced a screeching sound that was literally nauseating to anyone within earshot of the aircraft, and which could be heard for miles around the airport. (Machat)

Fairey Rotodyne was a good concept for city-to-city air travel in Europe, but it proved impractical for routine airline operations.

643 *Gimli Glider* was the name given to an Air Canada Boeing 767 that made a dead-stick landing on an abandoned airfield in Manitoba. A combination of errors caused an insufficient amount of fuel to be loaded on the aircraft. Between Montreal and Edmonton both engines flamed out at an altitude of 41,000 feet but the crew managed to glide to a safe landing on a racetrack that was RCAF Station Gimli's runway before it was closed. Although the nose gear didn't fully extend and failed on landing, there were no fatalities and only minor injuries incurred during evacuation of the aircraft cabin using slides. (Lewis)

644 Three classes of service on U.S. domestic aircraft have recently become the norm with major carriers: first class, economy, and "economy plus." But this concept was first introduced more than 50 years ago in August 1964 when United Air Lines introduced "Red, White and Blue" service on its Douglas DC-8 jetliners. First class (red) and what was then called coach (blue) were basically unchanged. Added was an in-between option (white) branded as "standard," with five-across seating. Remarkably, the difference between standard and coach fares on New York–Los Angeles flights was only $5.30 plus tax. (Proctor)

645 American Airlines responded to United's program with similar layouts on its 707s, but TWA demurred except in limited markets, whereas Convair 880s with their five-across coach configuration were marketed as the equivalent of United's "white" offering, but without the increased fare. United's effort followed a one-class, five-abreast "one class red carpet service" that debuted earlier in the year. Both American and United's plans, after failing to produce sufficient revenue, were abandoned. (Proctor)

646 ETOPS: When twin-engine jet airliners began to fly passengers over extended ocean routes procedures were established to ensure that diversion to emergency landing fields was designed and implemented. Extended Range Operational Performance Standards (ETOPS) was the name and abbreviation given to these new procedures. It wasn't long before the phrase "Engines Turning or People Swimming" appeared. (Lewis)

647 When a Seaboard World Douglas DC-8-63 landed at Marble Mountain Army Airfield in South Vietnam at 2:00 am by mistake they were advised to disassemble the aircraft and move it to DaNang, which was their original destination. Not wanting to go to that extreme they offloaded all passengers, cargo, and cabin crew and made a spectacular takeoff with just the flight crew onboard. (Lewis)

648 Douglas introduced its DC-8 jetliner with great fanfare, and plugged its "larger windows," no doubt a dig at those of the competing Boeing 707. The "Big Eight" boasted a 17⅛ x 20⅝–inch portal, or 253 square inches of viewing space per seat row. In the end, Boeing's double-window concept proved an advantage when seat pitch began shrinking. For the most part, it still allowed at least one window per row, whereas the DC-8 window viewing could be hidden by seat backs in tighter configurations. (Proctor)

649 Boeing's initial 707s featured two smaller windows per row, each measuring 9 x 12½ inches, a total of 112½ square inches. Multiplied by two, total viewing area was 225 square inches, indeed less than that of the DC-8. To counter the claim, Boeing offered a slight increase in window size, to 10 x 14 inches, and voilà: The resulting 280 square inches per pair exceeded that of the DC-8's single window per row. Several airlines selected the increase in window size, including United for its Boeing 720s, while other carriers switched over on later 707 and 720 orders. (Proctor)

650 According to Boeing historian Michael Lombardi, one of the most frequent questions the company receives is why its aircraft names begin and end with the number 7. Lombardi explained that Boeing's engineering department began dividing the model numbers into blocks of 100 with 300s and 400s for aircraft, 500s for turbine engines, 600 for rockets, and 700s assigned to jet transports. Company marketing people suggested 707 sounded better than 700, thus beginning the policy of beginning and ending models with 7. It continues to this day with the 787. (Proctor)

651 The current post-Boeing merger appellation of the former McDonnell Douglas MD-95 jetliner is the designation "717." However, the current post-Boeing merger appellation of the former McDonnell Douglas MD-95 at 717 built is not the answer. The original and sequential model number "717" was assigned in the early 1950s to the military development of the Boeing 707, the C/KC-135 Stratotanker. Specifically, the 717 was the non-tanker/all-freighter C-135 aircraft. Certain versions were also assigned the model number 739. So, just like the mysterious missing link Douglas DC-5, the Boeing numbering system for passenger airliners is still indeed unbroken and sequential. (Kodera)

652 Airlines today often widen fleet types to receive timely deliveries, and Eastern Air Lines' legendary Eddie Rickenbacker had no problem with multiple fleet types all the way back to the 1950s. Some carriers inherited varied types through mergers, but Eastern boasted airliners from different manufacturers that served basically the same missions. For example, Martin 404s, Convair 440s, and Lockheed Constellations from 649s to 1049Gs flying alongside Douglas DC-6s and DC-7s. In the Jet Age, Eastern flew the Douglas DC-8 and DC-9 and Boeing 720 and 727. (Proctor)

653 Even after Rickenbacker's departure, Eastern flew all the widebody types ever built, which included the twin-engine Airbus A300 and tri-jet Lockheed L-1011 TriStar, along with a few leased Boeing 747-100s and McDonnell Douglas DC-10-10 tri-jets. (Proctor)

654 The first scheduled turboprop airline service in the world was begun by British European Airways (BEA) on 18 April 1953 utilizing the new Vickers Viscount 701 airliner. The route was from London, England, to Nicosia, Cypress. (Kodera)

655 The first scheduled turboprop (and first jet) service in the United States was launched by Capital Airlines on 26 July 1955 between Washington, D.C., and Chicago, Illinois, also utilizing the Viscount, this one, though, the U.S.-certificated 745 model. The first commercial airline to operate in the United States carrying passengers in scheduled revenue service was the St. Petersburg–Tampa Airboat Line. On 1 January 1914, that company inaugurated air service using a Benoist flying boat capable of carrying a pilot and one passenger. (Kodera)

656 The first airline VIP "club" room was introduced by American Airlines in 1939 at the brand-new LaGuardia Airport in New York City. The room was originally a lounge for Mayor LaGuardia who, under financial pressure to pay for the new airfield, offered the space at a press conference when prompted by a reporter. American's station manager at the time snatched the property on the spot. The name given to the new club room was Admirals' Club, hewing to the airline's nautical aviation marketing theme. Following this, the airline built another club in Washington, D.C., followed by the rest of the system where warranted. (Kodera)

657 The wonder of jet propulsion was quickly adapted after World War II to an airliner design. Taking the lead in this development was the de Havilland Aircraft Company of Hatfield, England, which gave the aeronautical community the beautiful DH 106 Comet jetliner. With its four de Havilland–designed Ghost engines buried in its wing roots, the airplane, after several years of route proving, entered scheduled passenger service with British Overseas Airways Corporation (BOAC) on 2 May 1952, becoming the first operational jetliner in the world. (Kodera)

658 Lockheed's venerable turboprop transport, the C-130 Hercules, not only proudly served the armed forces of 70 different nations in its nearly 65 years of existence, but was also used by airlines as a freighter. Flown by Delta Air Lines in the United States and several international carriers, the commercial version of the C-130 featured a stretched fuselage and was designated the "L-100." Capable of carrying payloads in excess of 50,000 pounds at speeds of up to 360 mph, the L-100 also offered the convenience of a rear cargo ramp. (Machat)

659 The original seating configuration for the first U.S. jet airliner, the Boeing 707, was five abreast in a three-two configuration (this fuselage width being a direct transposition of the company's precursor KC-135 aerial tanker design). United Air Lines rejected this width as too narrow and insisted on six abreast, hence the choice of the Douglas DC-8, which was of this dimension. Boeing consequently widened the fuselage on its airplane, and this wooed American Airlines to purchase the 707, abandoning longtime supplier Douglas. (Kodera)

660 The first turbine-powered airliner to be lost in a fatal accident was in service for only 10 days. On the cold winter night of 3 February 1959, American Airlines "Flagship New York," a brand-new Lockheed L-188 Electra, crashed into the upper East River on final approach to Runway 22 at New York's LaGuardia Airport, the result of an altimeter problem in the cockpit. Of the 73 passengers and crew onboard, 65 lost their lives in the accident. (Machat)

Gleaming in the California sun, the factory fresh American Airlines Lockheed Electra Flagship New York *is prepared for delivery.*

661 3 February 1959 was also "the day the music died" when rock 'n' roll stars Buddy Holly, Richie Valens, and the Big Bopper perished in the crash of a Beechcraft Bonanza at Clear Lake, Iowa. News of both the American Electra crash and the Bonanza tragedy were carried on the front page of the *New York Times* the next morning. (Machat)

662 In an unbelievable coincidence, a third aircraft tragedy was narrowly averted that same night of 3 February 1959 when a Pan American Boeing 707-121 (N712PA) suffered a "jet upset" 35,000 feet over the Atlantic during a Paris–New York flight. An autopilot problem caused the jet to roll nearly inverted while diving toward the ocean's surface, but the crew managed to wrestle the jet under control, pulling out of the dive at 6,000 feet. The jetliner landed at Gander, Newfoundland, where significant structural damage to the aircraft was discovered. Legendary dancer Gene Kelly was in first class aboard that flight. (Machat)

663 Beginning in February 1966, the Federal Aviation Administration mandated that airliners of all sizes have a 3-inch-wide contrasting outline surrounding all doors and exits on the exterior of the airplane to assist emergency personnel in immediately finding these openings to expedite the rescue of passengers. However, on aircraft with integral air stairs behind and blocking the door, such as the Lockheed Electra or Convair Liner, no outline is required due to the impassability of the blocked area. This is why these aircraft have inconsistent markings. (Kodera)

664 From its 9 April 1967 maiden flight, Boeing's 737 twinjet continues to roll off the assembly line nearly 50 years later. Few recall its slow start and that Boeing considered canceling the program early on. Instead it became the company's best-selling airplane in terms of number sold and now accounts for more than 25 percent of the world's mainline airliner fleet. Affectionately dubbed "Fat Albert" by enthusiasts, for the early model's stubby fuselage, it will easily exceed a 10,000 production run. (Proctor)

665 Ultra-long-range jetliners operate scheduled segments nearing 18 hours duration. But these seemingly endless flights were eclipsed many years ago. On 1–2 October 1957, TWA 1649A Starliner Fight 801 remained in the air 23 hours, 19 minutes while flying 5,300 miles from London to San Francisco, the record for a scheduled land plane segment that stands to this day. (Proctor)

666 However, during World War II, Qantas Airways operated Consolidated PBY Catalina flying boats on a 3,500-mile nonstop route, Swan River in Perth, Western Australia, to Koggala Lake in Southern Ceylon (now Sri Lanka), as part of the Australia–England air link, spending up to 32 hours aloft. (Proctor)

667 All but one trunk carrier (National Airlines) operated the venerable Douglas DC-3, which dominated flying schedules until the end of World War II. American Airlines was first to put the type into regular service, on 25 June 1936, and became first to retire it, ironically, on 1 April 1949. Although a few carriers briefly operated

DC-3s acquired via mergers, the actual retirement dates were: Braniff, 17 April 1960; Continental, September 1965; Delta, 29 October 1960; Eastern, June 1956; Northeast, 16 December 1966; TWA, January 1953; United, 28 October 1956; Western, late 1958. (Proctor)

668 First jet airliner to exceed the speed of sound was, surprisingly, not Concorde but rather a Douglas DC-8 Series 43. The date was 21 August 1961 at Edwards AFB in California. The airplane, a standard passenger model that was destined for delivery to Canadian Pacific Airlines in November, was in a test flight regime at the time to validate a new leading-edge design from its manufacturer. Company test plot Bill Magruder placed the jetliner in a shallow dive from an altitude of 52,090 feet and reached a max speed of 1.012 Mach, or 660 mph, as he passed 41,088 feet. These speeds were verified by the accompanying chase planes from the Air Force, a Lockheed F-104 and North American F-100. Chuck Yeager was the first pilot to break the sound barrier in 1947. (Kodera)

669 In the English language, words starting with "q" are followed usually by the letter "u," but that is not the case with Australia's Qantas airline. *Qantas* isn't a word at all but an acronym for Queensland and Northern Territories Airways System. (Lewis)

670 Ironically, and continuing the blood rivalry between Juan Trippe and Howard Hughes, Pan American World Airways was first to put the Constellation into revenue service, operating a charter flight from New York to Bermuda on 20 January 1946. TWA followed shortly thereafter on 5 February with scheduled service from New York to Paris via Gander, Newfoundland, and Shannon, Ireland. (Proctor)

671 When re-engined with more advanced and more powerful 25,000-pound-thrust General Electric/SNECMA CFM-56 high-bypass-ratio turbofans, the stretched DC-8 "60 series" family became DC-8-71, -72, and -73 series, respectively. Many of these re-engined examples are still being flown today by several air freight carriers around the world as of this writing. (Lewis)

672 Much like the eyes in a portrait, cockpit windows form the "face" of any airliner. Boeing's family of modern airliners began with the Model 377 Stratocruiser, which had a total of 19 cockpit windows. Boeing's first jetliners, the 707, 727, and 737, all shared a 10-window cockpit design, while the 757, 767, and 777 aircraft all had 6-window configurations. The new 787 has only 2 large windows per side, or 4 total. (Machat)

A far cry from the complex multi-pane windshield architecture of the piston era is this streamlined wrap-around design on Boeing's 787.

673 Although almost every jet airliner flying today has only a two-person flight crew, the first jet airliner to fly scheduled transatlantic service had five men in the cockpit. In a compelling example of how modern digital avionics, satellite navigation, and automated flight control systems have changed the face of aviation, it is interesting to note that onboard Pan American World Airways' first Boeing 707-121s were a captain, co-pilot, flight engineer, navigator, and radio operator. (Machat)

674 SABENA is the name of Belgium's airline, but it is not a word. It's an acronym for Societé Anonyme Belge d'Exploitation de la Navigation Aérienne (French Belgian Corporation for Air Navigation Services). British passengers who were sometimes less than thrilled with the airline's inflight service or on-time performance referred to the acronym's definition as "Such a Bloody Experience, Never Again!" (Lewis)

675 In today's world of nonstop airline flights between almost any two cities in the world, it should be remembered that the first westbound transatlantic flights by jetliner from Europe had to stop and refuel at either Shannon Ireland, Goose Bay Labrador, or Gander Newfoundland, before arriving in New York. When El Al Israel Airlines introduced nonstop service from London to New York with the new turboprop Bristol Britannia in 1958, they proudly announced in their advertisements: "No Goose, No Gander!" (Machat)

676 If you book an airline flight to India, the time zones are 30 minutes different from anywhere else in the world. With the advent of travel schedules in the early twentieth century, Indian government authorities compromised with the two newly established time zones on either side of their nation and came up with a single time zone for the entire country 30 minutes ahead/behind Greenwich Mean Time. (Machat)

The world's first jumbo jet was the stretched McDonnell Douglas DC-8 Super 60 series, seen here in Flying Tigers colors in 1967.

677 The longest operated first-generation jet airliner is the Douglas DC-8, also quite literally the longest first-generation jetliner. In 1966, Douglas launched the "Series 61" with a fuselage stretch allowing for a 250-passenger capacity. Adding a modified wing and sleeker "flow-through" engine nacelles and "cut-back" pylons resulted in the Series 63. Combining the features of those two aircraft but with a fuselage only slightly longer than a standard DC-8's produced the ultra-long-range (for its time) Series 62. (Machat)

678 In a dramatic example of jet airliner utilization today, the total number of hours flown per airframe is more than double the highest time of 40 years ago. In 1979, the highest-time Douglas DC-8 had 65,000 hours in its logbook. The highest-time Boeing 767 today is American Airlines N351AA, which has about 115,000 hours and 20,000 cycles, while the highest-time 747s are with KLM/Southern Air with about 135,000 hours. (Proctor)

General and Sport Aviation

Envisioned as the ultimate dream of every military pilot returning home from World War II, ownership of private planes was expected to be a top priority in 1946. The U.S. Department of Commerce even predicted as many as 200,000 private aircraft being needed to meet the demand. What happened instead was a postwar recession, which eclipsed the dream of airplane ownership. Fast-forward to the mid-1960s, when general aviation soon reached, and then surpassed, those predicted levels of popularity. Today, the myriad aircraft of general and sport aviation possess performance numbers that were once considered world records.

LIGHT AND SPORT AIRCRAFT

679 The expected 200,000-airplane market for pilots returning home from World War II created the postwar boom in GA aircraft, with 55 different airplane types available in 1946. However, most veterans went back to school, established businesses, or started families, and by 1948, the light plane market was gone. (Machat)

Right echelon formation of Cessna's proud product line in 1957 included (from top) the twin-engine 310B, Skylane, Skyhawk, and 172 models.

680 Ads for GA aircraft closely paralleled those of the automobile industry with new models every year, annual color schemes, design changes, and colorful photos and illustrations emphasizing aircraft use for business and family. (Machat)

Company founder Donald Douglas poses with The Cloudster II, *a private plane for the general aviation market after World War II.*

681 After World War II, many military aircraft manufacturers designed light aircraft for the anticipated sales boom that never happened. North American created its own "mini-Mustang" with the Navion, and Douglas had its Cloudster II, while Lockheed had the Little Dipper (playing off its galactic naming theme). Not to be outdone, Republic built the RC-1 Thunderbolt Amphibian, prototype predecessor to the now-classic RC-3 Seabee, of which 1,063 were built. Factory fly-away price in 1947 for a brand-new 'Bee was $3,995. (Machat)

682 Although North American's Navion did not reach its sales potential after the war, new life was breathed into the type with a sleek, modified enclosed cabin and the addition of tip tanks for increased range. Built by the Navion Aircraft Company of Galveston, Texas, the newly named Navion Rangemaster was introduced in 1961 and offered an impressive 1,500-mile range at speeds of up to 200 mph. The aircraft had seats for five people and offered more luxury interior appointments than the original North American version. (Machat)

683 The year 1961 was a good one for America's light aircraft industry. Piper Aircraft of Vero Beach, Florida, introduced a new low-wing four-passenger airplane named the PA-28 Cherokee that was designed as a flight school trainer and replacement aircraft for the high-wing Colt and Tri-Pacer line, and a "middle step" between those models and the higher-performance PA-24 Comanche series. Offered with either 150- or 160-hp engines, the Cherokee sold for $10,995 fully equipped and offered cruising speeds of 110 to 130 mph. (Machat)

684 There is perhaps no greater example of how a basic airplane design can evolve into an entire family of airplanes than the Piper Cherokee. Only five years after its introduction in 1961, the Cherokee line had expanded to the 180-hp Cherokee 180C, the 235-hp Cherokee 235, the retractable-gear Cherokee Arrow, and the longer-fuselage, six-passenger Cherokee Six, creating a Piper dynasty still evident at flight schools worldwide today. (Machat)

685 Buying a shirt at Macy's? While you are there, pick up an airplane, why don't you? A real one. In 1945 and 1946 you could have done just that. Department stores across the country were suddenly selling light aircraft to over-the-counter customers, capitalizing on the predicted postwar flying craze by all those freshly minted military aviators. Stores with airplanes on their display floors included Macy's, Bamberger's, Marshall Field's, and Mandel Brothers selling real Ercoupes, Pipers, and Taylorcraft. A not-yet-certified Piper Skycycle at Wannamaker's in Philadelphia was retailing for $995. Unfortunately, this was all short-lived as the entire U.S. light plane market collapsed in 1947. (Kodera)

686 After World War II, the record year for most number of first flights of general aviation aircraft (and actually all types of aircraft) was 1956 when a total of 25 new or derivative aircraft types first flew. Such significant GA airplanes as the Forney update of the original Ercoupe, Piper PA-24 Comanche, Beechcraft Badger, Aero Commander 560E, and four-engine Cessna 620 were on that list. Cessna named that aircraft because it was "twice a 310." (Machat)

687 Naming civilian aircraft has always been a challenge as manufacturers' marketing departments tried to come up with names that conveyed speed or power, yet gave the airplanes an image of being "everyman's" airplane. The Howard DGA series comes to mind ("Damn Good Airplane") and of course the American Champion "Champ." That company's aerobatic Citabria serves as a good example also; Citabria is Airbatic spelled backward. (Machat)

Master illustrator Jo Kotula captures this dramatic view of a Piper Comanche departing Chicago's Meigs Field.

688 Artwork in advertising was governed by art directors, not pilots. Quite often, the aircraft depicted in ads were doing things in flight that were not accurate, or were shown in locations that would have been impossible in real life. (Machat)

689 Certain single-seat military airplanes such as the North American P-51 Mustang evolved into unique designs where twin fuselages were joined together to create a two-seat aircraft. Oddly enough, several general aviation aircraft went through similar iterations, although none of these designs advanced to full production status. Such aircraft types included the Piper Super Cub, Piper Tri-Pacer, Mooney Mark 22, Ercoupe, and V-Tail Beech Bonanza. (Machat)

690 Likewise, certain light single-engine aircraft were converted to twin-engine designs to augment their powerplants and allow carriage of greater payloads with more range. These aircraft include the North American Navion (Twin Navion), Republic RC-3 Seabee (UC-1 Twin-'Bee), and Beechcraft Twin Bonanza. The Piper Cherokee series later evolved into the twin-engine Seneca line. (Machat)

$5 TO SATISFY A DREAM

In the early 1960s, you could fly an airplane for $5 in a clever promotional campaign from Piper and Cessna.

691 To help enlist new pilots in the mid-1960s, Cessna and Piper flight schools offered introductory "You Can Fly!" lessons in Cessna 150s and Cherokee 140s for only $5. Five-dollar introductory flight coupons were printed in aviation magazine ads, and these 15-minute introductory rides gave prospective student pilots their first taste of taking the controls of an airplane. This resulted in many new "student starts" for young pilots attending the nation's growing flying schools. (Machat)

692 The dream of most young pilots and certainly that of airplane manufacturers was to own a personal airplane, perhaps even flying from one's own garage/hangar. Cessna Aircraft of Wichita, Kansas, has, over the years, come pretty darn close to achieving this goal and has been considered perhaps the most prolific of all the light aircraft manufacturers in the world. One production benchmark was passed by the airframe company back in 1975 as they rolled out from the line their 100,000th single-engine airplane, a first in the world's history of aircraft manufacturing. (Kodera)

693 Using media exposure to help market general aviation, many notable pilots such as Max Conrad, Jerrie Mock, and Jerrie Cobb set speed, distance, and endurance records, or made round-the-world flights in GA aircraft for publicity during the late 1950s. Using aircraft ranging from Conrad's Piper Comanche 250 to Cobb's Aero Commander 560F, these courageous pilots represented the everyday American with identities such as the "Flying Grandfather" or "Flying Housewife." (Lewis)

694 Homebuilt airplanes have been popular since humans learned to fly. One such enterprising designer was Robert Starr of Arizona who gave the world the smallest airplane to date, the *Starr Bumble Bee*. Measuring a mere 5 1/2 feet in wingspan and less than 9 feet in length, the Continental engine–powered mite flew first and last at Marana Air Park near Tucson on 2 April 1988. Engine failure caused the airplane to crash, but Starr survived to fly another day and kept building, giving us the *Bumble Bee II*. (Kodera)

695 The world's smallest airplane in the 1950s was the *Stits Sky Baby*, designed by homebuilt aircraft pioneer and founder of EAA Chapter 1, Ray Stits. Rumors were spread by competitors that Stits was so afraid of the 7-foot-wingspan airplane that he refused to fly it and hired another pilot, but nothing could have been further from the truth. Ray simply weighed too much to fly the miniscule aircraft and hired a 100-pound racing jockey who he taught to fly. (Machat)

Founder of EAA Chapter 1, Ray Stits poses with his **Stits Sky Baby,** *the world's smallest airplane in the 1950s.*

696 The ERCO Ercoupe is a low-wing, two-seat, twin-tail monoplane built by the Engineering and Research Corporation in the late 1940s and early 1950s. Using a novel flight-control system with interlinked rudder pedals, the airplane was marketed as easy to fly and virtually "stall-proof," although that was not always the case. However, the interlinked controls made the airplane a favorite of pilots with physical disabilities that rendered them unable to fly airplanes with standard controls. (Lewis)

697 Cessna's new twin-engine enhancement of their classic 310 model was the 310F Skyknight, powered by turbocharged engines and with a stretched fuselage to seat up to six people. With a cruising speed of 245 knots at altitudes up to 27,000 feet, the Skyknight took Cessna twins to new heights. Oddly enough, when the Douglas Aircraft Company named its F3D two-seat radar interceptor, it was also called the Skyknight to denote its mission as an all-weather night fighter. (Machat)

698 Perhaps one of the most popular homebuilt aircraft of the 1980s was the Burt Rutan–designed VariEze, a play on words for the original canard VariViggen design and the relative ease with which the aircraft could be built. When enough VariEzes arrived at the annual EAA fly-in at Oshkosh, Wisconsin, to warrant their very own display area, more than a dozen VariEzes were seen lined-up wingtip to wingtip. A sign had been prominently posted at the end of the row, appropriately reading "Eze Street." (Machat)

699 Beginning as a local fly-in at Rockford, Illinois, what is now the EAA Airventure at Oshkosh emanated from humble beginnings. Growing to more than 10,000 airplanes of all types parked and on display, with attendance as high as 800,000 people at its peak, the aeronautical experience called simply "Oshkosh" must be seen to be believed. It is the only place in the world you will ever see three airplanes landing simultaneously on the same runway: one near the threshold, one midfield, and one near the departure end of the strip. (Machat)

700 In a "tale of two Pipers," it is interesting to note that the combined production numbers for both the Cub (in all models) and the Cherokee family (all models) exceeds 50,000 aircraft

Piper introduced the modern, low-wing, all-metal Cherokee line in 1961. By 1965, the 180-hp four-seat model 180C was queen of the fleet.

since the beginning of their respective production runs. The J-3 Cub began production in 1938, and the Cherokee production run started in 1961, but both types certainly made their mark on aviation, training tens of thousands of pilots over the past eight decades. (Machat)

701 The Meyers 200 was a single-engine light plane designed by Al Meyers in 1955. It featured an exceptionally robust steel truss structure with record-setting performance. Meyers hand built the early examples with a small staff of craftsmen at his shop in Tecumseh, Michigan. The Meyers 200 set an around-the-world speed record, a 50-km speed record, and a 3-kilometer world record for its class. It was regarded as the fastest non-turbocharged piston engine single ever produced, and it never had an FAA-mandated Airworthiness Directive issued against it. (Frankel)

702 In 1966 the Aero Commander division of North American Rockwell, looking for a successful product to capture a share of the light aircraft market, bought the production rights to the Meyers 200, but Aero Commander overlooked the fact that no production tooling existed for the aircraft. When production was moved to Albany, Georgia, a corporate audit found that it was taking more than 10,000 man hours of labor to build each aircraft. Competitors were taking approximately 2,500 hours to build Beechcraft Bonanzas, Piper Comanches, or Cessna 210s. Aero Commander ceased production in 1968 having spent $4 million to produce just 78 examples worth a total of $3 million. (Frankel)

703 Aviation is full of unique phrases, one of which describes the wing of the original Piper Cherokee. Called the "Hershey Bar" wing, original Cherokees from the two-seat 140 model through the six-seat Cherokee Six, and the 235-hp retractable gear Arrow in between, had untapered wings that indeed resembled the exact shape of the classic candy bar. On later models renamed Warrior, Archer, and Lance, the wings were redesigned with tapered outboard wing sections. (Machat)

Predecessor to the Cherokee was the Piper Colt, a two-seat version of the larger Tri-Pacer, but with a smaller engine.

704 Speaking of phrases, Piper's trusty 150-hp four-seat Tri-Pacer and 108-hp two-seat Colt models sat fairly tall on their tricycle landing gear, which had a narrow tread for the main wheels. While this didn't pose problems on normal landings, cross-wind landings could be a bit, uh, "spirited." As a result, these two aircraft were known as the "flying milk stools." (Machat)

705 In the category of improbable first impressions is the notion that a balloon can cover any great distance while flying. However, in 1978 the first crossing of the Atlantic Ocean occurred between 11 August and 17 August, a total of 137 flight hours. The ship was known as *Double Eagle II*, a helium-filled balloon piloted by Ben Abruzzo, Maxie Anderson, and Larry Newman. Route of flight was from Presque Isle, Maine, to Ireland, England, and finally Paris, France. Astoundingly, the first 60 percent of the journey was flown at 20,000 feet. (Kodera)

706 A balloon also managed to cross the Pacific Ocean nonstop. Capitalizing on their success over the Atlantic, Ben Abruzzo and Larry Newman teamed up with Ron Clark and Rocky Aoki to tackle the longer distance from Nagashima, Japan, to Cavello, California. The total number of days was three, 9–12 November 1981, and total distance covered equaled 5,208 miles. (Kodera)

707 Not to be outdone, the hang-gliding community also dove into the distance act with incomprehensible distances covered simply by flying their unpowered aircraft on the winds and thermals of the world's geography. The farthest distance flown to date by a hang glider and pilot is 761 km (473 miles), which took place on 3 July 2012. The pilot, Dustin Martin, was towed to an altitude of 10,000 feet over Zapata, Texas, and released. He was flying alongside Jonny Drumond and beat him by just a couple of miles to claim the record. They both landed near Lubbock, Texas. (Kodera)

708 An ad for Schweizer sailplanes seen in a 1957 issue of *Flying* magazine claimed that the company's single-seat model 1-26 sailplane had an "engine" that produced 2 million horsepower! That's the dynamic energy of a cumulus cloud that equaled "the combined power of more than 20 thundering B-52 jet bombers." At that time, sailplanes had reached altitudes of more than 40,000 feet in mountain waves, and set distance records of more than 500 miles. (Machat)

709 By 1986, the U.S. altitude record for sailplanes had reached 49,000 feet in the Sierra Wave over the Owens Valley in California, and the U.S. distance record exceeded 1,000 miles set over the Appalachian ridge with a flight that launched from eastern Pennsylvania and reached Knoxville, Tennessee, before turning back to home base. Total time in the air was 14 hours. (Machat)

710 If you feel like pedaling your way above and across the landscape, designers at the Massachusetts Institute of Technology have an airplane for you: the Daedalus. A total of three airplanes were constructed at the MIT Lincoln Lab Flight Facility at Hanscom Field outside Boston, Massachusetts, by a team of undergraduate students, faculty, and recent graduates of MIT. It worked like a charm and holds the record for distance in a man-powered airplane by flying from Iraklion on the island of Crete to the island of Santorini. The flight also established official FAI world records for straight-line distance and duration for human-powered aircraft, all set on 23 April 1988. (Kodera)

Rutan-designed Voyager *braves stormy skies on its epic journey around the world in December 1986 nonstop and unrefueled inflight. (Craig Kodera)*

711 First nonstop unrefueled flight around the world was accomplished by Dick Rutan and Jeana Yeager flying their custombuilt *Rutan Voyager* aircraft. Departing from Edwards on 14 December 1986, and ending 9 days, 3 minutes, and 44 seconds later on 23 December, the flight set a flight-endurance record. The aircraft flew westerly 26,366 statute miles at an average altitude of 11,000 feet and dodged many areas of foul weather along its route. (Kodera)

712 Everyone loves watching the skilled aerobatic work performed by the various aerial demonstration teams around the world as they show their stuff at air shows. The Blades Aerobatic Team, a British civilian aerobatic team made up of former Red Arrows pilots, had a field day describing loops while in their four-plane formation. As a matter of fact, they beat the world's record by completing 26 consecutive formation loops with their low-wing aerobatic airplanes on 22 October 2011. (Kodera)

713 One of the longest-production runs for a light aircraft in history is a single-engine amphibian that began life in 1948 as the Colonial C1 "Skimmer." Evolving into the Lake La-4 in 1960, the four-place sport aircraft now featured a top speed of 130 mph, more power and longer range, along with the continued ability to operate from water or land-based airports. Later models included the turbocharged Lake Renegade and Seafury, before production ended in 2008, a continuous run of 60 years. (Machat)

714 In the "futuramic" sci-fi-loving 1950s, names sprang from Madison Avenue advertising agencies to every type of technology imaginable. General aviation was no exception, and in 1956, a well-known light plane manufacturer came up with the ultimate phrase for one of their easy-to-land single-engine four seaters. In a bit of a mixed message, this aircraft's "Land-O-Matic" landing gear ensured effortless aviating, and according to a nationally published ad, "makes flying practical for businessmen who don't have time to stay professional pilots." The airplane in question was the new Cessna 172. (Machat)

715 Since there have been airplanes and cars, clever inventors have tried to fuse the two and create a roadable aircraft, usually referred to as a "flying car." Moulton Taylor was a Navy pilot in World War II assigned to the Navy's then-new missile program, and after the war he designed his own airplanes. His concept for a flying car became a company and design called the Aerocar. It really did work quite well. As a car it pulled its wings behind it and one man could convert the vehicle to an airplane in approximately

5 minutes. Raising the rear license plate revealed a connect point for the pusher propeller driveshaft to attach to the drivetrain of the car's motor. Top speed was 60 mph for the car and 110 mph for the airplane. Although Taylor amassed orders for 250 Aerocars, only 6 were built. (Kodera)

716 On 17 August 1957, the Piper Aircraft Corporation hosted a fly-in and open house at its Lockhaven, Pennsylvania, manufacturing headquarters celebrating the 45,000th Piper airplane produced. The event was attended by nearly 700 aircraft that had flown in from every corner of the United States. Planes were landing at the rate of eight aircraft per minute, with as many as 40 airplanes in the pattern at once. Despite this frantic pace, not one airplane was even scratched at the airport. There was no control tower, either. (Machat)

717 In the 1950s, McCarren Field in Las Vegas, Nevada, claimed to be the world's only airport with a Ford Thunderbird crash wagon, boasting that no location on the entire airport was more than 90 seconds away from the T-Bird's garage. The car carried a two-way radio and 60 pounds of dry chemicals for fighting small aircraft fires. Apparently, that idea stayed in Vegas. (Machat)

718 If you thought JATO units were strictly for high-performance jet bombers, think again. Aerojet General, the Azusa, California–based company that manufactured JATO bottles for the military, marketed a line of takeoff-boosting JATO units for light business aircraft to assist with operations from hot, high airports. Priced between $2,500 and $3,000 were units for aircraft as small as a D-18 Twin Beech and as large as a Convair-Liner. Each unit weighed 144 pounds and produced 1,000 pounds of thrust. (Machat)

719 What a difference a decade makes. By the mid-1960s, Piper Aircraft Corporation was producing the single-engine Colt, the Cherokee in 5 different models, the Comanche in 2 models, plus the twin-engine Apache and Aztec, a total of 10 different aircraft

types. Only a decade earlier, in 1956, the company had only 3 airplanes in its line-up to sell, the 90- or 150-hp Super Cub, the 150-hp Tri-Pacer, and the top-of-the-line Apache. Factory prices for this trio were $4,750 for the Super Cub, $7,295 for the Tri-Pacer, and a whopping $34,000 for the Apache. (Machat)

720 On the cold, windy afternoon of 25 February 1961, NACA program director and champion sailplane competition pilot Paul Bikle launched an aerotow from California's William J. Fox Field in the Mojave Desert to set the world altitude record for sailplanes. Flying his custom-modified Schweizer 1-23E high-performance sailplane, Bikle climbed to 46,269 feet using the powerful Sierra Wave. While the record itself is impressive, Bikle began his climb from only 4,000 feet, making his 42,303-foot climb the still-unbroken "altitude gain" record to this day. (Machat)

721 After waiting nearly five years, a glider pilot from Riverside, California, finally had the perfect weather conditions to assault Paul Bikle's record. Owner of a local industrial metals business Robert Harris launched his Grob 102 Astir III from California City north of Edwards AFB, California, and harnessed the sheer power of the Sierra Wave above the Owens Valley to break Bikle's mark and climb to 49,009 feet. Although that record was broken by a two-seat sailplane in South America years later, Harris' record set on 17 February 1986 still stands for absolute altitude achieved by a single-seat sailplane, and highest altitude record in the United States. (Machat)

722 The normal operating envelope for a sailplane being towed to altitude by a piston-powered towplane is generally in the range of 65 to 70 knots, fast enough for the tow aircraft to maintain control, but slow enough to not overstress the glider in turbulence. However, in 1972, a glider distributorship in Long Beach, California, devised a safe FAA-approved method for towing sailplanes on high-altitude cross-country aerotows using a Beechcraft V35B Bonanza. The V35B would fly at 100 knots, but in relatively still air at 10,000 feet. This method was utilized for delivering new

View from the cockpit of a Czech Blanik L-13 sailplane during high-speed, high-altitude cross-country aerotow with a Beech Bonanza.

gliders to their owners in the United States, with the longest West Coast aerotow being from Long Beach to Eugene, Oregon. (Machat)

723 The records for longest production run and largest number built of any airplane in history belong to general aviation aircraft. The Beechcraft Bonanza has been in continuous production since 1947 with more than 18,000 built in various models, while Cessna 172s have been built since 1955 with more than 45,000 produced, although production was suspended for 10 years due to legal issues. Cessna's omnipresent 150 and 152 trainer series numbers 32,000 built. (Machat)

EXECUTIVE AIRCRAFT

724 Years before "light jet" aircraft such as the Cessna Mustang, Eclipse, or HondaJet were available, the first four-seat private jet plane available in the United States came from France. Built by Morane-Saulnier, the low-wing twin-engine MS-760 "Paris Jet" bore a slight resemblance to the Air Force's new Cessna T-37 jet trainer, but with two more seats. Powered by two 800-pound-thrust Turbomeca Marbore turbojets, the Paris Jet cruised at 400 mph, well above the speeds of existing executive twins. After a national tour in 1955, the aircraft was distributed by Beechcraft, and found several new U.S. owners. Purchase price was $300,000. (Machat)

Moraine-Saulnier Paris Jet was the first four-seat turbine-powered executive aircraft. This example was at Truckee, California, in 1974.

725 The Walt Disney Company was one of the first customers for Grumman's stunning new twin-turboprop executive transport named the Gulfstream. First flown in 1958, the Gulfstream was powered by Rolls-Royce Dart engines and carried up to 10 passengers in its comfortable cabin. The airplane cruised at nearly 300 mph, and taking a cue from the Air Force's presidential detail, Disney's airplane was named *Mickey One*. (Machat)

726 In the late 1950s, the used market for executive aircraft was red hot. Remember, this was just before the first executive jets (Sabreliner, Jetstar, Learjet, and Jet Commander), and the need for executive transportation and business travel in general was booming. In 1957, the popular aircraft types considered most in demand on the used airplane market were the Douglas DC-3, Grumman Mallard, Grumman Goose, and Aero Commander 560F. (Machat)

727 The first U.S. executive jet to fly was the Lockheed CL-329 JetStar in September 1957, designed for the Air Force's UTX competition as a twin-engine VIP transport to replace aging C-47s (DC-3) and C-118s (DC-6As). Powered by two Bristol Orpheus turbojets, the aircraft was conceived and designed in Lockheed's famed super-secret Skunk Works in Burbank, California. (Machat)

728 Vying for that same Air Force UTX contract in 1958 was the North American Aviation Corporation in Inglewood, California, with a smaller twin-engine executive transport design. Capitalizing on its famed F-86 Sabre and F-100 Super Sabre names, the new NAA bizjet was called the Sabreliner. After winning a coveted production contract, the aircraft was designated T-39 and flew in active service with the military for nearly four decades. (Machat)

729 The first executive jet to fly the Atlantic nonstop was Grumman Gulfstream II on 5 May 1968. The sleek 19-passenger twinjet flew from Teterboro, New Jersey, to London's Gatwick Airport, covering the 3,500-mile distance in 6 hours, 55 minutes. (Machat)

730 NASA converted a Gulfstream G-1159 (G-II) aircraft into a space shuttle trainer. The left seat was modified so it was almost identical to the shuttle cockpit while the right seat was retained in its original configuration. Clamshell thrust reversers were replaced with cascade reversers so they could be deployed in flight, and a pair of vanes were mounted below the fuselage to help simulate the flight characteristics of the shuttle. It was also necessary to extend both main gear to increase descent rates, but the nose gear was kept

in the retracted position to prevent uneven airflow to the two Rolls Royce 511-8 Spey engines. (Lewis)

731 When the Federal Aviation Administration (FAA) assigned a civilian identification to the Grumman Albatross aircraft little did it know it would cause confusion. The FAA assigned "G-111" to the civilian version of the Grumman HU-16 (SA-16) Albatross but didn't realize it would conflict with Grumman Gulfstream III (G-1159A) jet aircraft. When one Grumman Albatross filed a flight plan from Hawaii to the mainland officials met the G-III when it landed because they were very suspicious as to why it took 16 hours to make the flight when 5 hours would have been the usual time. (Lewis)

732 To demonstrate its long-range potential using a maximum standard fuel load, Boeing flew a 737-700 BBJ (Boeing Business Jet) on a nonstop round-robin flight across the United States, covering 6,252 nautical miles in 13 hours and 52 minutes. The trip was made on 23–24 April 1999, flown by Boeing's chief BBJ pilot, Michael Hewitt, and famed former United captain and bizjet entrepreneur Clay Lacy. (Machat)

733 Throughout modern aviation history, design crossover from the civil fleet to military aircraft has been used to great advantage. Cessna classics such as the twin-engine 310B became the U-3 (also known as the Blue Canoe for its tuna-shaped tiptanks), while the single-engine taildragger 185 morphed into the L-19 Birddog used as a Forward Air Controller (FAC) aircraft in Korea and Vietnam. Its successor was yet another Cessna product, the twin-boom pusher-puller O-2 Skymaster, which evolved from the model 337. (Machat)

734 Every era of executive aviation had an airplane that was considered "King of the Hill." The classic Beechcraft Staggerwing in the 1930s and equally classic Learjet 23 in the 1960s were the all-stars of executive transportation. Today, it would have to be the impressive flagship of the Gulfstream fleet, the 610-mph 8,053-mile-range G650 bizjet. (Machat)

HELICOPTERS

735 The first flight of a helicopter in the United States was made by Igor Sikorsky on 14 September 1939 at Stratford, Connecticut. Sikorsky flew his own design called the VS-300, with a single main rotor for lift and tail rotor for directional control. Although primitive by today's standards, the VS-300 was the seminal breakthrough design that led to the entire Sikorsky dynasty of military and commercial helicopters. (Machat)

736 With unmanned aircraft (formally known as unmanned aerial vehicles, or UAVs) in widespread use around the world today, it is interesting to note that the world's first remote-control flight of a "pilotless" helicopter was made in summer 1957 when an experimental Kaman Aircraft Corporation intermeshing blade 'copter was flown at Bloomfield, Connecticut, with no pilot aboard. Called a "robot helicopter" in the press releases, the craft took off vertically, hovered, and flew forward, backward, and sideways before landing, an impressive precursor of the digital age. (Machat)

737 We now know helicopters can fly the great oceans of the world, but did you know that a helicopter also flew into the stratosphere? The highest recorded flight of a rotary wing aircraft took place on 21 June 1972 above Istres, France. The daring pilot that day was Jean Boulet, who commanded a stripped-down version of an Aerospatiale SA315 Lama and achieved a total altitude of 40,820 feet. The aircraft's engine eventually flamed out, necessitating an auto rotation to the ground, which was its own world's record. (Kodera)

738 Tilt-rotor technology finally came of age with the Boeing V-22 Osprey in operational use today, but the first experimental tilt-rotor vehicle to fly successfully in 1956 was the Vertol VZ-2, a development of the earlier Model 76. This odd-looking T-tail craft had an open-frame fuselage and a Bell 47–like bubble cockpit with a slab wing and two turboprop engines that rotated 90 degrees to transition from vertical to horizontal flight, and back. (Machat)

739 In the first successful use of rotary wing aircraft to rescue stranded animals, helicopters operated by Louisiana wildlife workers were used to rescue 750 starving deer stranded on isolated patches of land at the mouth of the Mississippi River in 1957. The deer were airlifted to safety one at a time. (Machat)

740 The first nonstop flight across the United States by a rotary-wing aircraft was on 23 August 1954 utilizing a piston-powered twin-rotor Piasecki H-21 helicopter, which flew from San Diego, California, to Washington, D.C. (Kodera)

741 In yet another novel use of the relatively new helicopter in the 1950s, millions of dollars of valuable crops were saved from damage when 19 helicopters were used to blow excess rainwater off 2,000 acres of ripening cherry orchards in California's verdant central valley. Unusually heavy winter rains in 1957 threatened the crops. (Machat)

742 A longtime controversy centers around helicopter airlines and their history: Who was first? Both Los Angeles Airways and New York Airways claim the honor, but it is a matter of semantics. Los Angeles Airways was the first scheduled helicopter airline in the world (carrying mail only) starting 22 May 1947. New York Airways was the first scheduled passenger carrying airline, beginning 8 July 1952. (Kodera)

743 Airlines who at one time or another operated helicopter passenger and air mail service include Los Angeles Airways, New York Airways, San Francisco-Oakland Airlines, Chicago Airways, United Airlines, National Airlines, Mohawk Airlines, British European Airways, and Sabena Belgian World Airlines. (Kodera)

744 New York Airways employed the first African American airline pilot. Perry H. Young made his historic first flight on 5 February 1957. Young had previously made history as the first African American flight instructor for the U.S. Army Air Forces in World War II. (Machat)

New York Airways Boeing Vertol 107-II helicopter prepares to disembark its 25 passengers atop the Pan Am Building.

745 Flying helicopters from the rooftops of buildings began almost as soon as helicopters became practical mail-or freight-carrying aircraft. Passenger operations were another matter, and safety was always of paramount concern. New York Airways began operations from the rooftop heliport of the Pan Am Building in Midtown Manhattan in December 1965 with 25-passenger Boeing-Vertol 107 helicopters with service to and from Kennedy International Airport (JFK). One-way fare for the 18-mile 8-minute flight was $10. (Machat)

746 To avoid the risk of a catastrophic crash due to engine failure while flying from the Pan Am roof, a new takeoff procedure was devised that called for the 'copter to lift off and climb backward while ascending to 500 feet above the roof before turning left and heading out to JFK. This way, in the event of engine fail-

ure in one or both of its General Electric T58 turbines, the BV-107 could safely autorotate back to the rooftop. (Machat)

747 Despite all the concerns about a tragic flight accident happening on the Pan Am heliport, it was equipment failure while a helicopter was parked on the roof while boarding passengers that caused the first fatal accident. On 16 May 1977, a large bolt sheared in the right-main landing gear of a New York Airways Sikorsky S-61L, causing the 'copter to "capsize" onto its right side. The spinning rotor blades became shrapnel that caused four fatalities on the rooftop and the death of one woman walking on 42nd Street below. This accident forever ended flight operations from the Pan Am building. (Machat)

748 The first hoist rescue by helicopter occurred on 29 November 1945. The helicopter was a Sikorsky R-5 flown by Sikorsky Aircraft's chief test pilot Jimmy Viner, assisted by Army Air Forces Captain Jack Beighle. Two men were rescued from a stranded oil barge off the Connecticut shoreline. (Caruso)

749 One of the first major operational uses of a passenger-carrying helicopter overseas was SABENA Belgian World Airways' 12-passenger Sikorsky S-58 service to the 1958 World's Fair in Brussels. The 'copters were also used for gala sightseeing flights over the scenic Loire region of France. (Machat)

750 The first helicopter to gain a civilian certificate of airworthiness from the Civil Aeronautics Agency in the United States was the new and pioneering Bell model 47B-3. Perhaps no other helicopter in the world symbolized rotary wing aviation more than this little Bell aircraft for many, many years afterward. (Kodera)

751 Although turbine powerplants had been fitted to experimental helicopters or even existing rotary-wing airframes for flight test and evaluation, the world's first production turbine-powered helicopter was the five-place bubble-cockpit Sud Est SE. 3130 Alouette II. An immediate hit with the helicopter world, jet-powered

World's first production jet helicopter was the French Sud SE 3130 Alouette II. Twenty-five were built under license by Republic in the United States.

Alouettes became the new backbone of the industry, setting several altitude records and even being produced under license in the United States as the "Lark" built by Republic Aviation Corporation in Long Island, New York. Republic built 25 U.S.-registered Alouette IIs. (Machat)

752 The world's first floating heliport was installed in the waters off Pittsburg, Pennsylvania, to provide aerial access to downtown locations from various industrial areas surrounding the city proper. Service was inaugurated in winter 1956 with a Hiller 12E helicopter that landed and took off from the metal structure. (Machat)

753 A VIP version of the Alouette II was conceived as an upscale executive transport for corporate CEOs, government officials, and the like. With a drag-reducing faired tail cone enclosing the Alouette's open lattice-work tail boom and a sleek forward

cabin replacing the bug-like Plexiglas cockpit, this new adaptation of the SE. 3130 was called the "Gouverneur" (Governor). Despite its elegant external appearance, courtesy of legendary industrial designer (and French native) Raymond Loewy, the helicopter's performance was underwhelming due to the extra weight of all that external structure. The modern iteration of this idea can be found in today's brilliant Aerospatiale/Eurocopter AS350 Astar. (Machat)

754 In March 1958, fire engine manufacturer American LaFrance based in Elmira, New York, collaborated with Sikorsky Helicopters in Bridgeport, Connecticut, to develop the world's first "flying fire engine" using an S-58 helicopter equipped with a mechanical foam unit used to fight aircraft fires in situations where standard fire apparatus was insufficient. The helicopter's speed in reaching the site of an aircraft accident also made this concept very desirable. (Machat)

755 Light aircraft manufacturing titan Cessna Aircraft Company in Wichita, Kansas, entered the commercial helicopter game in 1962 with a novel design called the CH-1D Skyhook. With a nose-mounted engine and fuselage design resembling automobiles of that time, the five-seat craft was based on the company's earlier YH-41 developed for the U.S. Army in 1956 and seemed poised to make an impression on the domestic U.S. market. The 'copter was intended for use as a utility and executive transport. (Machat)

756 The Lycoming Division of the AVCO Corporation in Stratford, Connecticut, built the majority of both reciprocating and turbine powerplants for helicopters in the post–World War II era. Models powered by Lycoming engines included the Bell 47 and 204 Huey series, the Brantley B2, Hughes 300, Hiller 12 series, Kaman Huskie, and Boeing Vertol Chinook helicopters, among others. (Machat)

757 Lycoming's direct competitor for producing turbine helicopter engines was General Electric, which built the rugged and reliable T58 that powered such production helicopters as the Boeing Vertol 107 and HRB-1; Sikorsky S-61, S-62, and HSS-2; and the Kaman HU2K. The T58 produced 1,250 shaft hp and weighed little more than 100 pounds. (Machat)

Chapter 6

Aviation in the Media

For any aviation fan, aircraft and pilots in action on the big screen in Cinemascope was as good as it gets, especially while enjoying a giant tub of hot buttered popcorn in a cool "air conditioned" theater on a hot, humid summer day. After World War II, the novel idea of owning a TV set took on a whole new meaning when programs about aviation began to hit the airwaves. For air-minded kids on a Saturday morning, watching a Cessna 310 blaze out of the clear blue of the western sky was a right of passage.

TELEVISION

758 The highly successful *Star Trek* television and movie franchise started in 1966 on NBC television. The art director and designer of 23rd Century technology for those productions was a Hollywood craftsman named Walter "Matt" Jefferies, who was both an artist and private pilot. Matt needed a registration number for the *Starship Enterprise*, making it believably "military credible" in the program. He came-up with NCC-1701. Why? His personal airplane, a beautifully restored 1935 Waco YOC cabin class job, had the pre-1948 CAA registration numbering of NC17740 and he used what was readily at hand. According to Jefferies, the *Enterprise* was Starfleet's 17th starship design and it was the first in the series; therefore the ship had the number "1701." (Kodera)

Martin XB-51 (aka Gilbert XF-120) is ready for its close-up in the movie **Toward the Unknown** *filmed at Edwards AFB.*

Sky King's beautiful Cessna 310B was named Songbird, *one of three Cessna twins used in the Saturday morning TV classic.*

759 If you grew up in the 1950s and 1960s and loved airplanes, you watched the television series *Sky King* (taken from the radio serial of the 1940s). The show followed the adventures of America's favorite flying cowboy, Schuyler King, his niece Penny, and nephew Clipper. They operated from the Flying Crown Ranch in Arizona, a logo of which appeared on their airplane. (Kodera)

760 Three airplanes were used in the show, and all were named *Songbird*. The first was a twin-engine Cessna T-50 (UC-78) Bobcat, registered N67832. This airplane, known in aviation circles as the *Bamboo Bomber*, was replaced in 1956 with the swank new Cessna 310B, N6348A named *Songbird II*. This was and is the airplane most closely associated with the program today. But right at the end of the series came the new swept-tail Cessna 310D, N6817T named *Songbird III*. This final airframe still exists, based in Vacaville, California, and tours the annual air show circuit yearly in all its restored glory. (Kodera)

761 Sky King (played superbly by actor Kirby Grant) "flew" Cessna aircraft exclusively in the TV series, which lasted from October 1959 until September 1966. From episode 1 through 39, the World War II surplus UC-78B *Bamboo Bomber* was used, an aircraft owned by legendary movie pilot Paul Mantz and flown by his employees. Once dry rot was discovered in the airframe, the Cessna Aircraft Corporation loaned a new model 310B flown by their national sales manager to be used in episodes 40 through 72. (Keeshen)

762 Because of production budget restraints, stock footage of the flying scenes used in episodes of *Sky King* was sometimes flopped to show the *Songbird* making a left turn when in fact the airplane was turning to the right. If you look closely you can see that the "N" on the lower right wing is backward. (Keeshen)

Poor-quality but very rare photo of the Bell 47G-II used to promote the TV series Whirlybirds *in 1957.*

763 Soon after its introduction in the early 1950s, the ubiquitous Bell 47 helicopter became the backbone of light rotary-wing operations in the United States, and that 'copter was soon celebrated on the hit TV show *Whirlybirds*, which first aired in 1957. Starring Kenneth Tobey as senior pilot Chuck Martin and Craig Hill as his junior partner P. T. Moore, this weekly serial had our

heroes flying both the bubble-top Bell-47G-II and larger enclosed-cabin Model 47J Ranger in an endless variety of novel uses for those aircraft. Whether flying their choppers rescuing good guys or chasing bad guys, there always seemed to be a wise moral at the end of each episode. (Machat)

764 *Whirlybirds* originated from a 1956 episode of *I Love Lucy* called "Bon Voyage," where Lucy misses her chance to embark on the transatlantic ocean liner SS *Constitution* and talks the pilot of a Bell 47G into flying her out to the ship and hoisting her down onto the deck. The Desilu Studio (short for Desi Arnaz and Lucille Ball) decided to look into the potential of a new series using helicopters and entered into discussions with Bell Aircraft. The television show aired from 4 February 1957 through 18 January 1960 with a total of 111 episodes filmed. (Keeshen)

765 The hit television show *Steve Canyon* was adapted from Milton Caniff's famed newspaper comic strip *Steve Canyon*. The strip ran from January 1947 through June 1988, shortly after Caniff's death. The TV show was made up of 34 half-hour episodes and ran for one year starting in 1958. (Keeshen)

766 Colonel Stevenson B. Canyon, United States Air Force, became a household name when that show came on the air. Canyon's TV adventures celebrated the very best of the Air Force during the tense Cold War era. The odd choice for sponsorship of this television show aimed at preteen and teen male viewers was Chesterfield cigarettes. (Machat)

767 Naval aviation was highlighted on TV in the 1950s as well. *The Blue Angels* was produced in collaboration with the U.S. Navy, which insisted that each episode be as realistic as possible based on real-life exploits of the flight demonstration squadron as they performed at air shows and other public events. The TV show aired for only a single season from September 1960 until July 1961. In the show's episodes, actual footage of the team's Grumman F9F-8 Cougars and Grumman F-11F-1 Tigers was shown. (Keeshen)

768 The Moult Taylor Aerocar was a unique aircraft, the forward fuselage of which also served as a small, drivable two-place automobile. One of these machines, registered N102D, was sold to TV actor Bob Cummings, an experienced pilot and an Air Force Reservist in Southern California. In his first comedy television series, *Love That Bob*, he was constantly showcasing aviation in the various plot lines. The series ended in 1959, but his next show, *The New Bob Cummings Show*, proudly featured his Aerocar in episodes. (Kodera)

769 Other shows not exclusively devoted to aviation featured many good aviation stories, nevertheless. *Airpower* focused heavily on World War II, while the newsreel-like *You Are There* (narrated adeptly by Walter Cronkite) ran episodes on air disasters like the 1937 disaster of the German airship *Hindenberg*, or exploration of the supersonic "thermal thicket" with the Mach-3 Bell X-2. (Machat)

770 It is most interesting to note the TV personalities who made it big in Hollywood that also served proudly in the U.S Armed Services during World War II. For the U.S. Army Air Forces, it was George Gobel (instructor for fighter pilots), Gene Autry (transport crewman over "the Hump"), and Ed McMahon (flew L-19 Birddogs in Korea). (Machat)

MOVIES

771 The screenplay for the World War II classic *12 O'Clock High* was based on the novel written by former Army Air Forces officers Sy Bartlett and Bernie Lay Jr., who used their experiences in the 8th Air Force to write this fictional story based on real-life Colonel Frank Armstrong Jr. Armstrong was ordered to take command of the beleaguered 306th Bomb Group in England and whip it into combat shape. Using abandoned older sections of air fields in Alabama and Florida, director Henry King effectively re-created the look and feel of a World War II English airfield. (Keeshen)

772 Legendary movie pilot Paul Mantz was contracted to film the necessary air-to-air formation footage of B-17s flying his specially outfitted B-25 camera plane. In a famous scene from the film, Mantz "crash lands" one of the 12 B-17s acquired for the film. Since he did not have a co-pilot for this stunt, the bomber's four throttles were welded together. Once the B-17 hit the ground, Mantz killed the engines as the plane skidded in front of the cameras for about a quarter of a mile, with Mantz using the still-functioning wheel brakes on the retracted but still exposed main landing gear to steer the careening bomber to a stop. Movie-making at its best. (Keeshen)

773 Much like how the movie *China Syndrome* eerily foretold the meltdown of a nuclear reactor, only two weeks later at Pennsylvania's Three Mile Island nuclear powerplant in 1979, the movie *Toward the Unknown* ended with a climactic scene of the Bell X-2 flying on its way to Mach 3, then tumbling out of control due to "inertia coupling." Actual footage of the Earth filmed from onboard cameras during Chuck Yeager's violent tumble in the Bell X-1A in December 1953 was used to depict the X-2's descent. The movie premiered in New York on 27 September 1956. That same morning, the X-2 had flown to Mach 3, but then tumbled out of control and crashed at Edwards, killing test pilot Capt. Mel Apt. (Machat)

774 Centered around the flight test world of Edwards AFB in 1956, this film starred William Holden and Lloyd Nolan as Air Force test pilots, with Nolan playing the gruff flight test center commander, General Bill Banner, a character based on an actual center commander, General Al Boyd. As mentioned, the date the Bell X-2 crashed was 27 September 1956. Actor Lloyd Nolan passed away at the age of 83 on 27 September 1985. (Machat)

775 The fabled story is that during filming of *Toward the Unknown*, one of the greatest trades in movie history was consummated. The movie was filmed on base in February and March 1956, and Air Force Flight Test Center Commander Brigadier General J. Stanley Holtoner was envious of William Holden's 1954 Ferrari 375MM Pinin Farina Spyder. He offered to trade the movie star a supersonic flight in the ultra-rare two-seat North American TF-86F for a

William Holden, in the rear cockpit of a North American TF-86F Sabre, became the first actor to fly supersonic. Brigadier General J. S. Holtoner (right) was the pilot.

chance to drive the 415-hp Ferrari at top speed down the centerline of Edwards' 15,000-feet-long Runway 22. Holden always said he got the better end of the deal, becoming the first movie actor ever to fly supersonic. (Machat)

776 One of the great techniques in Hollywood aviation films was to use "stand-in" aircraft modified to resemble the airplane in the story, usually due to unavailability of the desired craft. Such was the case in *Toward the Unknown*. In the opening scenes, a new Convair F-102 jet interceptor is on fire and crashes in the desert at night. While the flying sequences indeed show an actual F-102, Warner Brothers had to avail itself of an earlier, cast-off (by this time in 1956) prototype airframe known as the Convair XF-92A for use in the close-up ground accident sequences. (Kodera)

777 The XF-92 was the prototype test article precursor to the F-102, but was decidedly different enough that a lot of camouflage was required to simulate the real McCoy. This included an overall grey paint job, the use of a serial number on the tail, which matched one of the YF-102A airplanes (clever subterfuge!), and construction of a mock-up simulated air intake beneath the cockpit canopy, unlike the -92, which had a single inlet in the nose. (Kodera)

778 The one-of-a-kind test article XF-92 was also painted in camouflage and used in the earlier Howard Hughes epic, *Jet Pilot* starring John Wayne and Janet Leigh. The delta-wing jet supposedly portrayed an enemy MiG fighter; so all in all, it certainly had its day in the limelight well after providing valuable research data for delta-wing configured high-performance aircraft. (Kodera)

Jet Pilot was an early Cold War caper featuring a young John Wayne and the vivacious Janet Leigh as a Russian fighter pilot. (Courtesy **Air Classics***)*

779 The RKO movie *Jet Pilot*, was a Howard Hughes production of intrigue, romance, and aviation during the infancy of the Cold War. Filmed in the early 1950s, the movie was intended to be a Jet-Age version of the earlier Hughes' production *Hells Angels,* but because of the billionaire movie mogul's incessant tinkering, the film was not released until 1957. By that time, nearly all the Air Force aircraft seen in the film were obsolete. Despite Leigh playing a Russian jet aviatrix defecting to the West, and Wayne playing the Air Force colonel who befriends her, the movie was panned by the critics as being too little too late. (Machat)

780 If you ever saw the classic 1963 comedy *It's A Mad, Mad, Mad, Mad World* with a stellar ensemble cast, you'll remember the hilarious scene where Buddy Hackett is "flying" (just barely) a Beech D-18 over the California desert near Palm Springs. In one of the greatest aviation stunts ever filmed, the Twin Beech bursts through a billboard after flying too low to the highway with only 10 feet of wingtip clearance on either side. Legendary stunt pilot Frank Tallman performed that maneuver, after having a large bull's-eye target painted dead-center on the back of the paper billboard, and sighting it through an F4U Corsair gunsight he'd acquired and mounted on the glareshield of the Twin Beech. (Machat)

781 The ubiquitous one-of-a-kind Capelis XC-12 Safety Plane was designed by fiery Greek entrepreneur Socrates Capelis of Oakland, California, in 1933, a direct challenge to the Douglas DC-1 and -2. Assembled with the help of aeronautics students at the University of California, Berkeley, one of the unique features of the airplane was that it was held together with PK fasteners screwed into the structure rather than conventional rivets. Unfortunately, the vibration of flight and engines caused the screws to have to be replaced or tightened after each flight, which from a safety standpoint was obviously unacceptable. (Kodera)

782 The Capelis XC-12 was sold to RKO studios in Hollywood and used as a grounded airplane only, to be filmed for special-effects flying sequences in films being created via miniatures. The airplane was available to all studios for rental at $100 per day, or $500 per week. Eventually scrapped around 1950 or so, the XC-12 was featured in no less than 19 films, including *The Flying Tigers* with John Wayne and, earlier, *Five Came Home*, in which it played a prominent part in the plotline. (Kodera)

783 *Wing and a Prayer* was produced by Twentieth Century Fox Film Corporation (1944, subtitled "The Story of Carrier X"), starring Dana Andrews and Don Ameche. The movie is loosely based on the story of an American aircraft carrier sent into enemy waters in the Pacific soon after the invasion of Pearl Harbor to mislead and distract the Japanese Navy while the USN prepares and sets the trap for the Battle of the Coral Sea and the Battle of Midway. (Keeshen)

784 The Navy Department arranged for Director Henry Hathaway along with a film crew of five to photograph actual carrier activities on the newly commissioned USS *Yorktown* (CV-10) during its shakedown cruise in the Gulf of Paria, a body of water between Trinidad and Venezuela. (Keeshen)

785 On the Fox Studios back lot, a 400-foot concrete and wood flight deck was built to duplicate *Yorktown*'s flight deck for exterior shots that included cat walks, arresting gear, landing areas, and replicas of 40mm guns. (Keeshen)

786 The Navy provided detailed reference photos and engineering drawings for the 36 sets built to re-create ready rooms, the captain's bridge, crew quarters, and other key operational spaces found aboard U.S. Navy aircraft carriers. (Keeshen)

787 The Navy sent 12 planes from Naval Air Station North Island, San Diego, that were more contemporary with 1943–1944 operations instead of aircraft used in 1942, when the story takes place. They include Grumman F6F Hellcat fighters, Grumman TBF Avenger Torpedo Bombers, and Curtiss SB2C Helldiver Dive Bombers. Also used were Grumman Wildcats to replicate Japanese Zeros, and a Curtiss-Wright CW-22 as a Japanese reconnaissance patrol plane. The newer aircraft were flown into Clover Field in Santa Monica and then taxied over to the movie studio on Pico Boulevard escorted by motorcycle policemen. (Keeshen)

788 The Fox back lot lake was used to film the battle scenes where remote-control Japanese ship models were used. To get the dive bomber pilot's-eye view of launching an attack onto the Japanese ships, a camera was set onto a platform suspended high above the miniature ship models and lowered down toward the water as a zoom lens was activated. (Keeshen)

789 The earliest known reference of the phrase "coming in on one wing and a prayer" originated in the 1942 film *The Flying Tigers*. Captain Jim Gordon, played by John Wayne, asks a hotel clerk about an expected flight of replacement pilots. The clerk replies, "Yes, sir, it was attacked and fired on by Japanese aircraft. She's coming in on one wing and a prayer." Later in 1943 the hit song "Coming In On a Wing and a Prayer" was released. (Keeshen)

Jimmy Stewart convincingly played Lindbergh in The Spirit of St. Louis, *being filmed here on Long Island in 1957. (Courtesy* Air Classics*)*

790 A momentous aviation film of the 1950s was Warner Brothers' *Spirit of St. Louis*, starring Jimmy Stewart as Charles Lindbergh. This performance almost did not happen. From Turner Classic Movies: "Originally the lead role of Lindbergh was offered to John Kerr, who had earned acclaim for his performance in the Broadway production of *Tea and Sympathy*. . . . Kerr turned the part down due to Lindbergh's notorious sympathies with the Nazi party. . . . Jimmy Stewart, who had long admired Lindbergh's aviation achievement and had served in the Air Force himself, was eager

to play the role but had a difficult time convincing studio head Jack Warner to accept the 47-year-old actor in the part of a 25-year-old man. "I need a star but not one that's pushing 50," Warner said. Warner then recommended that producer Leland Hayward tell James Stewart that he was too fat for the part. Stewart recalls, "I couldn't believe what I was hearing, but I wanted the part so badly I dieted. I'd never dieted before in my life. I started off at 170 pounds and in the end I was so thin I didn't even look like myself. In fact, I looked terribly ill. My face was gaunt and I had black rings under my eyes." Eventually Hayward convinced Warner to let Stewart have the part." (Kodera)

791 Charles Lindberg himself was quite impressed with Stewart in the role from the start, and noted the many small "aviator" subtleties about the way Jimmy Stewart as a professional pilot behaved in the cockpit of the replica *Spirit*. A perfect fit, and we can all be grateful to Jimmy Stewart for his perseverance. (Kodera)

792 Since Roosevelt Field on Long Island (Lindbergh's point of origin for his New York–Paris flight) had been plowed under and developed as a modern shopping center after World War II, filming for the 1957 Warner Bros. classic *The Spirit of St. Louis* had to be staged elsewhere. Substituting nicely for the 1927 vistas of Roosevelt Field was nearby Zahn's Airport, a somewhat dilapidated general aviation strip with old corrugated metal T-hangars that, from certain angles, looked amazingly like the structures that once housed Lindbergh's famous Ryan. (Machat)

793 Surprisingly, Jimmy Stewart's first aviation movie role was not as a pilot, but rather as an American aeronautical engineer named Theodore Honey in the 1951 Twentieth Century Fox production of *No Highway in the Sky*. Stewart's character works for the Royal Aircraft establishment dealing with the potentially catastrophic issue of metal fatigue on a new British airliner called the Rutland Reindeer (which looks suspiciously like a Republic Rainbow). In this film, the first of several prescient aviation movie plots borne out in real-life aircraft crashes, tails of two Rainbows fail in the movie due to metal fatigue after so many hours in the air. Within three years after the film's release, two British BOAC de Havilland Comets exploded in midair due to catastrophic structural failure traced to metal fatigue. (Machat)

794 Paramount Pictures released *Strategic Air Command* starring Jimmy Stewart and June Allyson in 1955. The first of a slew of movies about the role of the Air Force's Strategic Air Command and its nuclear bombers as the Cold War grew, this film depicted the rigors of Air Force life, giving the American public its first glimpse at SAC in the Jet Age. Stewart is brought back from the reserves to command USAF units flying the Convair B-36 and Boeing B-47. In real life, Stewart flew Consolidated B-24s in Europe, and retired from his Air Force Reserve career as a brigadier general. (Machat)

795 One of the most famous lines from *Strategic Air Command* is when Harry Morgan, playing the B-36's flight engineer, says to Jimmy Stewart, "It'll only be one takeoff and one landing," failing to mention that they'll be flying to Alaska and back in between. In a classic case of art imitating life, what was a routine operational mission had to be proven in early B-36 flight testing, and the longest-duration flight of the (at that time) six-engine piston-powered bomber was 33½ hours flown by Convair Chief Test Pilot Beryl A. Erickson, proving the aircraft's endurance to the Air Force in between his "one takeoff and one landing." (Machat)

796 Another famous line endlessly quoted by fans of the movie is the response Stewart gives to a flight line mechanic who admonishes General Ennis C. Hawkes (based on the gruff, cigar-chomping SAC Commander General Curtiss E. LeMay, and exquisitely played by Frank Lovejoy) for smoking a cigar next to his private Boeing VC-97 transport, warning that the aircraft might explode. Replies Stewart sardonically, "It wouldn't dare!" (Machat)

797 In stark contrast to playing a young Charles Lindbergh or dashing Air Force colonel, Jimmy Stewart's final role as an aviator was in the movie *Flight of the Phoenix*. Playing a grizzled veteran

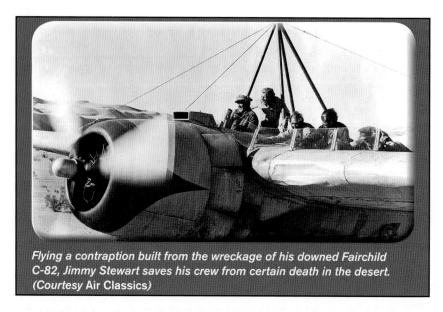

Flying a contraption built from the wreckage of his downed Fairchild C-82, Jimmy Stewart saves his crew from certain death in the desert. (Courtesy Air Classics)

"freight dog" pilot, Stewart is flying oil field workers to a desert destination in Africa when a dust storm forces his aging Fairchild C-82 Packet down for a crash landing. Over the next few weeks, the twin-tailboom airplane is rebuilt into an aerial contraption to fly the men back to civilization. (Machat)

798 Although the jury-rigged aircraft used for the movie's final moments actually flew, it claimed the life of legendary movie stunt pilot Paul Mantz in 1965 who along with equally famous movie pilot Frank Tallman had formed Tallmantz Aviation in 1961 at Santa Ana, California, to cater to the needs of the nearby Hollywood studios. Tallman flew in numerous films before he was also killed, in the crash of his Piper Aztec C while trying to land at Orange County Airport (now John Wayne Airport) at Santa Ana in 1978. (Machat)

799 The epic and pioneering movie *Wings* was produced in 1926– 1927 and released by Paramount Pictures on a budget of $2 million. Director William A. Wellman was hired because of his combat experience as a World War I aviator, and all the aerial scenes were shot at Kelly Field in San Antonio, Texas. The Allied aircraft

were contemporary Thomas-Morse MB-3s while German aircraft were Curtiss P-1 Hawks supplied by the Army Air Corps. Some 300 pilots were used in the filming, and an actual Fokker D-VII used in the film was purposely crashed and destroyed in the climactic ending scene. (Keeshen)

800 *Wings* won the very first Academy Award for Best Picture in 1929 and is the only fully silent film ever to do so. A new technology, "sound," would change movie making from then on. *Wings* also won an award for Best Engineering Effects, known today as "special effects" and all done by computer-generated imagery (CGI). (Keeshen)

801 *Test Pilot,* a Metro-Goldwyn-Mayer classic filmed in 1938, starred Spencer Tracy, Myrna Loy, and Clark Gable. The film featured several then-new aircraft types such as the prototype Boeing YB-17, which evolved into the legendary B-17 Flying Fortress; Gable's racer, the *Drake Bullet* (a modified version of the U.S. Army Air Corps Seversky P-35, itself an evolution of a racing plane); plus the test aircraft that sheds a wing in the film, the Northrop A-17. (Keeshen)

802 In a bit of life imitating art, it is interesting to see how many movie stars who made it big in Hollywood had served proudly in the U.S Armed Services during World War II. For the U.S. Army Air Forces, it was Clark Gable (B-17 gunner in Europe), Charlton Heston (B-25 radioman in the Aleutians), and Walter Matthau (B-24 radioman and cryptographer). (Machat)

803 Proving that movie characters don't always live happily ever after, *The Bridges at Toko-ri* is the story of LT Harry Brubaker, a dedicated World War II Navy veteran called back to fly Grumman F9F Panthers from a carrier during the Korean War. Brubaker, played by William Holden, is rescued from his crashed jet in the ocean by a faithful helicopter pilot, CPO Mike Forney, played by Mickey Rooney. After striking the Bridges at Toko-ri and a secondary target, Brubaker's jet is hit and leaking fuel. Unable to make it

William Holden and Mickey Rooney run for their lives as Rooney's rescue helicopter is overrun by North Koreans in **The Bridges at Toko-ri.** *(Courtesy* **Air Classics)**

back to the carrier, he crashes in North Korea and Forney attempts a rescue in his Sikorsky HO3S-1. As depicted in the above photo, the two pilots are pinned down and eventually killed by Communist soldiers. Brubaker's wife, Nancy, was played by Grace Kelly. (Machat)

804 The 1954 Paramount thriller *The High and the Mighty* is considered the progenitor of every modern aviation disaster movie ever made. Telling the tale of Dan Roman, John Wayne, a washed-up airline captain demoted to co-pilot after being involved in a fatal crash, the movie weaves its way through the lives of all the passengers flying to San Francisco from Honolulu, Hawaii. An inflight emergency halfway across the Pacific poses a potentially grave threat to the occupants of the DC-4, and its captain, played by a young Robert Stack, panics and descends to ditch the airliner at night. Roman springs into action and saves the day, however, making it to SFO with just barely enough fuel, but allowing all onboard to survive the harrowing ordeal. (Machat)

805 Speaking of washed-up pilots, this next film not only featured one of the best, but became the actual "donor" movie upon which a modern comedy classic was based. Called *Zero Hour!*, this

1957 Warner Bros. drama has World War II RAF pilot Ted Stryker saving a plane full of food-poisoned passengers and crew on yet another DC-4 flying from Ottawa to Vancouver, Canada. Stryker is their only hope of landing that airplane, and land it he does, but not before dealing with stormy weather, fogged-in alternates, and the fact that he flew Spitfires during the war, not transports. Read the next fact for the rest of the story. (Machat)

806 In 1980, an airplane disaster comedy (if that can be a category) was released by Paramount Pictures based quite literally on the previously mentioned *Zero Hour*, the rights to which were bought for $2,500 by the movie's writers and directors, Jim Abrahams, and David and Jerry Zucker. Such classic lines as "She handles like a wet sponge!" and "I sure picked the wrong day to quit smoking!" were lifted word for word from the 1957 movie and given a comedic spin in *Airplane!* (Machat)

807 Another interesting parallel in these two films is that the co-pilots were both played by former all-star athletes, Elroy "Crazylegs" Hirsch in *Zero Hour!* and Kareem Abdul Jabar in *Airplane!* The final ironic twist to this twin-movie story is that Stryker's commanding officer from the war is called to the control tower to talk him down to a safe landing. In *Zero Hour!* it's Sterling Hayden, but in *Airplane!* it is none other than Robert Stack, the cowardly captain from *The High and the Mighty*. (Machat)

808 During the tense Cold War years of the late 1950s and early 1960s, it seemed like America's movie-going audiences just couldn't get enough of the Strategic Air Command's Boeing B-52 Stratofortress with such box-office blockbusters as *A Gathering of Eagles* starring Rock Hudson and *Bombers B-52* starring Karl Malden. In both films, the B-52 was really the star of the show, with stunning Cinemascope sequences showing aerial refueling, MITO takeoffs (SAC alert minimum-interval takeoffs with a B-52 becoming airborne every 15 seconds), and breathtaking vistas of silver jet bombers flying over dramatic cloudscapes to surreptitiously promote SAC's sobering mission to the American public. (Machat)

Legendary movie pilot Frank Tallman did all the hair-raising flying for the barnstorming classic The Great Waldo Pepper. *(Courtesy Air Classics)*

809 *The Great Waldo Pepper*, written and directed by George Roy Hill and starring Robert Redford in the title role, gave audiences a fresh and insightful look at post–World War I aviation and the barnstorming antics of aviators in the roaring 1920s. Featuring plane-to-plane and car-to-plane transfers as seen in the above photo, the movie's aerial sequences were planned and flown by the great Frank Tallman, using hyper-accurate scale replicas of such famed aircraft of that era as the Sopwith Camel, Fokker Dr. 1, and countless Curtiss Jennies, most of which were crashed before the film's end. This Universal production set new standards for "live" flying sequences in the days before computer-generated imagery. (Machat)

810 The movie adaptation of Tom Wolfe's classic novel *The Right Stuff* tells the exciting and dramatic tale of America's aerospace industry during the salad days of the U.S. space program, and the inevitable rivalry between aircraft test pilots at Edwards AFB and NASA's first astronauts. Despite all these men being former test and fighter pilots, they were now relegated to "flying" Mercury space capsules launched atop Redstone and Atlas missiles, referred to by Air Force legend Chuck Yeager as being merely "Spam in a can." (Machat)

811 Yeager's side-kick, best friend, and technical mentor in the movie, as in real life, was fellow Air Force test pilot and flight test engineer Capt. Jack Ridley. In the movie, Ridley saws a broomstick in half to give Yeager the handle with which to close the door of the X-1, since Yeager had broken two ribs in a horse-riding accident the day before the flight. Ridley twirls the handle like a drumstick before giving it to Yeager in a bit of life imitating art. Ridley's character in the movie was adroitly played by Levon Helm, real-life drummer for the fabled Woodstock-era group The Band. (Machat)

812 Much of the beginning of the movie *The Right Stuff* involved Pancho Barnes and her "Happy Bottom Riding Club" located near the original Muroc site of Edwards AFB. In a clever bit of casting, the bright young-buck test pilots at the bar order a drink from a grizzled old "desert rat" bartender named Sam, and played in his best cameo role by none other than General Chuck Yeager himself. (Machat)

813 During the making of the great naval aviation epic *Top Gun* in 1985, director Tony Scott was filming scenes aboard the aircraft carrier USS *Enterprise* (CVN-65) at dusk. As the crew was filming a Grumman F-14 Tomcat being lifted to the flight deck on one of the super carrier's massive deck-edge elevators, the ship made a turn. Scott asked the ship's captain to turn the carrier back on course for best lighting, and when informed that the maneuver would cost an extra $25,000 to execute, Scott took out his checkbook and wrote that sum on a check that was immediately delivered to the bridge. (Machat)

814 One of the greatest aviation movies ever made did not have a single real airplane in it, the only aircraft footage being a computer-generated image of a lone NASA T-38 flyover. That movie was *Apollo 13*, starring Tom Hanks, Bill Paxton, and Kevin Bacon, and directed by Ron Howard. Perfectly capturing the essence of the Apollo space program and the cast-iron men who made all those lunar landings, the movie's space capsule interior scenes were filmed in a zero-G environment aboard a NASA KC-135 reduced-gravity simulator aircraft. (Machat)

815 *X-15* was a rather forgettable movie about North American's headline-grabbing rocket plane intended to inform the public

A young Charles Bronson is shown in the North American X-15 mock-up during filming of the movie X-15 at Edwards AFB. (Courtesy Air Classics)

about its accomplishments as well as being an enticing love story/ action drama. (Pick one.) This was the first screen role for an aspiring TV actress who first appears in the movie driving onto Edwards AFB in her silver Buick LeSabre convertible and then lighting up a cigarette. Believe it or not, the star was Mary Tyler Moore! Charles Bronson starred in this film that would have been totally forgettable had it not been for actual flight footage of the rocket plane in vivid Technicolor. (Machat)

816 Always playing the tough guy, as they used to say in Hollywood circles, Charles Bronson was no stranger to aviation. In World War II he served as a gunner with a B-29 crew and was wounded in action. (Machat)

Chapter 7

Pilots, Designers and Personalities

"Where do we get such men?" That question, asked about Navy pilots in the epic Korean War movie *The Bridges at Toko-ri*, could easily be applied to any aspect of aviation. During the height of the Cold War, courageous men flew dangerous missions skirting the edges of the Soviet Union and oftentimes never returned. Others sat in alert hangars 24 hours a day, seven days a week, ready to launch their strategic bombers against a nuclear foe. Other men and women had to envision, design, and build all these pioneering and record-shattering airplanes, but no matter what their respective roles in aviation, they were simply the best of the best.

817 The rivalry between Air Force test pilot Chuck Yeager and NACA test pilot Scott Crossfield was well-known. Yeager became "the first man to break the sound barrier" in the Bell X-1 in 1947. When Crossfield became "the first man to fly twice the speed of sound" in the Douglas D-558-II Skyrocket in 1953, Yeager bested him again one month later claiming the title of "first man to fly *faster* than twice the speed of sound" (Mach 2.44) in the Bell X-1A. Yeager made 36 flights in rocket-powered airplanes. Crossfield logged a total of 109. (Machat)

Representing the very best of flight test in the 1960s, Colonel Joe Cotton (left) and Lieutenant Colonel "Fitz" Fulton guided the XB-70 program to Mach 3.

NACA's Scott Crossfield was the first man to fly twice the speed of sound and had the most rocket flights of any pilot in the world.

818 Ben Rich, president of Lockheed's Advanced Design Projects Division, better known as the "Skunk Works," was quoted as saying "Do you know how we were able to build such revolutionary airplanes as the F-104, U-2, SR-71, and F-117 and make them work? We weren't afraid to fail!" (Machat)

819 The first time a woman pilot flew solo around the world was between 18 May and 20 June 1966. Flown by Shiela Scott of England, the 31,000-mile journey was made in a Piper Comanche 260 airplane with additional fuel tanks aboard. Her average speed during the planned easterly route was 166 mph. (Kodera)

820 The first solo flight across/above the North Pole was by Charles "Charlie" Blair on 29 May 1951 in a modified P-51C Mustang named *Excalibur III*. The flight plan called for a departure from Bardufoss, Norway, and an arrival at Fairbanks, Alaska. Above the pole a magnetic compass is next to useless so Blair, a captain for Pan American World Airways, devised an entirely new method of navigating by plotting sun lines to determine position. He proved his theoretical technique and 10 hours and 27 minutes later touched down at Fairbanks. He received the Harmon Trophy for his exploits, presented by President Harry Truman. (Kodera)

821 Charles Blair also holds other significant records: first intercontinental airmail to overfly the North Pole; fastest reciprocating engine, propeller-driven crossing of the Atlantic; and on the return flight from Fairbanks to New York another record was set for the first nonstop transcontinental solo crossing of the Alaska-Canadian route. Blair went on to found Antilles Air Boats and wooed and married the inimitable actress Maurine O'Hara. (Kodera)

822 Ben Epps, inventor, mechanic, and aviator, is considered to be the "Father of Aviation" in the state of Georgia. He was the first Georgian to build and fly an airplane. Over a 30-year career Epps was an innovator who instilled a love of flying in many young Georgians, including his own children. (Lewis)

823 Pat Epps, Ben's son, was instrumental in locating the two B-17 Flying Fortress bombers and six P-38 Lightning fighters forced to land in Greenland during World War II. One of the P-38s, *Glacier Girl,* was eventually recovered and rebuilt and is now flying in air shows around the country. (Lewis)

824 Colonel Norman D. Vaughn (an adventurer and explorer who accompanied Admiral Byrd to Antarctica on his 1932 expedition) was instrumental in rescuing the pilots and crews of six P-38 Lightning fighters and two B-17 Flying Fortress bombers that were forced to make emergency landings on a Greenland icecap during World War II. He also went back to Greenland in his 80s to help locate and recover those aircraft. A P-38 Lightning was recovered from its icy grave some miles away and 250 below the original icecap location. (Lewis)

825 Amelia Mary Earhart (1897–1937) was a pioneer female aviator and author; her accomplishments were overshadowed by her disappearance on an around-the-world flight in 1937. She took her first flying lesson on 3 January 1921 and purchased a second-hand biplane six months later. On 17 June 1928, she was the first woman to fly across the Atlantic Ocean. She flew with pilot Wilmer "Bill" Stultz and Louis "Slim" Gordon in the Fokker F7 *Friendship*.

While most people know Lindbergh made the first solo transatlantic flight, few realize that Amelia Earhart made the second only five years later.

On 20 May 1932, she became the first female to fly across the Atlantic Ocean solo. Three years later, on 11 January 1935, she flew solo across the Pacific Ocean from Honolulu, Hawaii, to Oakland, California. (Veronico)

826 Amelia Earhart was not only the first woman to fly across the Atlantic Ocean, but she was also the first person to fly solo across the ocean, five years to the day after Charles Lindbergh made his famous flight in 1927. Lindbergh flew from New York to Paris; Earhart's flight originated in Newfoundland and ended 15 hours later in Ireland after flying 2,000 miles. (Lewis)

827 In 1937, Earhart began her attempt to be the first woman to fly around the world, departing from Oakland, California, flying to Honolulu. There, she ground-looped her Lockheed Electra and was forced to return to California for repairs. On 1 June 1937, Earhart and navigator Fred Noonan took off from Miami, Florida, on the first leg of the around-the-world flight. After flying more than 22,000 miles, Earhart and Noonan disappeared on the leg between Lae, New Guinea, and Howland Island in the Pacific. (Veronico)

828 Amelia Earhart's tragic disappearance near the end of her round-the-world flight in July 1937 has spawned numerous theories: She ran out of fuel and crashed into the Pacific; she and Noonan landed near an island and became castaways; she and Noonan were spies for President Franklin D. Roosevelt and were captured by the Japanese. (Lewis)

829 Doug Matthews set several world records in his P-51D Mustang *The Rebel* on 30 May 2013. The records include time-to-climb to 9,000 meters (approximately 30,000 feet) in 18 minutes, 12,000 meters (approximately 40,000 feet) in 31 minutes, and maximum altitude of 42,500 feet. If approved by the FAI they will increase his list of records to 100, making him a member of the "100 Club," someone who has set a total of 100 records. (Lewis)

830 Royal Navy Captain Erik M. "Winkle" Brown flew 487 different types of aircraft, including captured German jet and rocket aircraft, during his career. He holds the world's record for the most aircraft carrier takeoffs (2,407) and landings (2,271) and was the first pilot to test the feasibility of landing a modified twin-engine de Havilland Mosquito on a carrier deck. He was the first pilot to land jet aircraft and aircraft with a tricycle landing gear aboard aircraft carriers. Captain Brown also managed to successfully recover from severe oscillations encountered while flying a de Havilland DH 108 Swallow, the same type aircraft that claimed the life of Geoffery de Havilland Jr. (Lewis)

831 Thomas Fitzpatrick became famous for flying an airplane from a field in New Jersey to a landing on a street in Manhattan on 30 September 1956. After an evening spent consuming a large quantity of spirits he made a bet that he could get from New Jersey to New York City in 15 minutes. He then proceeded to steal an aircraft at Teterboro airport and fly it to Manhattan where he landed on St. Nicholas Avenue and 191st Street. On 4 October 1958 he repeated his feat when someone expressed disbelief that he had done it the first time. This time he landed in front of a Yeshiva University building. Although he had only been fined $100 for his first offense he received six months in jail for his second. (Lewis)

832 James H. Brodie invented a system to allow light aircraft to land in areas where no suitable runways were available. His system could also be mounted on ships, making them light aircraft carriers able to launch and recover observation aircraft at sea. The system consisted of a trapeze cable apparatus mounted on the ground or on the side of a ship plus a hook mounted to the top of the aircraft to engage the cable. Brodie felt the system could be modified to handle even larger aircraft. (Lewis)

833 MAJ Charles Carpenter, aka "Bazooka Charlie," mounted bazookas on his L-4 "Grasshopper" aircraft and proceeded to destroy German tanks and armored vehicles during his tour in Europe during World War II. Also called the "Mad Major," he became adept at firing rockets from the wings of his observation aircraft and succeeded in damaging or destroying a large number of enemy vehicles. He was highly decorated for his efforts. (Lewis)

834 Maj. George A. Davis Jr. was our only fighter ace to be killed during the Korean War. He flew combat in World War II and the Korean War and was credited with a total of 21 kills. In addition to the 7 Japanese aircraft he shot down during World War II he is credited with 14 MiG aircraft in Korea. On his final mission Maj. Davis engaged 12 MiG 15 fighters when he saw them about to attack friendly aircraft. He was posthumously awarded the Medal of Honor. (Lewis)

835 Hans Fey, a test pilot for Messerschmitt, was directed to fly an Me 262 jet fighter from Schwabisch-Hall to a new location in Neuburg, but defected instead to Frankfurt, landing at Rhine-Main and delivering the revolutionary new aircraft directly into the hands of Allied forces. (Lewis)

836 Fritz Wendel set a world speed record in his Me 209 of 469 mph in 1939. The record stood for 30 years until, on 6 August 1969, civilian racing pilot Darryl Greenamyer established an absolute world air speed record for piston-engine aircraft of 483.041 mph. He flew a modified Grumman F8F-2 Bearcat over the

3-kilometer course, breaking the previous record established by Wendel in April 1939. (Lewis)

837 Walter Soplata developed his own private aircraft museum on his farm in Newbury, Ohio. Over a period of years starting in 1947 he brought surplus aircraft onto his property to preserve them because he didn't see much effort to save aircraft for future generations. His collection included an American Eagle biplane, Vultee BT-13, Goodyear FG-1D, and an F2G with an R-4360 engine used in air racing. He also had an XP-82 Twin Mustang, F7U Cutlass, and a Douglas AD Skyraider. (Lewis)

838 Douglas Corrigan flew his Curtiss Robin from New York to Ireland on 17 July 1938 even though he filed a flight plan from New York to Long Beach, California. According to Corrigan he ended up in Ireland due to a navigation error compounded by low clouds and poor visibility. He had requested approval to fly the Atlantic but was denied clearance because the authorities said his aircraft wasn't airworthy. He was dubbed "Wrong Way" Corrigan and never admitted he had flown to Ireland on purpose. (Lewis)

839 Automotive legend Ettore Bugatti designed and built an aircraft in 1939 called the Bugatti Model 100p. Painted a stunning bright royal blue color, the sleek V-tail monoplane with swept-forward wings was powered by two automobile engines mounted in the fuselage driving a pair of contra-rotating propellers. It was intended to be used in the Deutsch de la Meurthe Cup Race but World War II intervened and the airplane was never finished or flown. This ultra-modern for its time, one-of-a-kind aircraft is on display at the EAA Museum, Oshkosh, Wisconsin. (Lewis)

840 Hawaiian pineapple magnate James D. Dole created the Dole Air Race in August 1927, offering a $25,000 prize to the first person who successfully flew from Oakland, California, to the Territory of Hawaii. Dole also offered a prize of $10,000 for the second person to complete the flight. Of the 18 aircraft that entered the competition only 11 were certified, and of those, only 8 participated after

3 crashed during testing, all killing their pilots. Ten lives were lost before and during the race. Only two aircraft succeeded in reaching Hawaii. *Woolaroc*, piloted by Goebel and navigated by Davis, won first prize. Jensen and Schulter came in second flying the *Aloha*. (Lewis)

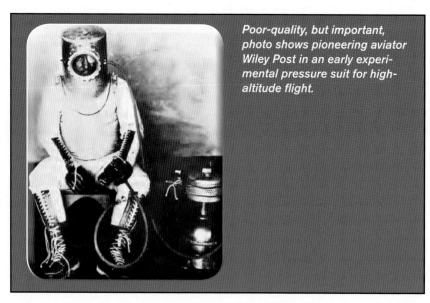

Poor-quality, but important, photo shows pioneering aviator Wiley Post in an early experimental pressure suit for high-altitude flight.

841 Flying high and above the weather has always been the calling of aviators, but how to do so without the pilot expiring in such an inhospitable environment? The answer, before pressurized cabins became reality, was to pressurize the aviator. Wiley Post, flyer and pioneering adventurer of aviation, worked with BFGoodrich Rubber Company to develop a pressure suit made from rubber. Looking like a deep-sea diving suit, the Post outfit allowed for the pilot's immediate personal surroundings to go no higher in altitude than 5,500 feet, regardless of airplane altitude. The suit worked just fine, allowing Post to climb his supercharged Lockheed Vega *Winnie Mae* all the way to 40,000 feet on 5 September 1934. (Kodera)

842 Not only higher but farther, that was Wiley Post again when in July 1933 he became the first solo flyer to circumnavigate the earth by air. He was gone for 7 days and 18 hours and stopped for fuel in Berlin, Germany; Moscow, Russia; Siberia; and Alaska. (Kodera)

843 The feat of flying a piston-powered airplane up to the edge of the stratosphere is amazing for that type of powerplant. Nevertheless, a world record, which stands to this day, belongs to one Lieutenant Colonel Mario Pezzi flying his Caproni Ca.161 biplane. The date was 22 October 1938 and the location was Montecelio, Italy. Incomprehensibly his non-supercharged engine continued to operate all the way to the astounding rarefied altitude of 56,850 feet. In the cockpit, Pezzi was ensconced in a pressure suit, which was filled not with air but with water. (Kodera)

Douglas C-54 Skymasters carried the brunt of food, coal, and materials during the Berlin Airlift, as well as candy.

844 COL Gail S. Halvorsen was a Douglas C-54 Skymaster and C-74 Globemaster pilot who flew both U.S. Air Force aircraft during the Berlin Airlift. In addition to his duties as a transport pilot during Operation Vittles when the Soviet Union blockaded West Berlin, he also became famous for dropping candy to beleaguered German children from his aircraft. Halvorsen is well known by the people of Berlin as the "Candy Bomber" and his efforts helped demonstrate the intent of Allied forces that Berlin would not be abandoned. (Lewis)

845 CAP James H. Howard was a member of the Flying Tigers before the United States entered World War II. He shot down 6 Japanese fighters before the AVG was disbanded and he joined the U.S. Army Air Forces. While flying his P-51 Mustang fighter named *Ding Hao* he fought off 30 German fighter aircraft while protecting a bomber formation. When he ran out of ammunition he dove at the German aircraft using a method learned with the AVG. During the fight he shot down 6 German planes and scared off others. Howard was awarded the Medal of Honor for his actions that day. (Lewis)

846 Bill Overstreet shot down a German Bf109 while flying his P-51C Mustang *Berlin Express*. The two planes were in a running dogfight when the German pilot flew over Paris hoping that the heavy German anti-aircraft artillery would eliminate Bill's airplane. The German's engine was hit and Bill stayed on his tail when the German pilot aimed his plane at the Eiffel Tower and, in a surprising maneuver, flew beneath it. Bill followed him and scored more hits in the process. The German crashed and Bill escaped heavy flak around Paris by flying low at full throttle over the Seine River until he had cleared the city's heavy anti-aircraft batteries. (Lewis)

847 Lieutenants George Welch and Kenneth Marlar Taylor were two U.S. Army Air Corps P-40 Tomahawk pilots stationed at Wheeler Field, Oahu, Hawaii, when the Japanese attacked Pearl Harbor on 7 December 1941. They managed to get their two P-40s airborne from Haleiwa auxiliary field during the attack and succeeded in shooting down several Japanese aircraft. Both were awarded the Distinguished Service Cross for their efforts and Taylor the Purple Heart medal for wounds received during the attack. Welch went to work for North American Aviation as a test pilot after the war and Taylor remained on active duty, retiring in 1971. (Lewis)

848 American fighter pilot Lou Curdes shot down both German and Italian aircraft before being shot down himself and placed in a POW camp. He succeeded in escaping and, as was the practice, transferred to the Pacific theater where he shot down Japanese aircraft. He also shot down one American aircraft, a C-47, when he noticed it was about to land on a Japanese field. To prevent the landing and ultimate capture he took careful aim and shot out both of the C-47's engines to force them to ditch. Flags of the aircraft he shot down include German, Italian, Japanese, and American. (Lewis)

849 The first licensed woman pilot in the United States was Harriet Quimby in 1911. (Kodera)

850 Originally known as the Women's Air Derby, the transcontinental air race for female pilots only was unceremoniously dubbed by the media of the day "the Powder Puff Derby." The rather pejorative name stuck, but the race was always a highly credible outlet for women aviators to make their marks on aviation, heretofore a man's endeavor. (Kodera)

851 First running of the Women's Air Derby was in 1929 and included such luminaries as the stellar Amelia Earhart, Pancho Barnes, Blanche Noyes, and Ruth Nichols. That first running was won by one Louise Thaden flying her Travel Air 4000. That airplane was the first to be equipped with the then-new NACA engine cowl, earning it the name Speedwing. (Kodera)

852 Jacqueline "Jackie" Cochran (1906–1980) was an air racer and record-setting pilot in the years before World War II. With war on the horizon, she proposed a women's flying corps to Eleanor Roosevelt who turned the idea over to Hap Arnold. Originally cool to the idea, when war broke out Arnold rekindled the thought of a women's flying corps. In July 1943, Cochran joined the Army Air Forces to oversee the Women Airforce Service Pilot (WASP) program. She was enshrined in the U.S. National Aviation Hall of Fame, Dayton, Ohio, in 1971. (Veronico)

Jackie Cochran, shown here with her mentor, USAF test pilot "Chuck" Yeager, held more world records than any other pilot.

853 Jacqueline Cochran was also the first woman pilot to exceed the speed of sound (Mach 1); this was in May 1953 flying a North American F-86 Sabre from Edwards AFB in California. Coach and instructor for this flight was none other than Chuck Yeager, the original sound barrier slayer, who accompanied her on the flight in a separate airplane. (Kodera)

854 Jacqueline Cochran indeed held many "firsts" records, including first woman to reach Mach 2, first woman to take off from an aircraft carrier, first woman to make a blind instrument landing, and the first woman to be inducted into the Aviation Hall of Fame. (Kodera)

855 Aviation entrepreneur Jim Bede captured attention in the aviation press for his revolutionary "airplane-in-every-garage" BD-5 homebuilt design. At only 12 feet in length Bede's BD-5J is listed by Guinness World Records as the smallest turbojet-powered aircraft flown by a pilot. (Lewis)

856 Famed aerobatic pilot and cameraman Art Scholl lost his life while filming an inverted spin in his Pitts S-2 aircraft. His aircraft failed to recover from the spin and plunged into the Pacific Ocean. The sequence was being recorded for use in the film *Top Gun* where an F-14 Tomcat entered a flat spin during a training exercise. Efforts to recover Art Scholl and his aircraft were unsuccessful. (Lewis)

857 U.S. Air Force pilot David Schilling was instrumental in developing the ability to deploy jet fighter aircraft across the Atlantic Ocean. On one of his flights he departed England and with the use of then-new aerial refueling crossed the Atlantic Ocean in just more than 10 hours, landing at an Air Force base in Maine. (Lewis)

858 Alan Eustace's goal was to fly higher and jump farther than any other balloonist in history. He achieved his dream on 24 October 2014 over Roswell, New Mexico, when his balloon reached an altitude of 135,889 feet. He was suspended beneath the structure rather than encapsulated in it. When he released himself his descent to earth lasted 15 minutes and stretched nearly 26 miles with peak speeds exceeding 821 mph, setting new world records for the highest free-fall jump and total free-fall distance of 123,334 feet. (Kodera)

859 The names Clyde Pangborn and Hugh Herndon are forever etched in the annals of long-range flight. *Miss Veedol*, a 1931 Bellanca CH-400, was the first aircraft to successfully cross the North Pacific Ocean from Misawa, Japan, to the hills in East Wenatchee, Washington. The flight took 41 hours and culminated in a belly landing because they had jettisoned the landing gear after leaving Japan. Pangborn and Herndon were awarded the Harmon Trophy plus a $25,000 prize for their efforts. *Miss Veedol*'s name was changed to *The American Nurse* and the aircraft was later lost without a trace over the Atlantic on a flight from New York to Rome. (Lewis)

860 Captain James "Robbie" Risner was credited with eight Mig kills while flying North American F-86 Sabre jets during the Korean War. On one of his missions he pushed his wingman out of enemy territory by placing the nose of his F-86 against the tail of the other Sabre. Although they were successful in reaching safety, after his wingman ejected he became tangled in his parachute lines and drowned. Risner went on to fly the F-105 Thunderchief in the Vietnam War, was shot down, and became a prisoner, but was eventually repatriated with others from the Hanoi Hilton. (Lewis)

861 Captain Joe Kittinger II set a new altitude record in 1960 when he rode a balloon gondola to 102,800 feet. He then proceeded to free fall from his gondola, making a second record for the highest skydive parachute jump. His record stood until 2012 when Felix Baumgartner broke Joe Kittinger's records by free falling from an altitude of 127,852 feet. During his free fall Baumgartner reached a speed of 843.6 mph, becoming the first person to exceed the speed of sound without the use of an aircraft. (Lewis)

862 Captain Joseph C. McConnell Jr. was the top-scoring U.S. jet ace of the Korean War with 16 kills to his credit and still holds the record of being America's top-scoring jet ace. He flew both F-86E and F-86F Sabre jets (named *Beautious Butch* after his wife) during his tour. McConnell was shot down during one mission, rescued from the Yellow Sea, and was back in combat the following day. After the war he lost his life testing an advanced model of the Sabre, an F-86H, when his flight controls failed. (Lewis)

863 How far has a human being fallen without a parachute and survived? There are two answers to this question. If it is meant as a pure free-fall event and striking the earth, then the answer is I. M. Chisov of the Soviet Air Force who in January of 1942 escaped his mortally wounded airplane with parachute, passed out due to hypoxia, fell 22,000 feet, hit a snowy mountainside, and slid to an eventual stop with severe injuries. He flew again three months later. (Kodera)

864 If we include falling while in a broken piece of airplane, then flight attendant Vesna Vulovic of Yugoslavia and the national airline, JAT, holds the record. Her DC-9 was blown apart by a bomb over Czechoslovakia on 26 January 1972. She and the fuselage segment that enshrouded her fell some 33,000 feet. She had severe injuries and was in a coma for 27 days but eventually was able to walk again and is leading a normal life. (Kodera)

865 Who was the earliest-born human to fly as an astronaut/cosmonaut? Soviet cosmonaut Georgy Beregovoy, born on 15 April 1921, beat the United States' John Glenn by three months (18 July 1921). Beregovoy flew on the Soyuz 3 mission in 1968, a prototypical docking mission, which was basically unsuccessful. A World War II pilot who flew bombers for the Soviet Union, he went on to become a test pilot and, later, deputy commander of the test flying unit for the entire Soviet air force. Just as with our space program astronauts, this flying and academic background prepared him for the role of cosmonaut. (Kodera)

866 Who was the oldest professional astronaut/cosmonaut to fly in space? Story Musgrave, born in 1935, flew in space up until 19 November 1996, making him 61 years and 3 months old on launch day. He flew on six different space shuttle missions and was the only astronaut to have flown on all five shuttle orbiters. He was a NASA astronaut for more than 30 years. Musgrave's career began as a pilot in the United States Marine Corps, and he has accumulated more than 18,000 flying hours to date. (Kodera)

867 The first woman to parachute from an airplane was "Tiny" Broadwick (*née* Georgia Ann Thompson) on 9 January 1914. She jumped from a Martin biplane at 1,000 feet wearing a Glenn Martin–designed "life pack" parachute. Some sources claim that she actually jumped earlier on 21 June 1913. (Caruso)

868 British engineer F. W. Meredith found the Meredith Effect in his research. The result of his studies indicated that energy from the transfer of heat as air passes through a radiator could be converted into an increase in thrust. Heat energy is generated by ambient air flowing through radiators, and a small amount of forward thrust can be obtained by careful design of the ducting. Aircraft such as the Supermarine Spitfire, Hawker Hurricane, North

American P-51 Mustang, and Douglas A-26 Invader all benefited from the Meredith Effect. (Lewis)

869 Major Robinson Risner established a record when he flew North American F-100F Super Sabre *Spirit of St. Louis II* across the Atlantic to Paris over the same route used by Charles Lindbergh 30 years earlier. Major Risner made the 3,680-mile flight in 6 hours 37 minutes while Lindbergh's required 33 hours, 30 minutes. His flight originated at McGuire AFB, New Jersey, and was officially timed from Floyd Bennett Field, New York, to Le Bourget Field in Paris, France. (Lewis)

870 Fitzhugh L. "Fitz" Fulton was an Air Force and NASA test pilot known for his outstanding flight test work on various multi-engine aircraft from the B-29s, B-50s, and B-52s that launched the X-Planes to the Boeing 747 that first carried the Space Shuttles. As a result, he was often referred to as the "Father of the Motherships." (Machat)

871 However, the soft-spoken Georgia native also flew just about every other type of aircraft imaginable, a total of 235 types in all. Never considering himself a true fighter pilot, he always spoke of his fighter aircraft experiences as "flying single-pilot airplanes." (Machat)

872 Geoffrey de Havilland built a series of aircraft and named them after moths. His first biplane, a DH.60, was designed so the wings could be folded against the fuselage similar to how moths fold their wings. He produced several more designs, also named after moths. His most famous moth was the DH.82 *Tiger Moth* that was used to train Royal Flying Corps and RAF pilots for World War II. Two other notable de Havilland designs were the *Wooden Wonder* DH.98 Mosquito and jet airliner DH 106 Comet. (Lewis)

873 In 1943–1944 Alexander Lippisch was designing a manned interceptor that would be powered by a Lorin-type ramjet. The unusual fuel for the engine would have been pulverized coal, to avoid the need for scarce liquid fuel. The aircraft itself was a delta dart shape with a reinforced structure to allow it to ram and destroy enemy bomber aircraft. (Veronico)

874 Clarence "Kelly" Johnson, Lockheed Aircraft's design wizard, didn't always get it right. The father of the P-80 Shooting Star, F-104 Starfighter, U-2 Dragon lady, and the SR-71 Blackbird hated the design of Lockheed's most successful aircraft, the C-130 Hercules. He wasn't at all happy with the bulky shape of the C-130 preliminary design and refused to sign the proposal for the C-130 to the U.S. Air Force. Fortunately, his judgment about the Hercules was overridden. (Veronico)

875 General Hap Arnold's personal Douglas C-41 was a one-of-a-kind aircraft. It was manufactured between the DC-2/C-39 series & DC-3/C-47 models. If current identification methods had been applied, it would have been called a VC-41. (Lewis)

876 American Airlines CEO Robert Crandall, affectionately given the nickname "Fang" by company employees, was famous for his claims of saving money. Widely reported was a $40,000 savings realized in 1987 by simply removing one olive from each salad served in first class. (Proctor)

877 Another of Crandall's claims to fame for frugality was replacing a night security guard in a company building with a watchdog. Later he replaced the watchdog with a recording of a dog barking. (Proctor)

878 Neil A. Armstrong (1930–2012) was an American naval aviator, test pilot, and astronaut who was the first human being to set foot on a celestial body. Armstrong was a naval aviator from 1949 to 1952, and joined the National Advisory Committee for Aeronautics (NACA) in 1955. NACA became the National Aeronautics and Space Administration (NASA) where Armstrong served as an engineer and test pilot flying the X-15 and hundreds of other types. He served as the command pilot of the Gemini 8 mission in March 1966 and was the spacecraft commander of the *Apollo 11*, NASA's first manned lunar landing mission. (Veronico)

Neil Armstrong suits up for his next flight in North American's X-15, assisted by Edwards AFB Chief Flight Surgeon Major Ralph Richardson.

879 Edwin E. "Buzz" Aldrin Jr. (b. 1930) is a graduate of the U.S. Military Academy at West Point, New York, class of 1951. Upon graduation he entered the U.S. Air Force and flew more than 65 missions during the Korean War and is credited with two aerial victories over MiG-15 fighters. He was selected to the astronaut corps in 1963 and assigned to the Gemini program. He flew as pilot of *Gemini 12* and later was assigned to the crew of *Apollo 11*. With Neil Armstrong, Aldrin left his footprints on the moon during the July 1969 lunar landing mission. (Veronico)

880 Edmund T. "Eddie" Allen (1896–1943) was a World War I pilot, and between the war years a freelance test pilot who made the initial flights of many important types ranging from the Northrop Alpha to the Boeing 314 Clipper and the Douglas DC-1. With war clouds on the horizon, Allen was hired at Boeing as chief of flight test, aerodynamics, and wind tunnel testing. He flew the maiden flights of the Stearman, B-17B, -C, -D, -E, and –F as well as the

XB-29. He also flew the Lockheed C-69 Constellation on its first flight (9 January 1943). Allen perished on 18 February 1943 trying to land the second XB-29 prototype at Seattle's Boeing Field while fighting two in-flight fires. (Veronico)

881 Henry H. "Hap" Arnold (1886–1950) graduated from the U.S. Military Academy at West Point, New York, in the class of 1907. In 1911, he was taught to fly by the Wright brothers and was a proponent of military air power. In March 1942, Arnold was promoted to commanding general of the Army Air Forces. At its peak, the Army Air Forces had more than 2.5 million men and 75,000 aircraft. Arnold was in command during the Allied victory over Germany and Japan. (Veronico)

882 Colleen Barrett served as president of Southwest Airlines after working as a legal secretary for the air carrier's founder, Herb Kelleher. She joined the airline, which was started in 1971, in 1978 and held positions of increasing responsibility, becoming chief operating officer in 2001. She served as president from 2004 to 2008. Barrett directed much of the carrier's success through the turbulent post-9/11 years, which saw Southwest Airlines grow at a tremendous rate. She was honored with the National Aeronautic Association's Wright Brothers Memorial Trophy in 2016. (Veronico)

883 William E. Boeing (1881–1956) founded the aviation company that bears his name. What would soon become the Boeing Airplane Company was formed in 1916 and received its first military orders for the Boeing Model 1 floatplane on the eve of World War I. Boeing's holding company, United Aircraft and Transport Corporation, owned United Aircraft Corporation (today's United Technologies Corporation), the Boeing Airplane Company, and United Air Lines. In 1934, Boeing was forced to break up the company amid charges of operating a monopoly. (Veronico)

884 Claire Lee Chennault (1893–1958) served in the U.S. Army's Signal Corps Aviation Section during World War I and progressed through the ranks during the inter-war years. In 1937 he

traveled to China to stand up the fighter units of the Chinese Air Force, and in 1941 he started to recruit pilots to serve in the American Volunteer Group. When war between the United States and Japan was declared, Chennault returned to serve with the U.S. Army Air Forces as commander of the 14th Air Force in China. After the war, Chennault served as president of Civil Air Transports (CAT), an airline using surplus C-46 and C-47 transports. (Veronico)

885 Geraldyn M. "Jerrie" Cobb (b. 1931) was named America's first female astronaut in 1959 and was the only woman to pass all three of the required sections of Mercury astronaut training. Cobb had learned to fly at age 12 and went on to set numerous aviation speed, distance, and altitude records in the late 1950s. She also flew humanitarian missions into the jungles of Brazil, Colombia, and Peru. She was inducted into the U.S. National Aviation Hall of Fame in 2012. (Veronico)

886 Major General Michael Collins, USAF, ret. (b. 1930) graduated from the U.S. Military Academy at West Point, New York, and was commissioned into the U.S. Air Force. He flew fighters in Europe before being accepted into the Test Pilot School at Edwards AFB, California, in 1960. Collins was accepted into the third group of astronauts and flew on *Gemini 10* and served as the command module pilot of *Apollo 11*. He was the first astronaut to have performed more than one spacewalk and is 1 of only 24 to have flown to the moon. In retirement, Collins served as director of the National Air and Space Museum, and later as undersecretary of the Smithsonian Institution. (Veronico)

887 Test pilot Albert Scott Crossfield (1921–2006) became the first human to fly at twice the speed of sound on 20 November 1953 while flying the Douglas D-558-II Skyrocket in the skies above Edwards AFB, California. As a pilot for the National Advisory Committee for Aeronautics (NACA), Crossfield reached a speed of 1,291 mph, or Mach 2.005. He left NACA in 1955, having flown more than 90 flights in the rocket-powered X-1 and D-558-II. While working for North American Aviation, Crossfield helped to design

A young Scott Crossfield poses with the Douglas D-558-2 Skyrocket, which he flew for the National Advisory Committee on Aeronautics (NACA).

and test the X-15 and flew the plane 14 times, reaching Mach 2.97 (1,960 mph) at 88,116 feet. (Veronico)

888 Aviation pioneer Glenn Hammond Curtiss (1878–1930) made the first pre-announced flight on 4 July 1908 in the *June Bug*. He also received pilot License Number 1 from the Aero Club of America on 8 June 1911. As an aircraft manufacturer demonstration pilot Eugene Ely, flying a Curtiss Pusher, made the first flight from a ship, the cruiser *Birmingham*, on 14 November 1910, and the first shipboard landing on the stern of the armored cruiser *Pennsylvania* on 18 January 1911. Curtiss sold his interest in his company in 1920 and retired to Florida where he was instrumental in the development of the cities of Hialeah, Opa-locka, and Miami Springs. (Veronico)

889 Benjamin Oliver Davis Jr. (1912–2002) is best known as the commander of the Tuskegee Airmen and America's first African-American general. A graduate of West Point, class of 1936, he was only the fourth African-American to graduate from the school. During World War II he commanded the 99th Fighter Squadron and the 332nd Fighter Group flying P-39s, P-40s, P-47s, and later

P-51s escorting bomber formations of the 15th Air Force in the Mediterranean Theater. Davis was instrumental in the integration of the armed forces beginning in 1948. During the Korean War, he flew F-86s as commander of the 51st Fighter-Interceptor Wing. He served stateside, in Europe, and in the Pacific before retiring from the Air Force on 1 February 1970. (Veronico)

James H. Doolittle pioneered many aspects of aviation, from air racing to fuel research and instrument flying.

890 James Harold "Jimmy" Doolittle (1896–1993) is best remembered as the leader of the 18 April 1942 Doolittle Raid, America's first retaliatory attack on the Japanese home islands. His military career began on 11 March 1918, when he was commissioned in the Signal Officers Reserve Corps as a lieutenant. Doolittle served as a flight and gunnery instructor during World War I and went on to be a test pilot and air racer. He won the 1925 Schneider Trophy Race flying a Curtiss R3C-2 floatplane, seen above, at a speed of 232 mph. (Veronico)

891 During the inter-war years, Doolittle was a pioneer in the development of instrument flying. World War II saw him lead the Doolittle Raid in April 1942, then take command of the 12th, 15th, and 8th Air Forces, respectively. He retired from the U.S. Army Air Forces on 10 May 1946, but continued his public service. He was instrumental in desegregation of the nascent U.S. Air Force and served as the chairman of the National Advisory Committee for Aeronautics (NACA, the forerunner of today's NASA). (Veronico)

Donald W. Douglas studied aeronautical engineering at MIT and founded the company that built the world's greatest passenger aircraft.

892 Donald Wills Douglas Sr. (1892–1981) entered the U.S. Naval Academy, but left to pursue an aviation engineering career before graduation. He then entered the Massachusetts Institute of Technology (MIT), where he earned a four-year degree in only two years. Upon graduation, MIT hired him as an assistant professor of aeronautics. In 1915, Douglas was hired as the chief engineer of the Glenn L. Martin Company In 1920, he formed the Davis-Douglas Company with millionaire David R. Davis. The company designed and built *The Cloudster*. (Veronico)

893 Davis sold his interest in the company to Douglas in 1921, and Douglas began building torpedo bombers for the U.S. Navy.

Ten years later, Douglas began work on the DC-1 and -2, revolutionizing the commercial air transport sector, and later dominating it with the DC-3. During World War II, the company built everything from SBD Dauntless dive bombers to license-built B-17 and B-24 bombers. In 1957, Douglas turned over the reins of the company to his son, Donald W. Douglas Jr., while remaining as chairman of the board of directors. He retired in 1967 when the company merged with McDonnell Aircraft Company. (Veronico)

894 Donald W. Douglas Jr. (1917–2004) was the son of the founder of Douglas Aircraft. He served in numerous positions while he learned the business and worked his way up within the company. During World War II, Donald Jr. served as the manager of flight test, and after the war as the director of the Flight Test Division. Appointed president of Douglas Aircraft in 1957, he took the company into the Jet Age with the introduction of the four-engine DC-8 and twinjet DC-9. In 1967, he guided the merger of the company founded by his father with McDonnell Aircraft. He retired in 1974. (Veronico)

895 Dr. Hugo Eckener (1868–1954) was an airship pioneer and captain of the record-setting dirigible *Graf Zeppelin*. Eckener was head of the Zeppelin Company following World War I and navigated the company through the 1920s and the restrictions of the Versailles Treaty on Germany and its war-related industries. In 1929, Eckener captained *Graf Zeppelin* on its around-the-world flight, and as a vocal opponent of the Nazi government, was forcibly retired. Eckener survived World War II and lived out his later years in Flensburg near the German border with Denmark. (Veronico)

896 Theodore Gordon "Spuds" Ellyson (1885–1928) was Naval Aviator Number 1, having learned to fly from Glenn Curtis in 1910–1911 at San Diego's North Island. He served at the U.S. Naval Academy at Annapolis and onboard the battleships *Kansas* (BB-21) and *Wyoming* (BB-32), and later commanded destroyers *J. Fred Talbott* (DD-156), *Little* (DD-79), and *Brooks* (DD-232). As a commander, Ellyson served in the Bureau of Aeronautics during the early 1920s. Ellyson perished when the aircraft he was flying, a Loening OL-7, crashed on the night of 27 February 1928 on a flight from Norfolk, Virginia, to Annapolis, Maryland. (Veronico)

897 Eugene Burton Ely (1886–1911) was granted U.S. pilot's License Number 17 on 5 October 1910, having learned to fly a biplane built by Glenn Curtis. On 10 November 1910, at Hampton Roads, Virginia, Ely flew a Curtiss Pusher biplane from a platform built over the bow of the light cruiser USS *Birmingham* (CL-2), and two months later, on 18 January 1911, landed the same plane on the stern of the armored cruiser USS *Pennsylvania* (ACR-4) in San Francisco Bay. Ely perished during an aerial exhibition on 19 October 1911 at Macon, Georgia. (Veronico)

898 Hal Farley flew A-4 Skyhawks with the U.S. Navy, then joined Grumman as a test pilot flying the F-14 Tomcat. After eight years and more than 1,000 hours in the Tomcat, Farley joined Lockheed and its Skunk Works. He was the test pilot for the prototype F-117A Stealth Fighter and has flown more than 600 hours in the type. Farley's callsign is "Bandit 117." (Veronico)

899 As a member of the 1960s Women in Space program, Wally Funk was selected as one of the Mercury 13 cadre of female astronaut candidates. At 20 years of age, Funk became a civilian flight instructor teaching military pilots at Ft. Sill, Oklahoma. Funk was subsequently the first female air safety investigator for the National Transportation Safety Board. Today she continues as an aviation ambassador and noted speaker. (Veronico)

900 Paul Edward Garber (1899–1992) was the first curator of the Smithsonian Institution's National Air and Space Museum and is responsible for assembling the early aircraft of the collection. Among the many historic aircraft and artifacts secured by Garber are the *Wright Flyer*, Lindbergh's *Spirit of St. Louis*, the B-29 *Enola Gay*, and many of the Axis aircraft from World War II. Garber saw the construction and opening of the museum's facility on the National Mall, which draws more than 8 million visitors per year. (Veronico)

901 Jane F. Garvey (b. 1944) has held positions of increasing responsibility in the transportation sector from the commissioner of the Massachusetts Department of Public Works, to the director of Logan International Airport in Boston, and deputy administrator of the Federal Highway Administration. Garvey was selected to serve as the administrator of the Federal Aviation Administration during the Bill Clinton presidency. Her term spanned 1997 to 2002, which included the terror attacks on the United States and its air transportation system on 11 September 2001. (Veronico)

902 Noted test pilot Robert J. Gilliland (b. 1926) was a 1949 graduate of the U.S. Naval Academy who joined the U.S. Air Force. After flight training he flew F-84s in Korea. He served as a test pilot at Eglin AFB, Florida, flying all types of Air Force aircraft. In 1960, Gilliland joined Lockheed, and two years later was accepted to fly the Skunk Works projects including the A-11, A-12, and YF-12A. On 22 December 1964, Gilliland, callsign Dutch 51, made the first flight of the SR-71A. He logged more than 6,500 hours and has flown more time at speeds above Mach 3 than any other pilot. (Veronico)

903 John Hershel Glenn Jr. (1921–2016) was one of the original Mercury astronauts, four-term senator from Ohio, and in later life an astronaut onboard the space shuttle. Glenn was commissioned in the Marine Corps in 1943 and flew 59 combat missions in F4U Corsairs with Marine Fighter Squadron 152 (VMF-152) in the Marshall Islands. During the Korean War, he flew combat with VMF 218 and later served as an exchange pilot with the U.S. Air Force flying F-86 Sabre jets. He scored three aerial victories over MiG fighters in the engagements. He then attended the Naval Test Pilot School at NAS Patuxent River, Maryland. (Veronico)

904 Glenn subsequently was assigned as project officer for the Vought F8U Crusader program. In that aircraft he made the first transcontinental flight at supersonic speed. He was then selected as one of NASA's Mercury Seven astronauts and performed a 4-hour, 55-minute three-orbit flight in the *Friendship 7* capsule on 20 February 1962, making him the third American in space, but

Marine Colonel John H. Glenn flew in World War II and the Korean War before being assigned as one of NASA's Mercury Seven Astronauts.

the first American to orbit the Earth. Glenn retired from the U.S. Marine Corps at the rank of colonel on 1 January 1965. At age 77, he flew a nine-day mission aboard Space Shuttle *Discovery* (STS-95) focusing on space flight and the aging process. Glenn passed away in 2016. (Veronico)

905 Virgil Ivan "Gus" Grissom (1926–1967) earned a mechanical engineering degree at Purdue University, then returned to military service with the Air Force where he earned his wings in 1950. He flew 100 combat mission in Korea with the 334th Fighter-Interceptor Squadron. In 1957, he earned his credentials as an Air Force test pilot and was assigned to Wright-Patterson AFB, Ohio. (Veronico)

906 After passing a rigorous battery of tests, Grissom and six others were selected as the first Project Mercury astronauts in April 1959. Grissom was launched into space on 21 July 1961 in his capsule christened *Liberty Bell 7*; his flight lasted 15 minutes and splashed down in the Atlantic Ocean. Shortly after landing while awaiting rescue by Navy divers, explosive bolts on *Liberty Bell 7*'s entry hatch blew, allowing water to flood the capsule. Grissom was able to swim free, but nearly drowned during the rescue. (Veronico)

907 Grissom was assigned to command the Gemini capsule *Molly Brown*, launched on 23 March 1965, with pilot John W. Young. This flight lasted five hours and covered 80,000 miles in three orbits of the planet. Grissom, Ed White, and Roger Chaffee were selected for the Apollo Earth-orbit mission, known as *Apollo 1*, slated for launch in October 1966. After a number of delays, tests continued, and on 27 January 1967, during the "plugs-out integration test," Grissom, Young, and White perished in an oxygen-fed fire in the pressurized capsule. (Veronico)

908 Air Marshall Arthur Travers Harris (1892–1984) served as air officer commander in chief (AOC-in-C) of the Royal Air Force Bomber Command. He implemented area bombing that devastated German cities and their people. Harris pushed for the 1,000-plane raid and launched the first such raid on Cologne on 30–31 May 1942. Area bombing raids on Dresden and Hamburg burned great areas of the cities, and deaths in Dresden were estimated at 25,000. (Veronico)

909 Bruce Hinds was a class of 1961 graduate of the U.S. Air Force Academy and served as a test pilot and test manager from 1967 to 1982. After retirement, he joined Northrop Aircraft (later Northrop Grumman) where he served as chief test pilot of the B-2 program, and the company's chief test pilot from 1982 to 1995. Along with U.S. Air Force B-2 Combined Test Force Commander Col. Richard S. Couch, Hinds made the first flight of the B-2 Stealth Bomber on 17 July 1989. The flight departed Air Force Plant 42 at Palmdale, California, and landed at Edwards AFB after 2 hours, 20 minutes in the air. Hinds is currently an aviation consultant. (Veronico)

910 Robert Anderson "Bob" Hoover (1922–2016) was known as the "pilot's pilot." Hoover began flying with the Army Air Corps and during World War II served as a test pilot flying aircraft that had been delivered to North Africa in crates. As a combat pilot with the 52nd Fighter Group, he was shot down over Sicily while flying a crippled Mk V Spitfire. He was interned in Stalag Luft 1 in

Considered the greatest air show pilot who ever lived, R. A. "Bob" Hoover worked for North American Aviation after serving in the Air Force.

Barth, Germany. Hoover escaped by stealing an Fw 190, and flew to freedom. After the war he served as a test pilot and was the back-up pilot for Chuck Yeager on the Bell X-1. (Veronico)

911 Entertainment, real estate, and aviation magnate Howard Robard Hughes Jr. (1905–1976) set a number of records (landplane speed record, 352 mph, on 13 September 1935; around-the-world record of 3 days, 19 hours, 17 minutes on 14 July 1938), was nearly killed in the crash of the XF-11 reconnaissance aircraft in 1946, designed and made the only flight of the Hughes HK-1 Hercules, owned Trans World Airlines, was the launch customer for the Lockheed Constellation and later the Convair 880 jetliner. Hughes later acquired Air West airlines that became Hughes Airwest, which was then acquired by Republic Airlines in 1980. (Veronico)

912 Test pilot Alvin M. "Tex" Johnston (1914–1998) recorded many aviation firsts while flying for Bell Aircraft and the Boeing

A. M. "Tex" Johnston flew for the Bell Aircraft Company before being hired by Boeing, where he piloted jet bombers and transports.

Company. During World War II, he flew for the Ferry Command and then transferred to Bell Aircraft where he flew the prototype and production versions of the P-39, P-63 Kingcobra, and America's first jet fighter, the P-59 Airacomet. After the war, he entered the National Air Races with a pair of P-39s, well prepared by factory mechanics. He easily won the Thompson Trophy Race at Cleveland, Ohio, setting a new speed record of 373 mph. While with Bell, he also flew the supersonic X-1 rocket plane. (Veronico)

913 In 1948 Johnston joined the Boeing Airplane Company and participated in testing the B-47 Stratojet. He made the first flight of the YB-52 Stratofortress, on 15 April 1952, with Lt.Col. Guy M. Townsend as co-pilot. Three years later, Johnston was demonstrating the 367-80 jetliner prototype in the skies over Seattle's Lake Washington when he barrel-rolled the airplane. Johnston stayed with the Boeing Company until 1968, when he left to join Aero Spacelines and its Guppy conversion program. His last career position was with Stanley Aviation Corporation. (Veronico)

914 Hugo Junkers (1859–1935) founded Junkers Flugzeug und Moterwerke AG and was a pioneer in the development of all-metal aircraft. His company built several designs during World War I; however, the F.13 (1919) and later Ju-52/3 (1932) were the aircraft of choice of many inter-war airlines. Junkers was a pacifist and was forced from the company he founded in 1934 and died one year later. The company went on to build many of Nazi Germany's best aerial weapons, including the Ju 87 Stuka dive bomber and Ju 88 medium/torpedo bomber. (Veronico)

915 Herbert David "Herb" Kelleher (b. 1931) and two other partners reportedly sketched out the concept for the company that would become Southwest Airlines on the back of a napkin in 1971. Low fares, point-to-point service to a city's secondary airports, and no frills was the basis for their airline concept that today flies to more than 100 cities and several international destinations, with approximately 3,800 flights a day using more than 720 Boeing 737 jetliners. Kelleher retired as CEO in May 2008. (Veronico)

916 Clay Lacy (b. 1932) was hired by United Airlines in January 1952 and served with the airline for more than 41 years. He flew nearly every type in the company's inventory: the Convair 340, all the company's Douglas types (DC-3, DC-4, DC-6, DC-7, DC-8, DC-10), as well as the Boeing 727 and Boeing 747. Lacy retired from United in 1992 with his pilot seniority number as "1." (Veronico)

917 Lacy was one of the first racing pilots when Unlimited Air Racing returned in 1964, and in 1968 he founded Clay Lacy Aviation, the West Coast's first business jet charter company. His charter company, based at Van Nuys, California, flew corporate executives and Hollywood movie stars in LearJets. His "Astrovision" camera system for the LearJet revolutionized aerial filmmaking, with Lacy's aircraft and system being used in countless commercials and more than 50 big screen movie productions. Lacy's charity work has been combined with numerous aviation record-setting flights, most notably his 1988 around-the-world flight in a Boeing 747SP. (Veronico)

918 Curtis Emerson LeMay (1906–1990) was a U.S. Army Air Forces and later U.S. Air Force general who was architect of the fire bombings of the Japanese home islands (1944–1945), the American response in the Berlin Airlift (June 1948–May 1949), and the evolution of the Strategic Air Command (SAC 1948–1957). LeMay was commissioned in the Air Corps Reserve in fall 1929, and his early exploits as a navigator have gone down in annals of air power history: He located the battleship *Utah* off the coast of California in an August 1937 exercise and intercepted the Italian ocean liner *Rex* in May 1938. (Veronico)

919 During World War II, LeMay commanded the 305th Bomb Group, 8th Air Force, then later the 3rd Air Division. In August 1944 he was sent to the China-Burma-India Theater as commander of the 20th Bomber Command, then the 21st Bomber Command in the Pacific. LeMay advocated for low-level bombardment of Japanese cities using incendiary bombs. (Veronico)

920 In 1948, when the Soviet Union attempted to starve the citizens of Berlin, LeMay sent C-54s into the city daily, with more than 500 flights bringing more than 5,000 tons of food and supplies each day. Later in the year, LeMay replaced General George Kenney as commander of the Strategic Air Command. His goal for SAC (circa 1949) was to destroy 70 enemy cities within 30 days. (Veronico)

921 LeMay served as the Air Force chief of staff from 1961, during the Cuban Missile Crisis, to 1965. His retaliatory stance in favor of bombing missile sites in Cuba was at odds with President John F. Kennedy's blockade strategy. In February 1965, now at odds with President Lyndon B. Johnson's Vietnam air war strategy, he was retired. In 1968, LeMay ran on Governor George Wallace's American Independent Party ticket as vice president. Wallace and LeMay finished the political race a distant third, with LeMay soon fading into retirement. (Veronico)

922 Charles Augustus Lindbergh (1902–1974) won the Orteig Prize for his nonstop trans-Atlantic flight from Roosevelt Field, New

While it was not his intent by any means, Lindbergh's historic solo New York-to-Paris flight thrust him into the public spotlight in 1927.

York to Paris, France, at the controls of the *Spirit of St. Louis*. Lindbergh married Anne Morrow in 1929 and the pair flew together throughout the globe in the 1930s, from Europe to Japan and China by way of Siberia. He was an Army Air Corps officer, air mail pilot, author, explorer, and aviation consultant. (Veronico)

923 During World War II, Lindbergh served as a consultant to Ford on its B-24 production, with United Aircraft/Vought on the F4U Corsair and with Lockheed flying the P-38 Lightning. As part of his consulting work, he flew 50 combat missions against the Japanese in the Pacific. After the war he consulted for both Pan American World Airways and the U.S. Air Force. He was very active in promoting environmental causes during the final years of his life. (Veronico)

924 Edward T. Maloney (1928–2016) was a pioneer in the warbird preservation movement and founded the Planes of Fame Air Museum, the first air museum west of the Mississippi River, in January 1957. He rescued many rare, one-of-a-kind aircraft from technical schools and movie theater backlots. He was derided during the early years of his collecting efforts, but as time went on and his collection of airframes became recognized for their rarity, perceptions changed. Maloney's vision of a living museum where warbirds were flown for the public grew into the annual Planes of Fame air show held each year in May. (Veronico)

925 James Smith McDonnell (1899–1980) graduated Princeton University in 1921 and continued his education, earning a master's degree in aeronautical engineering from the Massachusetts Institute of Technology in 1925. He worked for Ford Motor Company's Stout Metal Airplane Division, and later the Hamilton Metalplane Company and Huff Daland Airplane Company. During the Great Depression he worked for the Great Lakes Aircraft Company and the Glenn L. Martin Company In 1939 he founded McDonnell Aircraft Corporation, which would develop the jet-powered FH-1 Phantom (1945) and Phantom II (1958) as well as the Mercury (1958) and Gemini (1961) space capsules. McDonnell merged with Douglas Aircraft in April 1967. (Veronico)

926 William Lendrum "Billy" Mitchell (1879–1936) was a post–World War I advocate of air power and highly vocal in his belief that land-based and aircraft carrier–based aviation would defeat the battleship. The Navy provided the German battleship *Ostfriesland* as a target for Project B, initiated in February 1921. Dropping bombs in the water near the ship buckled its hull plates and sent it to the bottom. Later that year, Mitchell's bombers also sank the battleships *Alabama, Virginia*, and *New Jersey*. Following the September 1925 crash of the Navy's airship *Shenandoah*, Mitchell accused military leaders of "almost treasonable administration of the national defense." One month later he was court-martialed; the guilty verdict and subsequent sentence saw him suspended from duty for five years without pay. He was later restored to half pay, but Mitchell resigned his commission on 1 February 1926. (Veronico)

927 Thomas Albert Morgenfeld (CAPT, U.S. Navy, ret.) flew 90 combat missions in the F-8 Crusader over Vietnam between July 1972 and March 1973 with VF-191 onboard USS *Oriskany* (CV-34). He subsequently graduated from the U.S. Naval Test Pilot School (January 1975) and the Empire Test Pilot's School (December 1975). From there, he was appointed test director with VX-4 evaluating a number of foreign fighters smuggled into the United States (MiG-17, MiG-23, Su-22). After military service he joined Lockheed's Skunk Works serving as engineering test pilot, chief test pilot, and director of flight operations flying the YF/F-117, and prototype test pilot for the YF-22 and X-35. Morgenfeld has flown nearly 7,000 hours in more than 80 different aircraft types. (Veronico)

928 John Knudsen "Jack" Northrop (1895–1981) worked for several aviation companies in the 1920s and 1930s before establishing his own company, Northrop Corporation He worked for the Loughead Brothers' Lockheed Aircraft, worked on the Douglas World Cruiser aircraft, and for Ryan Aircraft worked on the *Spirit of St. Louis*. He returned to work for the Loughead Brothers before founding Avion Aircraft, which he sold at the height of the Great Depression. (Veronico)

929 With the backing of Donald Douglas and other partners, Jack Northrop founded the Northrop Corporation in 1932. Here, Jack Northrop designed and produced the Gamma and Delta all-metal, low-wing monoplanes. Northrop was a proponent of the flying wing concept and built many successful prototypes, which would culminate in the piston-powered XB-35 and jet-powered YB-49 flying wing bombers. The flying wing bombers were reportedly not stable enough as bombing platforms, and it would take another 40 years of technological advances before Northrop was vindicated with the B-2 Stealth Bomber. (Veronico)

930 Robin Olds (1922–2007) was a graduate of West Point (class of 1943) and an Army Air Forces and later Air Force pilot who attained 16 aerial victories in World War II and Vietnam. In Vietnam, as commander of the 8th Tactical Fighter Wing, Olds designed Operation Bolo to ambush North Vietnamese MiG-21 air defense fighters, which saw the loss of 10 enemy planes and suppressed their activity for nearly three months. Olds flew 107 combat missions in World War II and 152 during the Vietnam War. His MiG-killing F-4 Phantom, 64-0829, is displayed at the National Museum of the U.S. Air Force in Dayton, Ohio. (Veronico)

931 Hanna Reitsch (1912–1979) was a German test pilot known for setting more than 40 altitude and endurance awards and the first female helicopter pilot. She also flew the rocket-powered Me 163, among many other aircraft. During the closing days of World War II, as the Soviets approached the center of Berlin, Reitsch flew General Robert Ritter von Greim into and out of the city. After the war, when German citizens were able to fly again, she set a number of records in gliders. (Veronico)

932 Richard Stephen "Steve" Ritchie (b. 1942) graduated from the U.S. Air Force Academy in 1964. He flew 800 combat hours during 339 missions spanning two tours in Vietnam in the F-4 Phantom II. Along with his backseater, Ritchie is credited with downing five MiG-21 fighters. He attained the rank of brigadier general and was awarded the Air Force Cross, 4 Silver Stars,

10 Distinguished Flying Crosses, and 25 Air Medals during his military service. (Veronico)

933 Franklin D. "Frank" Robinson (b. 1930) worked for nearly every rotary-wing manufacturer, beginning in 1957 with Cessna Aircraft working on the CH-1 Skyhook. As helicopters matured, he worked for Umbaugh, McCulloch, Kaman, Bell, and Hughes before founding his own company, Robinson Helicopter Company, in 1973. Robinson saw the need for a small, low-cost helicopter, and the two-place R22 was born. The company now makes the R22, the four-place R44, and the five-place, turbine-powered R66 helicopters. The company delivered its 10,000th helicopter on 10 November 2011. (Veronico)

934 Elbert Leander "Burt" Rutan (b. 1943) is a revolutionary aircraft designer noted for a wide variety of aircraft, from the homebuilt VariViggen, VariEze, Long-EZ, and Quickie, to the record-setting *Voyager* (around-the-world unrefueled), Pond Racer (Unlimited Class air racer), GlobalFlyer (solo flight around the world, unrefueled), and SpaceShipOne and its mothership White Knight. With funding from Sir Richard Branson's Virgin Galactic, SpaceShipOne was the first privately funded, privately built, heavier-than-air manned vehicle to reach space. This achievement was awarded the Collier Trophy. Rutan retired from Scaled Composites in 2011. (Veronico)

935 Richard Glenn "Dick" Rutan (b. 1938) was an Air Force pilot who flew in the Vietnam War as a fast forward air controller, known as a FastFAC, flying F-100D Super Sabres. Rutan flew 325 combat missions, earning the Silver Star, 5 Distinguished Flying Crosses, 16 Air Medals, and the Purple Heart. Following his Air Force service, Dick Rutan joined Bert Rutan's Rutan Aircraft Factory as production manager and chief test pilot. On 14 December 1986, Dick Rutan and Jeana Yeager left Edwards on an around-the-world, unrefueled, nonstop flight. The plane landed 9 days, 3 minutes, and 40 seconds later. He was awarded the Presidential Citizen's Medal shortly after the flight. (Veronico)

936 Robert Forman Six (1907–1986) was one of the longest-serving airline CEOs, having formed Continental Airlines in 1937. He shaped the airline industry through its period of massive expansion from the 1940s to the 1970s. In 1936, Six took a loan of $90,000 and bought 40 percent of the Southwest Division of Varney Speed Lines and was named its general manager one year later. He moved the company's headquarters to Denver and renamed the carrier Continental Air Lines. During the war years, Continental performed aircraft modifications for the Army Air Forces. Six was outspoken against 1978 airline deregulation and soon after retired in 1982. (Veronico)

937 Deke Slayton (1924–1993) flew 56 combat missions as a B-25 pilot over Europe and 7 missions over Japan during World War II. Between World War II and service during the Korean War, Slayton earned an aeronautical engineering degree and worked at Boeing in Seattle. He was selected as one of the seven men to pilot the Mercury spacecraft, but a heart condition prevented him from a flight. He went on to lead the Astronaut Office and later flew on the Apollo-Soyuz mission in July 1975. He retired from NASA in 1982 and continued flying, including competing at the National Championship Air Races in the Formula One class. (Veronico)

938 William Bushnell Stout (1880–1956) was a successful automotive engineer who, in 1924, began the Stout Metal Airplane Company The company developed two designs and was acquired by Ford. The Stout 3-AT formed the basis of the Ford Trimotor. Stout worked for Ford until 1930, when he left to work full time at his Stout Engineering Laboratory. During the war, this company was sold to Consolidated Vultee Aircraft Corporation, where Stout became a company director. He designed a flying car and the sliding car seat among many other engineering innovations. (Veronico)

939 Paul Warfield Tibbets Jr. (1915–2007) was one of the U.S. 8th Air Force's first squadron commanders during the war in Europe, but he will forever be known as the pilot of the B-29 *Enola Gay* that dropped the world's first atomic bomb, on the city of Hiroshima, Japan. Among Tibbets' many accomplishments, he was deputy group commander of the 97th Bomb Group and flew the lead bomber on the first U.S. daylight raid over Europe on 17 August 1942. He returned to the United States to assist in the implementation of the B-29 Superfortress. Tibbets was named commander of the 509th Composite Group, which targeted Hiroshima (7 August 1945) and Nagasaki (9 August 1945) with atomic weapons. He later rose to the rank of brigadier general before retiring in 1966. (Veronico)

940 In 1927, Juan Terry Trippe (1899–1981) became the founder of the Aviation Corporation of the Americas, which soon grew

As founder of Pan American World Airways, Juan Trippe brought global air travel to the masses with one of the world's greatest airlines.

to become American flag carrier Pan American Airways. The airline was the first to fly across the Atlantic and Pacific oceans and ushered in the Jet Age as the launch customer for the Boeing 707 and later wide-body era with the 747 jumbo jet. The company's Clipper service to Asia captured the public's attention, carrying its first passengers on 21 October 1936. During his tenure, Trippe grew the company from its sole route from Florida to Cuba into a carrier with routes crossing 80,000 unduplicated air miles to 85 different countries. (Veronico)

941 Hungarian immigrant Steven F. Udvar-Házy (b. 1946; came to the United States in 1958) was one of the founding partners of International Lease Finance Corporation (1973–2010) and founded Air Lease Corporation in 2010. In 1999, Udvar-Házy gave approximately $65 million to the National Air and Space Museum as the founding donation for its expanded display hangar at the Dulles Airport in Virginia. The facility cost more than $310 million, bears Udvar-Házy's name, and displays more than 175 air and spacecraft along with thousands of artifacts. (Veronico)

942 Emily Howell Warner (b. 1939) was the first American female pilot hired in the modern aviation era, the first woman airline captain, and the first female FAA-designated pilot examiner. She was hired by Frontier Airlines in January 1973 and, at the time, was the only woman flying as a pilot at a major airline. She went on to fly for United Parcel Service and today is retired. She was enshrined into the National Aviation Hall of Fame in 2014. (Veronico)

943 Charles Elwood "Chuck" Yeager (b. 1923) flew P-51 Mustang fighters with the 363rd Fighter Group at RAF Leiston during World War II. He was shot down on 5 March 1944 and escaped back to England through Spain with the help of the French Resistance. Back in the air, on 12 October 1944 he became an "ace in a day," shooting down five German aircraft, and was one of the first pilots to down a jet-powered Me 262 fighter. He shot down 11½ enemy aircraft during the war. (Veronico)

944 Following the conflict, Yeager became a test pilot at Muroc AAF (now Edwards AFB) and was assigned to the Bell X-1 program. On 14 October 1947, while flying the X-1, he broke the sound barrier flying Mach 1.07 at 45,000 feet. Yeager later commanded squadrons in Europe and became the first commandant of the Air Force's Aerospace Research Pilot School at Edwards AFB. During the Vietnam War, he was in command of the 405th Tactical Fighter Wing based at Clark AFB, Philippines. Yeager was promoted to the rank of brigadier general on 22 June 1969 and retired from active duty on 1 March 1975. (Veronico)

945 Jeana Lee Yeager (b. 1952, and no relation to "Chuck") flew the first nonstop, unrefueled flight around the world with Dick Rutan in the Burt Rutan–designed *Rutan Voyager*. The aircraft departed Edwards AFB, California, on 14 December and landed on 23 December 1986, having been airborne for 116 hours and covering 24,986 miles. The flight set six world records and Yeager, the Rutans, and the *Voyager* team were awarded the Collier Trophy for the advancement of aviation with Yeager being the only female to have received the award at the time. (Veronico)

Chapter 8

Aircraft Models

From the earliest days of aviation, models of real airplanes were as close as anyone could get to flying. Seeing a three-dimensional representation of an early flying machine or Lindbergh's Ryan, a World War II bomber or fighter, or a modern jet creates a joy for any pilot or flight-minded enthusiast. In this section we bring you interesting facts about models of aircraft throughout history, beginning with a special section by our resident early-model expert, Jim Keeshen.

THE EARLY YEARS

946 Flying toys, gliders, kites, simple helicopters, and powered model airplanes had been in existence way before either Langley or the Wright brothers attempted their first flights.

947 The Englishman Sir George Cayley was flying model gliders in 1800. The first small engine-powered flight of a model was done indoors by William Henson in 1848; that model flew for a few seconds and covered a distance of 120 feet.

Aircraft manufacturers used models for promotion and marketing, such as this polished chrome Allyn Douglas C-133 Cargomaster.

948 Although George Cayley had proposed rubber as a source of power, it was the French who came up with a rubber-powered, heavier-than-air model airplane.

949 In 1871 the French scientist Alphonse Penaud demonstrated a small, rubber band–powered, heavier-than-air model that flew 131 feet. This flight was performed before the French Academy of Science with Penaud's planaphore model.

950 Penaud experimented with many configurations of flying models, and toy makers soon started creating and selling their own versions. The French became the leaders in offering flying toys at the turn of the twentieth century.

951 In the late 1800s and early 1900s rubber-powered models, besides being toys, became research tools to try and test different configurations of wings and surfaces to achieve sustained and inherently stable flight. These models provided a much cheaper way to experiment with flight than using full-size aircraft.

952 The flying helicopter was a popular toy that Bishop Milton Wright bought for his two sons, Wilbur and Orville, when they were young boys. It is reported that the boys made multiple copies of the toys.

953 But the Wright brothers were not the only ones to dabble in making their own flying toys; many other airplane enthusiasts (modelers) were trying their hands at building and flying models before any full-size airplane ever flew.

954 The first model airplane flying club, the Junior Aero Club of America, was started in 1907. It was sponsored by the Aero Club of America, which itself was started about 1902 but formally established in the summer of 1905 by an avid balloonist who wanted to promote the sport of aviation.

955 As a side note, the Aero Club of America issued the first five pilot's licenses in the United States in 1911. The licenses became a requirement by the U.S. Army for all its pilots up until 1914, but flying licenses were not required by law until after World War I.

956 Regional interest in airplane modeling was noted in the early days of aviation as more and more people saw airplanes flying overhead for the first time, inspiring them to take interest in these new and futuristic machines. Hotbeds of modeling activity in the early years were the Hempstead Plains on Long Island, New York, myriad towns throughout the Midwest, and areas such as Southern California where good weather was conducive to flying year-round.

957 The first model-airplane book was published by Francis A. Collins. *The Boy's Book on Model Airplanes* came out in 1910 and contains detailed instructions on how to build a flying model, with a list of materials that includes hard wood and nails.

958 At the beginning of the model airplane hobby industry, hobby shops as we know them today did not exist. Outlets where one could go and buy a kit to make a model airplane did not exist either. Supplies for hobby needs came from mail order companies with catalogs, much like the old Sears and Roebuck catalog/mail order system.

959 Long Island, New York, is considered the cradle of aviation in the United States. It stands to reason, therefore, that New York is also where the first model airplane supply companies were established. The first of these enterprises were in Brooklyn (technically a borough of New York City), and then were established in suburban Long Island.

960 The first two corporate model airplane companies were the White Aeroplane Company and the Aero Accessories and Supply Company, started in 1909 in Brooklyn, New York. Eventually the White Company moved to Wading River, Long Island, New York.

961 The Ideal Model Airplane and Supply Company started up in 1911 and would go on to be the leader and longest-lasting manufacturer of model airplanes.

962 The White Aeroplane Company offered wood (not balsa), propellers, wheels, fittings, chains, gears, silk fabric, liquid coating for covering, tubing, wire, pontoons, tools, gasoline and electric engines, and plans.

963 A gas engine weighed more than 3 pounds. The electric motors were offered for exhibition models that would be hung from a wire and fly in circles for display purposes.

964 Types of wood offered by the first model suppliers were poplar, ash, birch, white holly, bass, rattan, and bamboo. These made for heavy models, so it is safe to assume that the scale models were not easy to fly. But other non-scale flying models that were better flyers than the scale models were also offered.

965 The introduction of balsa wood as a building material came from a member of the New York Model Aero Club in 1911, John Carisi. He observed a boat builder on the docks of Long Island City easily chopping huge chunks of wood. When he investigated, he discovered an extremely light wood and asked if he could get a sample. The worker gave him a log of balsa wood about the size of a railroad tie, which Carisi brought back to his club and shared with his fellow modelers to make lighter airplanes.

966 In 1909–1910 the White Aeroplane Company offered the first scale model of the Bleriot Monoplane with a 36-inch wing span. Complete parts, securely packed, prepaid to any address in the United States or Canada cost $3. Or one could buy a completely built model shipped in a wooden box for $10.

967 Other non-scale models offered by the White Aeroplane Company included the Monster Butterfly with enlarged antenna used as a propeller. This toy, essentially a helicopter, "will ascend

to a great height and when its power is spent will descend with a graceful gliding motion."

968 Also available was the Percy Pierce Flyer, a simple, rubber-powered pusher made of a stick with propeller, wings, and canard, capable of flying 150 feet. Percy Pierce was a first-prize-winning contestant of an early model-airplane competition in New York who offered his design to the public through the White catalog.

969 The rest of the models offered by White were an ornathopter butterfly, an Aero Toy flying wing, the Bleriot Junior Model, and the Antoinette Junior Model, these last two being very simple stick tractor rubber-powered airplanes with fuselage lengths of 18, 24, 28, and 32 inches. One had a choice of silk or cotton wing coverings.

970 After 1912 the White Aeroplane Company moved to Wading River, Long Island, New York, and by 1914 it was either taken over or renamed the Wading River Manufacturing Company. This new company merged with the other earliest model company, the Aero Accessories and Supply Company.

971 Just like its predecessors, Wading River offered all the necessary individual parts and documents (plans) to make kits, including the package deals of a complete kit with all the parts necessary to make one model for $4 to $7, depending upon model type, and models completely built for $10 to $15.

972 For reasons not known today, Wading River and Ideal companies somehow shared the same group of scale models offered for sale. These scale models included the Bleriot, Nieuport Monoplane, the Curtiss Hydroaeroplane, the Langley Tandem Monoplane, the Antoinette Monoplane, and the Wright Flyer.

973 Even the stock of accessories was basically the same. What distinguished them from each other were the offerings of sports models from different contest winners that the companies contracted and represented as part of their line of airplane models.

974 The Ideal Model Aeroplane and Supply Company started up in 1911 at 82–86 West Broadway, New York, and offered basically the same building materials but a slightly different number of sports models, including a few "A" frame rubber-powered airplanes (the Speed-O-Plane, the Long Distance Flyer, and the Cecil Peoli Racer). At that time, Ideal included two of the same scale models that the other supply companies offered: the 3-foot Wright Biplane and the Bleriot Monoplane in either knocked down or completed versions.

975 Ideal would become the leader of the model supply business by 1914, and the scale models offered were increased. Over the next few years the Nieuport Monoplane, the Curtiss Hydroaeroplane, the Langley Tandem Monoplane, and the Antoinette Monoplane were added to the list. The Nieuport had a wing span of 32 inches and the rest had 36-inch wing spans.

976 Ideal, like the other model supply companies, was a mail-order catalog service. But it was the first to offer a retail counter service, at its New York City factory, where any model builder could walk in and buy their model needs.

977 Eventually the Ideal Company would continue as a wood scale-model manufacturer into the 1930s, 1940s, and 1950s. They went on to produce plastic models when the plastic craze took over in the mid-1950s. During this period they changed their name to ITC (Ideal Toy Company).

978 As with aviation itself, World War I and the 1927 crossing of the Atlantic by Lindbergh sparked the model airplane hobby business. Two kinds of models were commercialized: "stick and tissue" rubber- or gas-engine-powered flying models, and "solid" display models carved from wood.

979 After those two historical events many model airplane companies sprung up or grew larger. These included companies such as Megow, Cleveland, Peerless, Comet, Scientific, Hawk, and

Strombecker. The line of stick and tissue scale and sports flying models were much more extensive than the solid scale models.

980 The popularity of building, flying, and competing model airplanes was encouraged by the many model airplane clubs that existed throughout the United States and around the world. Prizes abounded for setting records of speed, altitude, endurance, and distance. However, World War II brought an end to these competitions, causing all countries and clubs to end flying events.

981 However, in 1942 at the beginning of U.S. involvement in World War II, solid display models came into great demand. The Navy Bureau of Aeronautics (BuAer) ordered mass production of 1/72-scale solid models. While waiting for companies to gear up, the Navy turned to the citizen population, commissioning high schools across the United States to turn out 1/72-scale solid models of every Axis and Allied aircraft involved in the war.

982 By the mid-1930s model gas engines were sufficiently developed and somewhat affordable to the hobby. This new power source became the popular form of building and flying model airplanes, basically utilizing reinforced stick and tissue construction but built larger to handle the weight and power of the engine. Model airplane engines were expensive and there was always the chance that the model would catch a thermal and fly out of sight, losing the plane and engine. From a cost perspective, by far the most affordable hobby was the rubber-powered model airplane.

THE WONDERFUL WORLD OF PLASTIC

983 In 1952 the Aurora plastic model company came out with its 1/48-scale Lockheed XF-90 and Grumman F9F Panther, which were thought to be pirated copies of the recently released Hawk kits. To secure proof of any future misdeeds by Aurora, Hawk had its name spelled out with rivets in Morse code on their other planes. (Keeshen)

Topping Models of Akron, Ohio, produced hundreds of thousands of solid display models like this classic Grumman F9F-8T Cougar.

984 For aircraft manufacturers in the 1950s and 1960s, Topping Models, originally based in Akron, Ohio, produced the best "non-factory model shop" replicas in the business. Although basic in shape and markings, these models were produced by the thousands and could be found in executive offices of major companies across the United States. Produced in various scales depending on the use of the model, Toppings are now collectible and rare examples in perfect condition can command exceedingly high prices. (Machat)

985 The Topping X-15 was one of the best and was produced with two slightly different stands, each with a rocket-exhaust-colored plastic rod that was inserted into the exhaust cone to display the model "climbing into outer space." The model's clear plastic base was engraved with the North American logo but was molded so that the exhaust rod had two different angles: a steep climb angle representing the X-15's altitude records and a flatter angle for the rocket plane's speed records. (Machat)

986 By 1956, Revell models had become the industry leader by producing accurate, detailed models of cars, ships, planes, and armor, coupled with stunning artwork on the box tops. That year, the company introduced a new series of models called "S" kits. Arguably the best plastic models of that era, "S" kits today are prized collectibles. The "S" stand for styrene plastic. (Machat)

Factory build-up of the Revell Nike Hercules "S" Kit shows figures for scale, and the nuclear warhead–equipped missile ready to launch.

987 With so much emphasis on the dreaded Soviet nuclear threat during the Cold War, not to mention the Cuban Missile Crisis of October 1962, missile kits were all the rage for teenage model builders at the time. To best show the dramatic scene of a pending missile launch right there in your own living room, model manufacturers often employed veritable armies of women to build kits for display in the windows of the thousands of hobby shops dotting the United States. These now-rare factory build-ups are highly valued collector's items today. (Machat)

988 Without realizing it, Revell Models of Venice, California, created the world's first "limited edition" model kit by destroying the master molds used to produce their American Airlines Lockheed Electra "S" kit in 1961. A slow seller (and ironically now a prized collectible), Revell's Electra kit became a prime candidate for conversion to the P-3 Orion anti-submarine patrol aircraft, much like Lockheed did with the real aircraft. When modelers realized that Revell's American Electra could never be re-issued, prices for that kit began to skyrocket. (Machat)

989 Revell's Electra kit is also the textbook example of how model companies used premature information in designing a kit that became inaccurate by the time the model was released for sale. Early artist renderings showed the aircraft with a large black radome, yet the actual airplane had an orange nose with only a small black dot radome. Having used the only available color scheme reference material when the model was first designed, the wrong radome was incorporated into the kit. (Machat)

990 The words "SCALED FROM OFFICIAL BLUEPRINTS" are emblazoned proudly on the box top of every Revell "S" kit, but on the American Electra, the model manufacturer got caught yet again: A single, odd-looking larger window is molded into the right-hand forward fuselage. Upon examination of Lockheed's marking drawing showing the color scheme of the actual airplane, the forward right-hand emergency exit is missing because that assembly is painted separately before being installed in the airplane.

The model followed the drawing precisely and was incorrect as a result. (Machat)

991 One of the greatest joys of model building was comparing your finished model with the kit's box top painting to see how close the two matched in appearance. Below is an Aurora "Famous Fighters"–era box top and build-up of the World War II North American T-6 Texan Advanced Trainer. (Machat)

A favorite aspect of model building in the 1950s was comparing your finished model to the box art. Aurora's T-6 was painted by Mort Kunstler.

992 In the mid-1950s, several U.S. model manufacturers developed a brilliant marketing scheme that took only 40 years to come to fruition. By bundling several individual 79¢ or 98¢ kits into a single large box by subject (fighter aircraft, bombers, navy ships, etc.), the gift set was created. Usually purchased by a family for birthdays or Christmas presents, these giant kits were very expensive for their day, costing up to $4.95 when a gallon of gasoline cost 29¢. Forty years later when the model collecting hobby turned red-hot, gift sets began to command insane prices. Rare examples found in perfect condition can bring as much as $1,500 today. (Machat)

993 As each new and exciting airplane took flight in the Fabulous Fifties, plastic-model manufacturers rushed kits of those aircraft into production for immediate release and distribution throughout the United States. Inevitably, the same aircraft would be duplicated at the same time in kits by different model companies, and examples of these are countless. One airplane, however, stands out for being released in model form by every major kit manufacturer in the United States within just a few years of its first flight, the Mach-2 delta-wing Convair B-58 Hustler. Models of the B-58 were produced by Revell, Monogram, Aurora, Lindberg, and Comet. (Machat)

Revell promo photo shows the box and factory build-up of their Republic F-105B Thunderchief "S" kit released in 1957.

994 Operating features were all the rage for aircraft models of the Cold War era, with opening canopies, movable control surfaces, retractable landing gear, and bomb bay doors that opened and closed "just like the real thing." Certain Monogram kits such as the Republic F-105, Douglas B-66 Destroyer, and Convair B-58 Hustler featured small plastic "bombs" that either were dropped or jettisoned by a spring-loaded plug. This was obviously well before child safety laws took effect beginning in the 1970s. (Machat)

995 With truth in advertising legislation in full swing by the mid-1970s, model manufacturers fell under the wrath of consumers who took issue with the claims made on model box tops. If a P-51 was shown firing its guns on the cover, would the guns actually fire on the model? One well-known box top artist told the story of having to re-paint the cover of a Navy aircraft carrier kit that showed crew figures running on the flight deck because there were no human figures in the kit. (Machat)

Moult Taylor's Aerocar created quite a sensation in the 1950s and is the only truly successful "flying car" ever built.

996 *The New Bob Cummings Show* featured the star's own Moult Taylor Aerocar in episodes of the TV program. Taylor of course being the consummate marketeer, asked Cummings to endorse the aircraft and to include his likeness on the model kit of the Aerocar, which itself was produced by the Gladen Company as yet another marketing tool. How different the aviation world would be today if Moult Taylor had been successful with his fabulous flying automobile. (Kodera)

The undisputed "king of model box art" was the great Jack Leynnwood, whose aircraft, ships, and cars came alive on Revell and Aurora box tops.

997 Legendary Los Angeles illustrator Jack Leynnwood produced a total of 625 model box top paintings primarily for Revell, as well as for Aurora and K&B Slot Cars. Adding supreme authenticity to his artwork was the fact that Leynnwood had been a flight instructor during World War II and had flown numerous military fighters, including the P-40, P-51, and his personal favorite, the P-38. He owned a North American T-6 Texan after the war and flew ultralights in his later years. (Machat)

998 Although it didn't impact a model's authenticity, oftentimes something shown on the box art was completely fictitious. On Revell's Academy Series Douglas D-558-2 Skyrocket kit, the hybrid jet/rocket aircraft is shown taking off from the dry lakebed of a mountainous "secret western test site," obviously Edwards. The scene shows a large yellow-and-black-striped wind tetrahedron in the background, which would never happen, as there are no manmade obstructions on the runways of Rogers Dry Lake. The base's real tetrahedron was located abeam the control tower. (Machat)

999 On Revell's French Caravelle jet airliner cover, both Scandinavian Airlines System (SAS) and Swissair Caravelles are shown at an airport in a famous European city with a noted architectural landmark shown in the background: the Eiffel Tower in Paris. But Leynnwood's visual "trick" on this cover was that the landing gear on the Swissair Caravelle in the background is completely missing; the airplane is literally hovering in mid-air. (Machat)

1000 For young model builders in the 1950s as well as grown collectors today (usually the same people), Revell "S" kits represent the gold standard in plastic modeling of that era. The precision with which these kits were designed, engineered, and manufactured was unlike that of any other company, with stellar Dick Kishady and Jack Leynnwood box art being the icing on the

One of the best-engineered "S" kits from Revell was its stunning Convair F-106A Delta Dart issued in 1958.

cake. Of the many excellent kits produced at that time, the 1958 release of the Convair F-106A Delta Dart has to be among the best. With Revell's new "flush rivet detail" and a host of operating features, it was like having a real miniature F-106 right in your room. (Machat)

1001 On the cover of Revell's famed B-52 with X-15 kit, the exotic black rocket plane is shown being launched from its mothership above a lime-green cloud deck. As magnificent as this Leynnwood illustration is to the casual observer, it contains many visual "tweaks" that he gave to his paintings to grab a young viewer's attention. For instance, the X-15 is rocketing directly away from its launch pylon under power, much like a missile being launched instead of being dropped; the B-52's rear fuselage is shortened dramatically to allow the entire tail to be shown on the box top; and the launch is taking place above a solid cloud deck that completely obscures the ground, something that was never allowed in actual X-15 operations. (Machat)

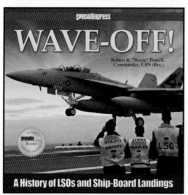